Critics of
State Education

Critics of
State Education

Edited by
George H. Smith and
Marilyn Moore

CATO INSTITUTE
WASHINGTON, D.C.

eBook ISBN: 978-1-944424-43-5
Print ISBN: 978-1-944424-42-8

Library of Congress Cataloging-in-Publication Data available.

Printed in the United States of America.

CATO INSTITUTE
1000 Massachusetts Avenue, N.W.
Washington, D.C. 20001
www.cato.org

TABLE OF CONTENTS

Preface

This book is a collection of writings by principled opponents of state education.

All selections are in the public domain. While some of the writers, such as Joseph Priestly, William Godwin, and Herbert Spencer, are well known, their opposition to state education may not be. The contributions of some of the most eloquent critics, however—Edward Baines, Jr., Edward Miall, and others—have been largely overlooked. We think they deserve to be more widely read.

We wish to thank Aaron Powell of the Cato Institute for his support and encouragement. We also wish to thank Dr. Daniel E. Cullen and Mrs. Paula Bramsen Cullen of the Chicago-based Opportunity Fund.

—GHS
—MM

Introduction

George H. Smith

I

Around the 12th century BCE, Dorian tribes, warlike nomads of uncertain origin, settled in southern Greece. By 800 BCE, these tribes had established political dominion in the territory of Laconia. The resulting state, Lacedaemon, was ruled by Sparta, a powerful city in the Eurotas Valley.

Before long the Spartans turned their gaze to the neighboring land of Messenia. After two long and arduous wars, the Spartans conquered the Messenians and enslaved them. Known as "helots," these slaves were assigned with parcels of land to individual Spartans, thereby supporting the Spartans and freeing them for other activities. Helots were treated with extreme brutality. Each year Sparta ceremoniously declared war against them, which made the murder of helots a permissible act of war.

The specter of a helot revolt was ever present. An earthquake in 464 BCE nearly devastated Sparta, and the ensuing uprising was barely contained. Thucydides recorded the Spartan fear of the helots during the Peloponnesian Wars (431–404 BCE), when "fear of their numbers and obstinacy" guided Spartan "policy at all times having been governed by the necessity of taking precautions against them."[1] This persistent threat helped to transform Spartan culture, which had shown promise in earlier centuries, into an austere militaristic society in which individuals were compelled to serve the state.

Sparta subordinated the individual to the demands of the state. This subordination would be unremarkable were it not for the praise that Sparta would later receive from some 17th- and 18th-century political philosophers who wanted to establish a republican form of government.

We might wonder what lesson political philosophers with liberal tendencies thought they could learn from the Spartan model, other than viewing it as a negative model that teaches us which policies a free society should avoid. For what, then, was Sparta praised? Certainly not for its cultural or philosophical achievements. As the Greek historian Werner Jaeger put it, "No Spartan name occurs in the long roll of Greek moralists and philosophers." Jaeger continued:

> However, Sparta has an unchallengeable place in the history of education. Her most characteristic achievement was her state; and the Spartan state is the first which can be called, in the largest sense, an educational force.[2]

---

[1] Thucydides, *The History of the Peloponnesian War*, trans. Richard Crawley, rev. R. Feetham (Chicago: Encyclopedia Britannica, 1952), book 4, chapter 80 (467).

[2] Werner Jaeger, *Paideia: the Ideals of Greek Culture*, vol. 1 (New York: Oxford University Press, 1962), p. 79.

As the French historian H. I. Marrou wrote about Sparta: "Education was entirely subordinated to the needs of the State and completely in the State's hands. . . . The Spartan ideal was the ideal of a barrack-room sergeant-major."[3] He explained:

> The ideal was an absolute patriotism, the devotion to the State carried to the supreme limit of death. The only standard of goodness was what served the interest of the city; whatever helped to increase the greatness of Sparta was right.[4]

Marrou pointed out that the Spartan model inspired German militarists from the time of Bismarck to the Nazi Third Reich. This influence is understandable, but more puzzling was that of the Spartan model on those post-Renaissance intellectuals with liberal proclivities. As those intellectuals looked back on Sparta, they saw something other than brutal totalitarianism. They saw a planned, well-ordered society where individual goals were subordinated to the common good, a society where education was controlled by the state and where civic virtues were instilled in children at an early age.

Plato and Aristotle, though by no means unqualified admirers of Sparta, endorsed the Spartan principle of state education (while disagreeing with its content), and their endorsements played major roles in elevating the Spartan model to pride of place in the

---

[3] H. I. Marrou, *A History of Education in Antiquity,* trans. George Lamb (Madison: University of Wisconsin Press, 1956), pp. 19, 24.

[4] Ibid., p. 22.

modern era. Plato's blueprint of an authoritarian society called for a state system of centralized education supervised by a minister of education. "In this conception," wrote the Greek scholar Ernest Barker, "Plato was definitely and consciously departing from the practice of Athens, and setting his face towards Sparta." Plato's aim was "to combine the curriculum of Athens with the organization of Sparta."[5]

Plato's view of the relationship between the child and the state reflects the Spartan influence, as we see in this passage from *The Laws*: "Education is, if possible, to be, as the phrase goes, compulsory for every mother's son, on the ground that the child is even more the property of the state than of his parents."[6]

Aristotle also preferred the Spartan approach over Athenian free-market education. Although Aristotle criticized Plato's obsession with uniformity in some respects, he agreed that uniformity in education is good because it promotes civic virtue. "The citizen should be molded to suit the form of government under which he lives," wrote Aristotle, which means that "education should be one and the same for all." Aristotle rejected the educational *laissez-faire* of Athens in which "everyone looks after his own child separately, and gives them separate instruction of the sort which he thinks best."[7]

---

[5] Ernest Barker, *Greek Political Theory: Plato and His Predecessors* (Abingdon, Oxon, U.K.: Routledge, 2010), pp. 211, 214.

[6] Plato, *Laws*, trans. A. E. Taylor, in *The Collected Dialogues of Plato*, ed. Edith Hamilton and Huntington Cairns (New York: Pantheon Books, 1961), section 805d (1376).

[7] Aristotle, *Politics*, trans. Benjamin Jowett (Chicago: Encyclopedia Britannica, 1952), section 1337b (542).

Aristotle clearly understood the broader philosophical under-pinnings of the Spartan model:

> Neither must we suppose that any one of the citizens belongs to himself, for they all belong to the state, and are each of them a part of the state, and the care of each part is inseparable from the care of the whole. In this particular as in some others the Lacedaemonians are to be praised, for they take the greatest pains about their children, and make education the business of the state.[8]

A Latin translation of Aristotle's *Politics* appeared around 1260. Plato's *Republic*, previously known to Western Europeans second-hand, became available in the mid-15th century and sparked a flurry of interest among Renaissance humanists.

Plato and Aristotle were not the only classical writers to infuse a passion for the Spartan model into European culture. Another important source was the Greek biographer Plutarch. His book *Parallel Lives* was translated into Latin in 1470 and later into English and other languages. As Elizabeth Rawson noted in *The Spartan Tradition in European Thought*, Plutarch "was one of the chief sources of laconism [admiration of Sparta] for the Renaissance, when the *Parallel Lives* were the staple reading of schoolboys and statesmen."[9]

Plutarch lived centuries after the events he wrote about, so the accuracy of his account is open to question. But the Sparta known

---

[8] Ibid.

[9] Elizabeth Rawson, *The Spartan Tradition in European Thought* (London: Oxford University Press, 1969), p. 112.

to Renaissance humanists and later philosophers was the Sparta described by Plutarch. And that account, accurate or not, is the one that influenced generations of European intellectuals, especially those who constructed their own versions of utopian societies:

> There is scarcely a detail of the constitution of Sparta and the way of life Plutarch described that failed to be picked up and incorporated into some seventeenth- or eighteenth-century utopia. While historical Athens left the memory of a rather easygoing society devoted to the arts but contaminated with moral faults, Sparta in its period of obedience to the laws of Lycurgus was the archetype of the most upright commonwealth. The civic virtues of the Spartans and their sense of duty were praised, and the military success made their constitution worth emulating.[10]

According to Plutarch, Spartan laws were originally framed by Lycurgus—a possibly mythical figure who would become the prototype for various utopian schemes in which a single man, a wise lawgiver, invents and implements the legal system of an ideal society.

Plutarch described Sparta "as a sort of camp" in which "no one was allowed to live after his own fancy" but was required to serve "the interest of his country" instead. Lycurgus understood that a rigorous and comprehensive system of state education, by

---

[10] Frank E. Manuel and Fritzie P. Manuel, *Utopian Thought in the Western World* (Cambridge, MA: Belknap Press, 1979), p. 97.

imprinting one's duty to serve the state "on the hearts" of Spartans from an early age, was the "best lawgiver."[11]

As part of his grand educational scheme, Lycurgus instituted state control over marriage—an idea that found favor with Plato and later utopian writers. "Lycurgus," Plutarch explained, "was of a persuasion that children were not so much the property of their parents as of the whole commonwealth."[12] The case for eugenics follows logically from this premise. After all, the owners of dogs and horses take special care to procure fine breeding, so why should women—who "might be foolish, infirm, or diseased"— be allowed to choose their own mates and thereby endanger the quality of state-owned children?

Spartan boys were taken from their parents at age seven and placed under the close supervision of government educators. "The whole course of Spartan education was one continued exercise of a ready and perfect obedience."[13] Although many later advocates of state education rejected the militaristic and totalitarian emphasis of Spartan education, they were enthusiastic about the potential implicit in the Spartan model. They believed the same means could be adapted to serve ends other than obedience to a totalitarian state. If a system of state education were to focus on the civic virtues needed for a *free* society, such as a respect for individual rights and obedience to a *limited* government, then surely this would be a good thing.

---

[11] *Plutarch's Lives of Illustrious Men*, trans. John Dryden, rev. A. H. Clough (Boston: Little, Brown, and Company, 1878), pp. 39, 34.

[12] Ibid., p. 35.

[13] Ibid., p. 36.

II

The place is Athens during the fifth century BCE. Hippocrates greets his friend Socrates with exciting news: the renowned Protagoras—a sophist (teacher of wisdom)—is in Athens. Protagoras charges a considerable fee for his educational services, but Hippocrates is happy to pay the celebrated teacher and sage.

But Socrates (as written by Plato) cautions his friend. A sophist is an educational entrepreneur—"a merchant or peddler of the goods by which a soul is nourished." Socrates then articulates what is probably the first market-failure argument against free-market education in the history of western thought. Most consumers are poor judges of educational quality, so they need experts to dictate their educational choices:

> We must see that the Sophist in commending his wares does not deceive us, like the wholesaler and the retailer who deal in food for the body. These people do not know themselves which of the wares they offer is good or bad for the body, but in selling them praise all alike, and those who buy from them don't know either, unless one of them happens to be a trainer or a doctor. So too those who take the various subject of knowledge from city to city, and offer them for sale retail to whoever wants them, commend everything that they have for sale. But it may be, my dear Hippocrates, that some of these men also are ignorant of the beneficial or harmful effects on the soul of what they have for sale, and so too are those who buy from them, unless one of them happens to be a physician of the soul. If then you chance to

be an expert in discerning which of them is good or bad, it is safe for you to buy knowledge from Protagoras or anyone else. But if not, take care you don't find yourself gambling dangerously with all of you that is dearest to you. Indeed, the risk you run in purchasing knowledge is much greater than that in buying provisions.[14]

Plato attributes this argument to Socrates, but it concurs with Plato's own views. It exhibits Plato's characteristic hostility to the sophists; indeed, his many allusions to the earnings of the sophists (31 in all) suggest that their entrepreneurial skills contributed to Plato's wrath. His castigation of the sophists, even to the point of calling them intellectual prostitutes, was hypocritical, considering that Plato also made his living as a professional teacher. This inconsistency has led one Greek scholar to suggest that "the pressure of professional competition" underlay Plato's disdain.

The sophists, wrote H. I. Marrou, "were professional men for whom teaching was an occupation whose commercial success bore witness to its intrinsic value and its social utility."[15] They traveled from city to city and engaged in collective tutoring that might extend over a period of several years. Sophists brought about a "veritable revolution" in Greek education, adapting well to the educational free market in fifth-century Athens.[16]

---

[14] *Protagoras,* trans. W. K. C. Guthrie, in *The Collected Dialogues of Plato,* ed. Edith Hamilton and Huntington Cairns (New York: Pantheon Books, 1961), sections 313d–314a (313).

[15] Marrou, *History of Education in Antiquity,* p. 49.

[16] Ibid., p. 59

Some sophists commanded large fees, but fierce competition lowered the fees of many teachers to the point where the Greek educator Isocrates could charge only one-tenth of the fee collected by the illustrious Protagoras. Predictably perhaps, Isocrates complained that "blacklegs" (i.e., competitors) were undercutting his price by more than half.[17] Duly offended at the verdict of a competitive market, Isocrates alleged that those who appear to sell instruction "for much less than its value" were obviously peddling an inferior product.[18]

Plato's argument that average people are not competent judges of educational quality was closely linked to his dislike of Athenian democracy, which he regarded as little more than mob rule. Plato harbored a deep distrust of the common man in politics and in every activity that requires special training. Derogatory references abound in the Platonic dialogues to the "nondescript mob," the "ignorant multitude," "the great beast," and so forth.

This distrust of Athenian democracy is the major reason that Plato attacked the sophists and Athenian free-market education. Educational entrepreneurs give the public what it wants and so cater to ignorance and vulgar desires. As Plato says in the *Republic*: "Each of these private teachers who work for pay, whom the politicians call Sophists . . . inculcates nothing else than these opinions of the multitude which they opine when they are assembled, and calls this knowledge wisdom."[19] The sophist

---

[17] Ibid., p. 49.

[18] Isocrates, *Against the Sophists*, in *Readings in the History of Education*, ed. Ellwood Cubberley (Cambridge, MA: Riverside Press, 1920), p. 14.

[19] Plato, *Republic*, trans. Paul Shorey, in *The Collected Dialogues of Plato*, ed. Edith Hamilton and Huntington Cairns (New York: Pantheon Books, 1961), section 493a (729).

panders to "the motley multitude." He must "give the public what it likes," but will public demand coincide with what "is really good and honorable"? No, says Plato; any such notion is "simply ridiculous."[20]

Plato does not deny the ability of a free market to educate the people. Education flourished in Athens, but, according to Plato, it was not the right kind of education. Athens lacked the political unity of Sparta, and her people indulged in the corrupting luxuries that attend every society that is based on commerce. It was principally because of these flaws that Athens had suffered a devastating defeat at the hands of Sparta during the Peloponnesian Wars.

Moreover, there were no educational experts in Athens with the power to dictate her intellectual and cultural developments, so, according to Plato, she was degenerating into tyranny, which was widely regarded as the corrupted form of democracy. Specially educated guardians—men of spotless virtue trained in the art of governing a city-state—should rule virtually without limit. A true knowledge of philosophy is accessible only to this elite; philosophy "is impossible for the multitude."

Plato's basic argument against free-market education would be repeated, in one form or another, by later champions of state education. Consider these remarks by the American sociologist Lester Frank Ward, who has been called the "father" of the American welfare state. In his influential two-volume work, *Dynamic Sociology*, Ward advocated a comprehensive system of state

[20] Ibid., section 493d.

education because such a system would shield professional educators from "the caprices" of "heterogeneously minded patrons." He wrote:

> The secret of the superiority of state over private education lies in the fact that in the former the teacher is responsible solely to society. As in private, so also in public education, the calling of the teacher is a profession, and his personal success must depend upon his success in accomplishing the result which his employers desire accomplished. But the result desired by the state is a wholly different one from that desired by parents, guardians, and pupils. Of the latter he is happily independent.[21]

Ward's argument for educational experts who will operate without interference by parents—ignorant, narrow-minded consumers who will neither understand nor desire the kind of education needed for the greater social good—would become a mainstay of the American Progressive movement during the early 20th century.

The jurisdiction of Plato's rulers is staggering—medicine, physical exercise, even "law-abiding play."[22] But I needn't list every detail as long as we understand the chain of reasoning employed here: Education, broadly conceived, includes everything that

---

[21] Lester Frank Ward, *Dynamic Sociology*, 2nd ed. (New York: Appleton, 1897), pp. 589–90.

[22] Plato, *Republic*, trans. Paul Shorey, in *The Collected Dialogues of Plato*, ed. Edith Hamilton and Huntington Cairns (New York: Pantheon Books, 1961), section 424e (666).

influences the character of human beings. Thus, if education is a vital and indispensable function of the state, then the state has a right—indeed, a duty—to supervise *every* aspect of a person's life. Because of Plato's comprehensive notion of education, there is scarcely any aspect of human life that his state, with its stranglehold on education, does not control.

Aristotle explicitly repudiated the notion of limited government that was defended by some of his contemporaries. He quoted the sophist Lycophron as saying that a government exists "for the sake of alliance and security from injustice" and that laws should serve as "a surety to one another of justice."[23] Aristotle disagreed. Rather than confine itself to this negative function—the enforcement of justice—the state should actively promote the good life.

To promote the good life and maintain social order, the state should inculcate civic virtue. Those "who care for good government take into consideration virtue and vice in states. Whence it may be further inferred that virtue must be the care of the state which is truly so called."[24] This concern with civic virtue was the basis for Aristotle's plan for a comprehensive system of state education, one that explicitly rejected the Athenian model in favor of the Spartan model.

The Spartan model was frequently invoked during the 18th century by those philosophers who believed that the fundamental purpose of education should be to "form valuable citizens to the

---

[23] *The Politics of Aristotle,* trans. Benjamin Jowett (Oxford: Clarendon Press, 1885), p. 83.

[24] Ibid.

state" (as the *philosophe* Baron d'Holbach put it).[25] With the rise of nationalism, children were seen as future citizens and patriots whose education must be carefully supervised to ensure proper results. "Thus," wrote Charles Duclos in 1750, "it is patent that in Spartan education, the first task was to form Spartans. In the same way, the sentiments of citizenship must be inculcated in every state; among us, Frenchmen must be formed, and in order to create Frenchmen, we must first work to form men."[26]

Montesquieu, in his immensely influential *Spirit of the Laws* (1748), set the stage for a good deal of Enlightenment thinking about children, the state, and education. If a democratic republic is to survive, it must imbue its citizens with civic virtue—"a love of the laws and of our country," a love that elevates the public interest above private interests. Montesquieu praised Spartan education for its ability to produce virtuous citizens, and he left no doubt that producing citizens should be the central task of education in a republic: "Everything therefore depends on establishing this love in a republic; and to inspire it ought to be the principal business of education."[27]

Another formative influence on Enlightenment thought was Jean-Jacques Rousseau. In *A Discourse on Political Economy*, Rousseau echoed Plato's objections to free-market education.

[25] Holbach, *The System of Nature*, vol. 1, trans. H. D. Robinson (Boston: J. P. Mendum, 1889), p. 131. On the rise of nationalism in the 18th century, see Hans Kohn, *The Idea of Nationalism* (New York: Macmillan, 1948), pp. 187–259. Cf. François de la Fontainerie, *French Liberalism and Education in the Eighteenth Century* (New York: McGraw-Hill, 1932).

[26] Quoted in Keith M. Baker, *Condorcet: From Natural Philosophy to Social Mathematics* (Chicago: University of Chicago Press, 1975), p. 286.

[27] Baron de Montesquieu, *The Spirit of the Laws*, trans. Thomas Nugent (New York: Hafner, 1949), p. 34.

The state should not "abandon to the intelligence and prejudices of fathers the education of their children, as that education is of still greater importance to the State than to the fathers." Public education is needed to ensure that citizens "will do nothing contrary to the will of society." Children should be taught "to regard their individuality in relation to the body of the State, and to be aware, so to speak, of their own existence merely as part of that of the State."[28]

The claim that children belong to the state, which echoes the Spartan model defended by Plato and Aristotle, was common in the 18th century. We even find it in some early American advocates of state education. In 1786, for example, Benjamin Rush (the "father" of American psychiatry) wrote: "Let our pupil be taught that he does not belong to himself, but that he is public property."[29] Similarly, in the 19th century a California superintendent of public education wrote that children "belong not to the parents, but to the State, to society, to the country."[30]

III

The relationship between school and state in American liberal thought has a checkered past. Many traditional heroes of American individualism, such as Thomas Paine and Thomas Jefferson, upheld some role for government in education, however minor that role is

---

[28] Jean-Jacques Rousseau, *A Discourse on Political* Economy, trans. G. D. H. Cole (London: J. M. Dent & Sons, 1913), pp. 269, 268.

[29] Benjamin Rush, *A Plan for the Establishment of Public Schools and the Diffusion of Knowledge in Pennsylvania* (1786), in *Theories of Education in Early America 1655–1819*, ed. Wilson Smith (Indianapolis and New York: Bobbs-Merrill, 1973), p. 247.

[30] John Swett, *History of the Public School System of California* (San Francisco: A. L. Bancroft, 1876), p. 115.

by today's standard. Even William Leggett, the radical Jacksonian and *laissez-faire* advocate who opposed nearly all kinds of government intervention, made an exception in the case of education.[31]

Radical individualism in America was a different matter. Josiah Warren, often regarded as the first American anarchist, warned in 1833 that national aid to education would be like "paying the fox to take care of the chickens," and said he feared the consequences of placing control of education in the hands of single group.[32] Gerrit Smith, a radical abolitionist who supported John Brown, upheld the separation of school and state. "It is justice and not charity which the people need at the hands of government," Smith argued. "Let government restore to them their land, and what other rights they have been robbed of, and they will be able to pay for themselves—to pay their schoolmasters, as well as their parsons."[33] William Youmans (an admirer of Herbert Spencer and a founder and editor of *Popular Science Monthly*) favored leaving education to "private enterprise."[34] And the Spencerian John Bonham vigorously attacked "the one true system" of Horace Mann that would impose a dulling uniformity and would extirpate diversity in education.[35]

[31] See William Leggett, *A Collection of the Political Writings of William Leggett*, vol. 1, ed. Theodore Sedgwick, Jr. (New York: Taylor and Dodd, 1840), pp. 80–81.

[32] Quoted in William O. Reichert, *Partisans of Freedom: A Study in American Anarchism* (Bowling Green, OH: Bowling Green State University Popular Press, 1976), p. 70.

[33] Quoted in Octavius Brooks Frothingham, *Gerrit Smith: A Biography* (New York: G. P. Putnam's Sons, 1878), p. 184.

[34] *Popular Science Monthly*, May 1887, pp. 124–27.

[35] John M. Bonham, *Industrial Liberty* (New York: G. P. Putnam's Sons, 1888), pp. 286–326.

The most thorough arguments against state education appeared in the writings of British (classical) liberals during the 1840s and 1850s. Calling themselves "Voluntaryists"—a label originally embraced by those who called for the complete disestablishment of the Church of England—these liberals launched a sustained campaign against state education in England that, though it was doomed to failure, produced a remarkable body of literature that has been largely ignored by historians.

The British Voluntaryist movement grew from the ranks of Dissenters, or Nonconformists (i.e., non-Anglican Protestants). After the Restoration of Charles II in 1660, Dissenters who refused to subscribe to the articles of the Established Church of England faced severe legal disabilities. Oxford and Cambridge were effectively closed to them, as were other conventional channels of education. Dissenters therefore established their own educational institutions, such as the dissenting academies of the 18th century, which one historian has described as "the greatest schools of their day."[36]

Until 1833, elementary education in England progressed without substantial state aid or interference. Free education on an ambitious scale had been undertaken by Dissenters, or Nonconformists, with the establishment, in 1808, of the British and Foreign School Society (originally called the Royal Lancasterian Society). Funded primarily by Dissenting congregations, the society used the monitorial system, which employed abler students

---

[36] Irene Parker, *Dissenting Academies in England* (Cambridge, U.K.: Cambridge University Press, 1914), p. 45.

to help teach their classmates, to bring education to the working classes without government assistance.[37] These efforts motivated Anglicans to form the National Society, which established competing free schools for educating the poor.

Over the next decade, government funds were made available to both Dissenters and Anglicans. Each pound from voluntary contributions was matched by the government, up to £20,000 per annum. Because the Anglican schools were receiving more contributions than the Dissenting schools, the former received most of the government funds, so Dissenters began to learn the hard way that government aid to education would serve the prevailing orthodoxy.

Even by 1839, when the Melbourne administration proposed to increase aid to £30,000 pounds per annum, relatively few Dissenters expressed opposition. Most Dissenters approved of, or silently accepted, state funding if it did not favor one religious group over another and if it did not entail state interference. The one Dissenting deputy who argued that education "is not a legitimate function of the government" could find no support among his peers,[38] and a meeting of Dissenting ministers in 1840 expressed its "satisfaction" with government aid for education.

All this changed in 1843 after Sir James Graham, home secretary under the Peel administration, presented a bill to the House of Commons titled *A Bill for Regulating the Employment of Children and Young Persons in Factories, and for the Better Education of Children in*

---

[37] For a history of the British and Foreign School Society, see Henry Bryan Binns, *A Century of Education* (London: J. M. Dent, 1908).

[38] R. W. Dale, *History of English Congregationalism* (London: Hodder & Stoughton, 1907), p. 652.

Factory Districts. Among other things, the bill required factory children to attend school for at least three hours each day, five days per week, and it placed effective control of those schools (to be financed largely from local rates) in the hands of the Established Church of England.[39] "The Church has ample security," wrote Graham, "that every master in the new schools will be a Churchman, and that the teaching of the Holy Scriptures, as far as the limited exposition may be carried, will necessarily be in conformity with his creed."[40]

Dissenting opposition to Graham's bill was swift and severe. It "set the whole country on fire," according to one observer.[41] *Eclectic Review*, a leading Dissenting journal, declared:

> From one end of the empire to the other, the sound of alarm has gone forth, and the hundreds of thousands who have answered to its call have astonished and confounded our opponents. The movement has been at once simultaneous and determined. The old spirit of the puritans has returned to their children, and men in high places are in consequence standing aghast, astonished at what they witness, reluctant to forego their nefarious purpose, yet scarce daring to persist in the scheme.[42]

[39] See J. T. Ward and J. H. Treble, "Religion and Education in 1843: Reaction to the Factory Education Bill," *Journal of Ecclesiastical History* 20, no. 1 (1969): 79–110. A thorough account of this bill is also contained in Dale, *History of English Congregationalism*, pp. 654–59.

[40] Charles S. Parker, *Life and Letters of Sir James Graham*, vol. 1 (London: John Murray, 1907), p. 344.

[41] Dale, *History of English Congregationalism*, p. 661.

[42] *Eclectic Review*, n.s. 13 (January–June 1843): 698.

Thousands of petitions with over 2 million signatures were presented to the House in opposition to the Factories Education Bill, whereupon Graham submitted amendments in an effort to appease the Dissenters. But to no avail. Petitions against the amended clauses contained nearly another 2 million signatures, and the measure was withdrawn.

It was during this agitation that support by Dissenters for state aid to education (provided it did not involve interference) transformed into opposition to all such aid. Edward Baines, Jr.—editor of the *Leeds Mercury*, the most influential provincial newspaper in England—described the transition:

> The dangerous bill of Sir James Graham, and the evidence brought out of the ability and disposition of the people to supply the means of education, combined to convince the editors of the *Mercury* that it is far safer and better for Government not to interfere at all in the work; and from that time forward they distinctly advocated that view.[43]

The Voluntaryist philosophy crystallized quickly. In meetings of the Congregational Union held in Leeds (October 1843), Baines articulated the basic arguments against state education that he would develop in more detail over the next 20 years.[44] The Congregational Union officially declared itself in favor of

---

[43] Edward Baines, Jr., *Life of Edward Baines* (London: Longman, Brown, Green, and Longmans, 1851), p. 315.

[44] Dale, *History of English Congregationalism*, pp. 659–60.

voluntary education.[45] An education conference held at the Congregational Union in Leeds (December 1843) resolved that "all funds confided to the disposal of the central committee, in aid of schools, be granted only to schools sustained entirely by voluntary contributions."[46]

By 1846 the majority of Congregationalists and Baptists supported voluntary education.[47] Leading newspapers and journals of the Dissenters—such as the *Leeds Mercury*, the *Nonconformist*, and the *Eclectic Review*—argued the case for Voluntaryism. Many Voluntaryists were active in the Anti–Corn Law League (which led a successful campaign to abolish import tariffs on grain), and they applied the principles of free trade to education. Voluntaryists energetically disputed reports that purported to show the deplorable condition of voluntary schools,[48] and they accused government

---

[45] R. Tudor Jones, *Congregationalism in England, 1662–1962* (London: Independent Press, 1962), p. 212.

[46] Dale, *History of English Congregationalism*, p. 661.

[47] This was the opinion of R. W. Dale (ibid., p. 633), a prominent Dissenter who opposed Voluntaryism. An article in *The British Quarterly Review* (probably written by Robert Vaughan) questioned whether Voluntaryism was as widespread among Dissenters as its supporters claimed: "We doubt much if there will be a single county union of Congregationalists in England that will not present considerable difference of judgment in reference to this question." Among the supporters of state education Vaughan listed were "Churchmen in England and Scotland; Free churchmen and Methodists in both countries; the bulk of Dissenters north of the Tweed, and a considerable number south of it; together with the whole body of British Catholics;—all our great political parties, moreover,—Tories, Whigs, Radicals, and the Chartist and Working Classes." Robert Vaughan?, "The Education Controversy," *British Quarterly Review* 6 (August–November 1847): 544–45.

[48] See Edward Baines, Jr., *The Social, Educational, and Religious State of the Manufacturing Districts* (New York: Augustus Kelly, [1843] 1969).

committees of misrepresenting facts and distorting evidence to buttress their case for government interference.[49]

Not all Dissenters supported Voluntaryism, of course; some Nonconformist journals, such as the *British Quarterly Review*, attacked Voluntaryism vigorously. In addition, some Manchester free-trade advocates (most notably Richard Cobden) were active in the movement for state secular education, creating a serious rift among British liberals. Indeed, in 1848 Cobden remarked that "education is the main cause of the split among the middle-class Liberals."[50]

> In Leeds the question was whether the State should intervene at all, while in Manchester it concerned the form that intervention should take. . . . Leeds imposed a prescriptive ban upon state education per se; Manchester sought to define the proper goals of a state education scheme that was both necessary and desirable.[51]

One important Voluntaryist was Herbert Spencer (1820–1903), the leading libertarian philosopher of his day. Although Spencer became an agnostic, he was home-schooled in Dissenting causes by his father and uncle. "Our family was essentially a *dissenting* family," Spencer wrote in later life, "and dissent is an expression of

---

[49] See, for example, Henry Richard, "On the Progress and Efficacy of Voluntary Education, as Exemplified in Wales," in *Crosby-Hall Lectures on Education* (London: John Snow, 1848), pp. 171–224.

[50] John Morley, *The Life of Richard Cobden* (London: T. Fisher Unwin, 1906), p. 495.

[51] Derek Fraser, *Urban Politics in Victorian Cities: The Structure of Politics in Victorian Cities* (Leicester, U.K.: Leicester University, 1976), p. 272.

antagonism to arbitrary control." Much of Spencer's first political article, written in his early 20s and published in the *Nonconformist* in 1842, was devoted to a critique of state education, and it possibly influenced the birth of the Voluntaryist movement in the following year.[52]

Other prominent Dissenters who campaigned for Voluntaryism were Joseph Sturge (1793–1859), a Quaker pacifist who played an important role in the antislavery movement; Samuel Morley (1809–1886); Andrew Reed (1787–1862); Henry Richard (1812–1888); Edward Miall (1809–1881); and the previously mentioned Edward Baines, Jr. (1800–1890). Of these men, Miall and Baines

---

[52] Herbert Spencer, "The Filiation of Ideas," in *The Life and Letters of Herbert Spencer*, ed. David Duncan (London: Williams and Norgate, 1911), p. 537. Spencer's series of articles, *The Proper Sphere of Government*, appeared in 12 parts, beginning on June 15, 1842. Did Spencer's critique of state education contribute substantially to the Voluntaryist movement? According to Raymond Cowherd, "Spencer constructed a new political platform to combine economists, Radicals, and Dissenters. . . . The political events of 1843, seeming to confirm Spencer's conclusions, impelled the Dissenters towards a more extreme voluntaryism." Raymond Cowherd, *The Politics of English Dissent* (New York: New York University Press, 1956), pp. 157–58. Cf. G.I.T. Machin, "The Maynooth Grant, the Dissenters and Disestablishment, 1845–1847," *English Historical Review* 82, no. 322 (1967): 66. Machin agreed that Spencer "provided the extreme Voluntaries with a political philosophy." Unfortunately, neither Cowherd nor Machin provided documentation to show that Spencer's early writing had a significant impact on the Voluntaryist movement. Spencer indicated that Edward Miall (editor of the *Nonconformist*) was impressed enough to say that "if the *Nonconformist* had had a more extensive circulation he should have been happy to have offered me a share in the editorship"; Spencer, *Life and Letters*, p. 38. Miall recommended Spencer to Thomas Price as a possible contributor to the *Eclectic Review*, to which Spencer contributed an article on education. (The article was accepted but never published.) Thus, it is safe to say that the young Spencer was admired by leading Dissenters who were to become prominent in the Voluntaryist causes, but I have been unable to find any proof of direct influence.

were the most important. Edward Miall founded and edited the *Nonconformist*, one of the most important Dissenting periodicals of its day. Miall was a tireless campaigner for both the separation of church and state and the separation of school and state. Edward Baines, Jr.—for many years editor of the influential *Leeds Mercury*—was the driving force behind Voluntaryism after 1843. Through Baines's many pamphlets and articles, which combined theoretical arguments with detailed statistics, the case for Voluntaryism reached a wide audience throughout Britain.[53]

IV

Liberty was a basic concern of all Voluntaryists. Dissenters saw themselves in the tradition of John Milton, Algernon Sidney, and John Locke—defenders of individual rights and foes of oppressive government. Religious liberty in particular—freedom of conscience—was viewed as the great heritage of the Dissenting tradition, any violation of which should call forth "stern and indomitable resistance."[54]

---

[53] In 1845, when the Committee of the British and Foreign School Society decided to continue accepting government aid, Sturge (a successful businessman) withdrew his support, stating that "a small annual Government grant may make the recipient subservient to the State"; see Henry Richard, *Memoirs of Joseph Sturge* (London: S. W. Partridge, 1864), pp. 336–39. On Miall, see Arthur Miall, *Life of Edward Miall* (London: Macmillan, 1884); William H. Mackintosh, *Disestablishment and Liberation* (London: Epworth Press, 1972); and David M. Thompson, "The Liberation Society," in *Pressure from Without in Early Victorian England*, ed. Patricia Hollis (London: Edward Arnold, 1974), pp. 210–38. On the younger Baines, see Derek Fraser, "Edward Baines," in *Pressure from Without*, ed. Patricia Hollis (London: Edward Arnold, 1974), pp. 183–209. Cf. Fraser, *Urban Politics*.

[54] *Eclectic Review*, n.s. 13 (January–June 1843): 576.

Liberty should not be sacrificed for a greater good, argued the Dissenting minister and Voluntaryist Richard Hamilton: "There is no greater good. There can be no greater good! It is not simply means, it is an end."[55] Education is best promoted by freedom, but should there ever be a conflict, "liberty is more precious than education." "We love education," Hamilton stated, "but there are things which we love better."[56] Edward Baines agreed that education is not the ultimate good: "Liberty is far more precious." It is essential to "all the virtues which dignify men and communities."[57]

The preservation of individual freedom, according to most Voluntaryists, is the only legitimate function of government. The purpose of government, wrote Herbert Spencer in "The Proper Sphere of Government" (1842), is "to defend the natural rights of man—to protect person and property—to prevent the aggressions of the powerful upon the weak; in a word, to administer justice." Edward Miall agreed that government is "an organ for the protection of life, liberty, and property; or, in other words, for the administration of justice."[58]

Government, an ever-present danger to liberty, must be watched with vigilance and suspicion. "The true lover of liberty," stated the

[55] Richard Winter Hamilton, *The Institutions of Popular Education* (London: Hamilton, Adams, 1845), p. 266.

[56] Richard Winter Hamilton, "On the Parties Responsible for the Education of the People," in *Crosby-Hall Lectures on Education* (London: John Snow, 1848), p. 77.

[57] Baines, *Letters to the Right Hon. Lord John Russell, on State Education* (London: Ward & Co, 1847), p. 76.

[58] Herbert Spencer, "The Proper Sphere of Government," in *Political Writings*, ed. John Offer (Cambridge University Press, 1994) p. 7.

Eclectic Review, "will jealously examine all the plans and measures of government."

> He will seldom find himself called to help it, and to weigh down its scale. He will watch its increase of power with distrust. He will specially guard against conceding to it any thing which might be otherwise done. He would deprecate its undertaking of bridges, highways, railroads. He would foresee the immense mischief of its direction of hospitals and asylums. Government has enough on its hands—its own proper functions—nor need it to be overborne. There is a class of governments which are called paternal. . . . They exact a soulless obedience. . . . Nothing breathes and stirs. . . . The song of liberty is forgotten. . . . And when such governments tamper with education, the tyranny, instead of being relieved, is eternized.[59]

Government is "essentially immoral," wrote Spencer in *Social Statics*, and with this many Voluntaryists agreed. A government has only those rights delegated to it by individuals, and "it is for each to say whether he will employ such an agent or not." Every person, therefore, has "the right to ignore the state."[60] The source of political authority is the people, argued Hamilton, and the people may revise or even "outlaw the State."[61]

Voluntaryists' concern for liberty can scarcely be exaggerated. Schemes of state education were denounced repeatedly as

---

[59] *Eclectic Review*, n.s. 20 (July–December 1846): 291.

[60] Herbert Spencer, *Social Statics* New York: Schalkenbach, [1851] 1954), pp. 185–86.

[61] Hamilton, "On the Parties Responsible," p. 82.

"the knell of English freedom," an "assault on our constitutional liberties," and so forth. Plans for government inspection of schools were likened to "government *surveillance*" and "universal *espionage*" that display "the *police* spirit." And compulsory education was described as "child-kidnapping." Educational freedom is "a sacred thing" because it is "an essential branch of civil freedom." "A system of state-education," declared Baines, "is a vast intellectual police, set to watch over the young at the most critical period of their existence, to prevent the intrusion of dangerous thoughts, and turn their minds into safe channels." [62]

Contrary to later historians, who were to portray Voluntaryism as a battle for narrow sectarian interests, the Voluntaryists insisted that crucial moral and political principles were at stake. "The crisis involves larger interests than those of dissent," stated the *Eclectic Review*. The threat that state education poses to individual freedom is sufficient ground to "take up a position of most determined hostility to it." [63] The Voluntaryists often drew parallels between educational freedom, on the one hand, and religious freedom, freedom of the press, and other civil liberties, on the other hand. As Baines noted, "We cannot violate the principles of liberty in regard to education, without furnishing at once a

[62] *Eclectic Review*, n.s. 13 (January–June 1843): 581; *Eclectic Review*, n.s. 21 (January–June 1847): 507; Baines quoted in n. s. 21, page 363; Baines, *Letters to Russell*, p. 124; *Eclectic Review*, n.s. 20 (July–December, 1846): 303; Baines quoted in *Eclectic Review*, n.s. 21 (January–June, 1847): 363; and Baines, *Letters to Russell*, p. 72.

[63] *Eclectic Review*, n.s. 21 (January–June 1847): 507.

precedent and an inducement to violate them in regard to other matters." He continued:

> In my judgment, the State could not consistently assume the support and control of education, without assuming the support and control of both the *pulpit* and the *press*. Once decide that Government money and Government superintendence are essential in the schools, whether to insure efficiency, or to guard against abuse, ignorance, and error, and the self-same reasons will force you to apply Government money and Government superintendence to our periodical literature and our religious instruction.[64]

Baines realized that a government need not carry the principle inherent in state education to its logical extreme, but he was disturbed by a precedent that gave to government the power of molding minds. If, as the proponents of state education had argued, state education was required to promote civic virtue and moral character, then "where, acting on these principles, could you consistently stop?" He asked:

> Would not the same paternal care which is exerted to provide schools, schoolmasters, and school-books, be justly extended to provide mental food for the adult, and to guard against his food being poisoned? In short, would not the principle clearly justify *the appointment of the Ministers of Religion, and a Censorship of the Press?*[65]

[64] Baines, *Letters to Russell*, pp. 73–74.
[65] Ibid., p. 8.

Baines conceded that there were deficiencies and imperfections in the system of voluntary education, but freedom should not be abrogated on this account. Again he pointed to the example of a free press. A free press has many "defects and abuses"; certainly not all the products of a free press are praiseworthy. But if liberty is to be sacrificed in education in order to remedy deficiencies, then why not regulate and censor the press for the same reason? Baines employed this analogy in his brilliant rejoinder to the charge that he was an advocate of "bad schools":

> In one sense I am. I maintain that we have as much right to have wretched schools as to have wretched newspapers, wretched preachers, wretched books, wretched institutions, wretched political economists, wretched Members of Parliament, and wretched Ministers. You cannot proscribe all these things without proscribing Liberty. The man is a simpleton who says, that to advocate Liberty is to advocate badness. The man is a quack and a *doctrinaire* of the worst German breed, who would attempt to force all minds, whether individual or national, into a mould of ideal perfection,—to stretch it out or to lop it down to his own Procrustean standard. I maintain that Liberty is the chief cause of excellence; but it would cease to be Liberty if you proscribed everything inferior. Cultivate giants if you please, but do not stifle dwarfs.[66]

---

[66] Edward Baines, Jr., "On the Progress and Efficiency of Voluntary Education in England," in *Crosby-Hall Lectures on Education* (London: John Snow, 1848), p. 39.

Freedom of conscience was precious to liberal Dissenters, and they feared government encroachment in this realm, even in the guise of "secular" education. The *Eclectic Review*, using arguments similar to those of Baines, stressed the relationship between religious freedom and educational freedom. Advocates of state education claimed that parents have the duty to provide their children with education and that the state has the right to enforce this duty. But parents have a duty to provide religious and moral instruction as well. "Are we then prepared to maintain . . . that government should interpose, in this case, to supply what the parent has failed to communicate? . . . If sound in the one case, it is equally so in the other."[67]

To the many state-school advocates who pointed to the Prussian system as a model, Baines retorted: "Nearly all the Continental Governments which pay and direct the school, pay and direct also the pulpit and the press. They do it consistently."[68] This is the potential "despotism" that Baines feared and loathed.

V

A common prediction of Voluntaryists was that government would employ education for its own ends, especially to instill deference and obedience in citizens. The radical individualist William Godwin, author of *Enquiry Concerning Political Justice* (1793), was among the first to express this concern. The "project of a national education ought uniformly to be discouraged," he wrote, "on account of its obvious alliance with national Government

---

[67] *Eclectic Review*, n.s. 13 (January–June, 1843): 579.

[68] Baines, *Letters to Russell*, p. 8.

[which] will not fail to employ it to strengthen its hands, and perpetuate its institutions."[69]

With the consolidation of Dissenting opposition to state education, the Godwinian warning was frequently repeated and elaborated on. This passage from the *Eclectic Review* is typical:

> It is no trifling thing to commit to any hands the mould-ing of the minds of men. An immense power is thus communicated, the tendency of which will be in exact accordance with the spirit and policy of those who use it. Governments, it is well known, are conservative. The tendency of official life is notorious, and it is the height of folly, the mere vapouring of credulity, to imagine that the educational system, if entrusted to the minister of the day, will not be employed to diffuse amongst the rising generation, that spirit and those views which are most friendly to his policy. By having, virtually, at his com-mand, the whole machinery of education, he will cover the land with a new class of officials, whose dependence on his patronage will render them the ready instruments of his pleasure.[70]

Government education, this writer feared, would produce "an emasculated and servile generation." A possible advance in literacy

[69] William Godwin, *Enquiry Concerning Political Justice and Its Influence on Morals and Happiness*, vol. 2, 3rd ed., ed. F. E. L. Priestley (Toronto: University of Toronto Press, [1797] 1946), p. 302.

[70] *Eclectic Review*, n.s. 13 (January–June 1843): 580.

would be purchased at the price of man's "free spirit." Elsewhere the *Eclectic Review* compared state schools to "barracks" and their employees to "troops." "The accession of power and patronage to that government which establishes such a national system of education, can scarcely be gauged."[71] Teachers paid by a government will owe allegiance to that government.

> What a host of stipendiaries will thus be created! And who shall say what will be their influence in the course of two generations? All their sympathies will be with the powers by whom they are paid, on whose favor they live, and from whose growing patronage their hopes of improving their condition are derived. As constitutional Englishmen, we tremble at the result. The danger is too imminent, the hazard too great, to be incurred, for any temporary stimulus which government interference can minister to education. We eschew it as alike disastrous in its results and unsound in its theory—the criminal attempt of short-sighted or flagitious politicians, to mold the intellect of the people to their pleasure.[72]

Indoctrination is inherent in state education, according to Edward Baines. State education proceeds from the principle that "it is the duty of a Government to train the Mind of the People." If one denies to government this right—as defenders of a free press and free religion must logically do—then one must also deny the

[71] *Eclectic Review,* n.s. 20 (July–December 1846): 291.
[72] *Eclectic Review,* n.s. 21 (January–June 1847): 359.

right of government to meddle in education. It "is not the duty or province of the Government to train the mind of the people," argued Baines, and this "principle of the highest moment" forbids state education.[73]

Herbert Spencer agreed. State education, he wrote in *Social Statics* (1851), will inevitably involve indoctrination.

> For what is meant by saying that a government ought to educate the people? Why should they be educated? What is the education for? Clearly, to fit the people for social life—to make them good citizens. And who is to say what are good citizens? The government: there is no other judge. And who is to say how these good citizens may be made? The government: there is no other judge. Hence the proposition is convertible into this—a government ought to mold children into good citizens, using its own discretion in settling what a good citizen is and how a child may be molded into one.[74]

Indoctrination was an issue that troubled even some proponents of state education. A case in point is William Lovett, the Chartist radical who is frequently praised as an early champion of state education. In his *Address on Education* (1837), Lovett maintained that it is "the duty of Government to establish *for all classes* the best possible system of education." Education should be provided "not as a charity, *but as a right*." How was the British government

[73] Baines, *Letters to Russell*, pp. 7, 10.
[74] Spencer, *Social Statics*, p. 297.

to discharge this duty? By providing funds for the erection and maintenance of schools. Lovett desired government financing *without* government control: "we are decidedly opposed to placing such immense power and influence in the hands of Government as that of selecting the teachers and superintendents, the books and kinds of instruction, and the whole management of schools in each locality." Lovett detested state systems, such as that found in Prussia, "where the lynx-eyed satellites of power . . . crush in embryo the buddings of freedom." State control of education "prostrates the whole nation before one uniform . . . despotism."[75]

Several years later Lovett became less sanguine about the prospect of government financing without government control. While still upholding in theory the duty of government to provide education, he so distrusted his own government that he called on the working classes to reject government proposals and to "commence the great work of education yourselves." The working classes had "everything to fear" from schools established by their own government, so Lovett outlined a proposal whereby schools could be provided through voluntary means, free from state patronage and control.[76]

We see a similar concern with indoctrination in the work of the celebrated philosopher John Stuart Mill. Mill contended that education "is one of those things which it is admissible in principle that a government should provide for the people," although

---

[75] William Lovett, *Life and Struggles of William Lovett*, vol. 1, ed. R. H. Tawney (New York: Alfred A. Knopf, 1920), pp. 139–43.

[76] William Lovett and John Collins, *Chartism: A New Organization for the People* (New York: Humanities Press, [1840] 1969), p. 63 ff.

he favored a system in which only those who could not afford to pay would be exempt from fees.[77] Parents who failed to provide elementary education for their children committed a breach of duty, so the state could compel parents to provide instruction. But where and how children were taught should be up to the parents; the state should merely enforce minimal educational standards through a series of public examinations. Thus did Mill attempt to escape the frightening prospect of government indoctrination. At this point, he began to sound like an ardent Voluntaryist:

> That the whole or any large part of the education of the people should be in State hands, I go as far as any one in deprecating. . . . A general State education is a mere contrivance for moulding people to be exactly like one another: and as the mould in which it casts them is that which pleases the predominant power in the government . . . in proportion as it is efficient and successful, it establishes a despotism over the mind, leading by a natural tendency to one over the body.[78]

Dissenters who favored state education were also sensitive to the problem of indoctrination, but many thought that the danger could be avoided by confining state schools to secular subjects. The Voluntaryists disagreed, and they repudiated all attempts at compromise. Government aid, however small and innocent at first, was bound to be followed by government strings. Government aid is "a *trap* and a *snare*," declared the *Eclectic Review*. It is "a wretched

---

[77] John Stuart Mill, *Principles of Political Economy*, vol. 2, 5th ed. (New York: Appleton, 1899), p. 574.

[78] John Stuart Mill, *On Liberty*, ed. David Spitz (New York: Norton, 1975), pp. 98–99.

bribe" that, if accepted, "will have irretrievably disgraced us."[79] The question is not, "How can we obtain Government money?" wrote Algernon Wells, "but, How can we avoid it?" Wells continued with a fascinating observation:

> [Dissenters] must ever be equally free to act and speak. They must hold themselves entirely clear of all temptation to ask, when their public testimony is required— How will our conduct affect our grants? The belief of many Independents is that, from the hour they received Government money, they would be a changed people— their tone lowered—their spirit altered—their consistency sacrificed—and their honour tarnished.[80]

Perhaps Edward Baines, Jr., best summarized the sentiment of the Voluntaryists: "When Governments offer their arm, it is like the arm of a creditor or a constable, not so easily shaken off: there is a handcuff at the end of it."[81] The lesson was clear. Educational freedom is incompatible with state support. If government control and manipulation of education are to be avoided, financial independence and integrity must be maintained.

VI

Another recurring theme of Voluntaryism was the need for diversity in education. Voluntaryists warned that state education

---

[79] *Eclectic Review*, n.s. 20 (July–December 1846): 297–98.

[80] Algernon Wells, "On the Education of the Working Classes," in *Crosby-Hall Lectures on Education* (London: John Snow, 1848), p. 65.

[81] Baines, *Letters to Russell*, p. 120.

would impose a dulling uniformity that would result, at best, in mediocrity. This lack of diversity in education was a primary concern of the 18th-century Dissenter Joseph Priestley. Education is an art, and like any art it requires many "experiments and trials" before it can approach perfection, he noted. To bring government into education would freeze this art at its present stage and thereby "cut off its future growth." Education "is already under too many legal restraints. Let these be removed." The purpose of education is not simply to promote the interests of the state but rather to produce "wise and virtuous men." Progress in this area requires "unbounded liberty, and even caprice." Life—especially human life—requires diversity to improve. Variety induces innovation and improvement. "From new and seemingly irregular methods of education, perhaps something extraordinary and uncommonly great may spring." The "great excellence of human nature consists in the variety of which it is capable. Instead, then, of endeavouring, by uniform and fixed systems of education, to keep mankind always the same, let us give free scope to everything which may bid fair for introducing more variety among us."[82]

Godwin expressed similar concerns. State institutions resist change and innovation. "They actively restrain the flights of mind, and fix it in the belief of exploded errors." Government bureaucracies entrench themselves and resist change, so we cannot look to them for progress. State education "has always expended its energies in the support of prejudice.[83]

[82] Joseph Priestley, *Priestley's Writings on Philosophy, Science, and Politics*, ed. John A. Passmore (New York: Collier, 1965), pp. 306–9.

[83] Godwin, *Enquiry Concerning Political Justice*, vol. 2, pp. 298–99.

The deleterious effects of intellectual and cultural uniformity were also of great concern to Herbert Spencer, who developed a theory of social progress based on increasing social diversity. National education "necessarily assumes that a uniform system of instruction is desirable," and this Spencer denied. Unlimited variety is the key to progress. Truth itself—"the bright spark that emanates from the collision of opposing ideas"—is endangered by a coerced uniformity. The "uniform routine" of state education will produce "an approximation to a national model." People will begin to think and act alike, and the youth will be pressed "as nearly as possible into one common mould." Without diversity and competition among educational systems, education will stagnate and intellectual progress will be severely retarded.[84]

According to Spencer, it is because individuals vary widely in their capacities, needs, and skills that we need a variety of educational systems from which to choose. The flexibility of competing systems allows the individual something suited to his or her individual requirements. This flexibility is provided in a free market where teachers are answerable to the public. Conversely, in a state system, teachers are "answerable only to some superior officer, and having no reputation and livelihood to stimulate them," they have little motivation to consider the individual needs of their students. Education becomes uniformly gray. Hence "in education as in everything else, the principle of honourable competition is the

[84] Herbert Spencer, "The Proper Sphere of Government," *Nonconformist*, October 19, 1842, p. 700.

only one that can give present satisfaction or hold out promise of future perfection."[85]

Edward Baines also warned that a uniform state education would obstruct progress. It would serve to "stereotype the methods of teaching, to bolster up old systems, and to prevent improvement." If we left education to the market, we would see continual improvements. "But let it once be monopolized by a Government department, and thenceforth reformers must prepare to be martyrs."[86] Algernon Wells made a similar point:

> How to teach, how to improve children, are questions admitting of new and advanced solutions, no less than inquiries how best to cultivate the soil, or to perfect manufactures. And these improvements cannot fail to proceed indefinitely, so long as education is kept wide open, and free to competition, and to all those impulses which liberty constantly supplies. But once close up this great science and movement of mind from these invigorating breezes, whether by monopoly or bounty, whether by coercion or patronage, and the sure result will be torpor and stagnancy.[87]

---

[85] Ibid. Spencer's contempt for uniformity remained with him throughout his life. In 1892, he complained of "a mania for uniformity, which I regard as most mischievous. Uniformity brings death, variety brings life; and I resist all movements towards uniformity." In 1897, Spencer again referred to the "mania everywhere for uniformity," and he argued that "competition in methods of education is all essential and anything that tends to diminish competition will be detrimental." Spencer, *Life and Letters*, pp. 315, 404.

[86] Baines, "On the Progress and Efficiency," pp. 42–43; Baines, *Letters to Russell*, p. 53.

[87] Wells, "On the Education of the Working Classes," p. 60.

The *Eclectic Review*, protesting that the "unitive design" of state education "would make all think alike," continued with a chilling account of uniformity:

> All shall be straightened as by the schoolmaster's ruler, and transcribed from his copy. He shall decide what may or may not be asked. But he must be *normalized himself.* He must be fashioned to a model. He shall only be taught particular things. The compress and tourniquet are set on his mind. He can only be suffered to think one way. . . . All schools will be filled with the same books. All teachers will be imbued with the same spirit. And under their cold and lifeless tuition, the national spirit, now warm and independent, will grow into a type formal and dull, one harsh outline with its crisp edges, a mere complex machine driven by external impulse, with it appendages of apparent power but of gross resistance. If any man loves that national monotony, thinks it the just position of his nature, can survey the tame and sluggish spectacle with delight, he, on the adoption of such a system, has his reward.[88]

Auberon Herbert also cautioned against the "evils of uniformity." Like his mentor Herbert Spencer, he thought that "all influences which tend towards uniform thought and action in education are most fatal to any regularly continuous improvement."[89] Imagine the effect of state uniformity in religion, art, or

[88] *Eclectic Review*, n.s. 20 (July–December 1846): 290.

[89] Auberon Herbert, *The Sacrifice of Education to Examination* (London: Williams & Norgate, 1889), p. 191.

science. Progress would grind to a halt. Education is no different. "Therefore, if you desire progress, you must not make it difficult for men to think and act differently; you must not dull their sense with routine or stamp their imagination with the official pattern of some great department."[90]

As a former member of parliament, Herbert was especially sensitive to the difficulty of implementing change in a bureaucratic structure. A free market encourages innovation and risk taking. An innovator with new ideas on education can, if left legally unhampered, solicit aid from those sympathetic to his views and then test his product on the market.

> But if some great official system blocks the way, if he has to overcome the stolid resistance of a department, to persuade a political party, which has no sympathy with views holding out no promise of political advantage, to satisfy inspectors, whose eyes are trained to see perfection of only one kind, and who may summarily condemn his school as "inefficient" and therefore disallowed by law, if in the meantime he is obliged by rates and taxes to support a system to which he is opposed, it becomes unlikely that this energy and confidence in his own views will be sufficient to inspire a successful resistance to such obstacles.[91]

---

[90] Auberon Herbert, "State Education: A Help or Hindrance," *Popular Science Monthly*, September 1880, p. 68.

[91] Ibid., pp. 68–69.

VII

Voluntaryists prized social diversity (or what we call today a "pluralistic society"), and they believed that state education would impose the dead hand of uniformity. Rather than giving to government the power to decide among conflicting beliefs and values, they preferred to leave beliefs and values to the unfettered competition of the market. One must appreciate this broad conception of the free market, which includes far more than tangible goods, if one wishes to understand the passionate commitment of many liberals to competition and their unbridled hatred of governmental interference. They believed that coercive intervention, whatever its supposed justification, actually served special interests and enhanced the power of government. The various campaigns against government were therefore seen as battles to establish free markets in religion, commerce, education, and other spheres.

British libertarians had a long heritage of opposition to state patronage and monopoly, reaching back to the Levellers of the early 17th century. The Voluntaryists, like their libertarian ancestors, believed that government interference in the market, whatever its supposed justification, actually serves special interests and enhances the power of government, thereby furthering the goals of those within the government. The various struggles against government intervention were seen by Voluntaryists as battles to establish free markets in religion, commerce, and education. It was not uncommon to find the expression "free trade in religion" among supporters of church-state separation; when the editor of the *Manchester Guardian* stated in 1820 that religion should be a "marketable commodity," he was expressing the standard libertarian position.[92]

When fellow free traders, such as Richard Cobden, supported state education, the Voluntaryists took them to task for their inconsistency. Those who embrace free trade in religion and commerce but advocate state interference in education, argued Thomas Hodgskin (senior editor of *The Economist*) in 1847, "do not fully appreciate the principles on which they have been induced to act."[93] "We only wonder that they should have so soon forgotten their free-trade catechism," wrote another Voluntaryist, "and lent their sanction to any measure of monopoly."[94]

Before free traders ask for state interference in education, Hodgskin argued, "they ought to prove that its interference with trade has been beneficial." But this, by their own admission, they cannot do. They know that the effect of state interference with trade has always been "to derange, paralyze, and destroy it." Hodgskin maintained that the principle of free trade "is as applicable to education as to the manufacture of cotton or the supply of corn." The state is unable to advance material wealth for the people through intervention, and there is even less reason to suppose it capable of advancing "immaterial wealth" in the form of knowledge. Any "protectionist" scheme in regard to knowledge should be opposed by all who understand the principle of competition. *Laissez-faire* in education is "the only

[92] Quoted in Norman Gash, *Reaction and Reconstruction in English Politics, 1832–1852* (Oxford, U.K.: Clarendon Press, 1965), p. 64, n. 1.

[93] *The Economist*, April 3, 1847, p. 380.

[94] *Eclectic Review*, n.s. 22 (July–December 1847): 598.

means of ensuring that improved and extended education which we all desire."[95]

The *Eclectic Review* posed the basic question: Can education "be best produced by monopoly or by competition?"—and it came down unequivocally on the side of competition. Education is a "marketable commodity," and demand for it is "as much subject to the principles and laws of political economy, as are corn or cotton." Government intervention, in education as elsewhere, causes market distortions.

> How will it affect the balance between the demand and the supply; disturb the relations of the voluntary teacher, and misdirect the expectations and confidence of the market? Let a private teacher attempt to come into competition with such accredited and endowed agents of an incorporate system . . . and he will find himself in the same state with a merchant who ventures to trade without a bounty in competition with those whose traffic is encouraged by large public bounties.[96]

Voluntaryists predicted that state aid to education would drive many voluntary schools out of business. Market schools would find themselves unable to compete with schools financed from taxes, and philanthropists who had previously contributed to education would withhold their funds, believing that, because

[95] Thomas Hodgskin, "Shall the State Educate the People?" *The Economist*, April 3, 1847, p. 381.

[96] *Eclectic Review*, n.s. 22 (July–December 1847): 592, 596, 607.

the state would provide education anyway, there was no need for charitable support. As state aid increased, market education would diminish, and this consequence would be used to support the contention that voluntary education had failed.

An educational bureaucracy, however tiny at its inception, would grow rapidly. An educational orthodoxy with employees answerable to the government would emerge. Costs would increase, and productivity would decrease. "Public servants," wrote one Voluntaryist, "are sustained at the largest cost, and always are subject to the least responsibility." The principle of the market, to produce "the best article . . . at the cheapest price," would disappear in a state system. In an educational free market, on the contrary, a "real and effectual discipline" is exercised over educators by consumers.[97] Free-market schools must either satisfy their customers or go out of business.

In calling for *laissez-faire* in education, Voluntaryists squared off against the major economists of their day, most of whom advocated some role for government.[98] John Stuart Mill, for example, opposed leaving education to the market: "In the matter of education, the intervention of government is justifiable, because the

[97] Ibid., pp. 609, 611.

[98] On the classical economists and state education, see William Miller, "The Economics of Education in English Classical Economics," *Southern Economic Journal* 32, no. 3 (1966): 294–309; Mark Blaug, "The Economics of Education in English Classical Political Economy: A Re-examination," *Essays on Adam Smith*, ed. Andrew S. Skinner and Thomas Wilson (Oxford, U.K.: Oxford University Press, 1975), pp. 568–99; and E.G. West, *Education and the State* (London: Institute of Economic Affairs, 1965), pp. 111–25.

case is not one in which the interest and judgment of the consumer are a sufficient security for the goodness of the commodity." Mill continued:

> The uncultivated cannot be competent judges of education. Those who must need to be made wiser and better, usually desire it least, and if they desired it, would be incapable of finding the way to it by their own lights. It will continually happen, on the voluntary system, that, the end not being desired, the means will not be provided at all, or that, the persons requiring improvement having an imperfect or altogether erroneous conception of what they want, the supply called for by the demand of the market will be anything but what is really required.[99]

Voluntaryists responded impatiently to this elitist argument. They had encountered the same argument many times before during their campaigns for religious freedom. With man's eternal soul at stake, defenders of a state church maintained that religion is far too important to be left to the untutored judgment of the masses. "It is the old dogma," wrote the dissenting minister Algernon Wells, "the people can know nothing about religion and it must be dictated to them."[100] Wells contended that the argument from incompetence, if used to defend state education,

[99] Mill, *Principles of Political Economy*, vol. 2, pp. 573, 577.
[100] Wells, "On the Education of the Working Classes," p. 77.

must also justify state interference in religion. The fact that some fellow libertarians failed to understand the ominous implications of Mill's argument obviously annoyed the Voluntaryists.

In *Social Statics* (1851), Herbert Spencer dismissed Mill's argument as "a worn-out excuse" that had been repeatedly trotted out to justify "all state interferences whatever."

> A stock argument for the state teaching of religion has been that the masses cannot distinguish false religion from true. There is hardly a single department of life over which, for similar reasons, legislative supervision has not been, or may not be, established.[101]

Spencer questioned whether parents are as incompetent to assess education as Mill alleged. Parents, far more than government, are concerned about the welfare of their children, and uneducated parents can seek advice from others whom they trust. Even granting problems in this area, however, it does not follow that the state should intervene. As a market for mass education developed, Spencer believed that consumers would gain the knowledge that comes with experience and thereby become more sophisticated in their choice of products. Social improvement takes time, and Spencer thought that "this incompetence of the masses to distinguish good instruction from bad is being outgrown."[102]

---

[101] Spencer, *Social Statics*, p. 300.
[102] Ibid., p. 302.

Spencer contended that Mill's argument is based on a false premise. Even if the interest and judgment of consumers are insufficient to guarantee educational quality, Mill assumed that the "interest and judgment" of a government *are* sufficient security. Mill, in other words, assumed that an identity of interests exists between rulers and the people they govern.

Spencer ridiculed this tacit belief. The English government desired "a sentimental feudalism," a country where "the people shall be respectful to their betters" and an economy "with the view of making each laborer the most efficient producing tool." The interests of a government differ from the interests of the people, and "we may be quite sure that a state education would be administered for the advantage of those in power rather than for the advantage of the nation." Hence, even if we concede some inadequacies in free-market education, the problems inherent in state education are more serious and dangerous.[103]

As for the rejoinder that this objection may apply to current governments but not necessarily to an ideal government that may someday exist—a government that would presumably have the best interests of the people at heart—Spencer pointed out that Mill's argument from incompetence depends on consumers "as they now are," not on consumers as they might be in an ideal society. We should therefore consider Mill's alternative—government—"as it now is," not as it *should* be in a hypothetical paradise.

[103] Ibid., pp. 303–4.

It will not do, notwithstanding that it is all too often done, to point out problems that might arise in an imperfect market and then offer government as a solution—as if that government were itself perfect, and as if government intervention will not generate its own unique and serious problems. Spencer was inviting Mill to descend from the clouds of political theory and take a hard look at the real world of governments. All things considered, in matters of education "the interest of the consumer is not only an efficient guarantee for the goodness of the things consumed, but the best guarantee."[104]

[104] Ibid., p. 301.

1

From An Essay on the First Principles of Government

Joseph Priestley

The Second Edition, corrected and enlarged (London: J. Johnson, 1771)

The most important Voluntaryist of the eighteenth century was the Englishman Joseph Priestley (1733-1804), an accomplished and highly regarded amateur scientist who is best known for his discovery of oxygen. (He also invented soda water.) Priestley, a Nonconformist minister who called himself a "liberal Unitarian," was one of the most remarkable polymaths of the eighteenth century. A friend of Benjamin Franklin and other leading scientists, Priestley wrote over 150 books on an astonishing range of subjects, including philosophy, science, theology, grammar, European history, the history of Christianity, and new methods of education.

Priestley also wrote one of the finest and most consistent libertarian tracts of the eighteenth century, *An Essay on the First Principles of Government* (1771), which included a previously published piece, *Remarks on Dr. Brown's Code of Education.* It is here that we find Priestley's trenchant criticism of state education. This is the part from which our selection is taken. Dr. John Brown was a popular author who wrote several books bemoaning the supposed decadence of English culture. In *Thoughts on Civil Liberty,* Brown repeatedly invoked the Spartan model of uniform and compulsory state education as a remedy for England's problems. Priestley, who believed that diversity and competition are essential preconditions of progress (most notably the progress of knowledge), would have none of this. Sparta was "the worst government we read of" in the ancient world, "a government which secured to a man the fewest of his natural rights, and of which a man who had a taste for life would least of all choose to be a member."

Priestley understood that there must exist some fixed rules in every society, but, as an advocate of limited government, he maintained that governmental institutions, which ultimately rely on force, should be kept to the minimum required to maintain "the tolerable order of society." Within this legal framework all social institutions—including religious, commercial, and educational activities—should be left free to develop spontaneously: "It is an universal maxim, that the more liberty is given to every thing which is in a state of growth, the more perfect it will become. . . ."

In his preface to *History and Present State of Electricity* (1767), Priestley maintained that the history of science provides the best example of the progress of human knowledge. It is here that "we see the human understanding to its greatest advantage, grasping the noblest objects, and increasing its own powers, by acquiring to itself the powers of nature, and directing them to the accomplishments of its own views; whereby the security and happiness of mankind are daily improved."

Like many Enlightenment thinkers, Priestley believed that knowledge would continue to progress indefinitely, so long as proper conditions were maintained. But unlike those many Enlightenment thinkers who recommended state education, Priestley regarded educational *freedom* as essential to progress. As he put it in *An Essay on the First Principles of Government*:

> If we argue from the analogy of education to other arts which are most similar to it, we can never expect to see human nature, about which it is employed, brought to perfection, but in consequence of indulging unbounded liberty, and even caprice in conducting it. . . . From new, and seemingly irregular methods of education, perhaps something extraordinary and uncommonly great may spring. At least there would be a fair chance of such productions; and if something odd and eccentric should, now and then, arise from this unbounded liberty of education, the various business of human life may afford proper spheres for such eccentric geniuses.

According to Priestley, "one method of education would only produce one kind of men; but the greater excellence of human nature consists in the variety of which it is capable. Instead, then, of endeavouring, by uniform and fixed systems of education, to keep mankind always the same, let us give free scope to every thing which may bid fair for introducing more variety." This emphasis on diversity and freedom as essential preconditions of educational progress would later become a major theme in the writings of nineteenth-century Voluntaryists.

SECTION IV: "In what manner an authoritative code of education would affect political and civil liberty."

Having considered the nature of civil liberty in general, I shall treat of two capital branches of which it consists. These are the rights of education, and religion. On these two articles much of the happiness of human life is acknowledged to depend; but they appear to me to be of such a nature, that the advantage we derive from them will be more effectually secured, when they are conducted by individuals, than by the state; and if this can be demonstrated, nothing more is necessary, to prove that the civil magistrate has no business to interfere with them.

This I cannot help thinking to be the shortest, and the best issue upon which we can put every thing in which the civil magistrate pretends to a right of interference. If it be probable that the business, whatever it be, will be conducted better, that is, more to the advantage of society, in his hands, than in those of individuals, the right will be allowed. In those circumstances, it is evident, that no friend to society can deny his claim. But if the nature of the thing be such, that the attention of individuals, with respect to it, can be applied to more advantage than that of the magistrate; the claim of the former must be admitted, in preference to that of the latter.

No doubt, there are examples of both kinds. The avenging of injuries, or redressing of private wrongs, is certainly better trusted in the hands of the magistrate than in those of private persons; but with what advantage could a magistrate interfere in a thousand particulars relating to private families, and private friendships? Now I think it is clear, that education must be ranked in the latter class, or among those things in which the civil magistrate has no right to interfere; because he cannot do it to any good purpose. But since Dr. Brown has lately maintained the contrary, in a treatise, intitled, *Thoughts on civil liberty, licentiousness, and faction*, and in an *Appendix relative to a proposed code of education*, subjoined to a *Sermon on the female character and education*. I shall in this section, reply to what he has advanced on this subject, and offer what has occurred to me with relation to it.

Lest it should be apprehended, that I mistake the views of this writer, I shall subjoin a few extracts from the work, which contain the substance of what he has advanced on the subject of education. He asserts, "That, the first and best security of civil liberty consists, in impressing the infant mind with such habits of thought and action, as may correspond with, and promote the appointments of public law." In his appendix, he says, that, "by a code of education, he means a system of principles, religious, moral, and political, whose tendency may be the preservation of the blessings of society, as they are enjoyed in a free state, to be instilled effectually into the infant and growing minds of the community, for this great end of public happiness."

In what manner the security of civil liberty is to be effected by means of this code of education, may be seen in the following description he gives of the institutions of Sparta. "No father had a right to educate his children according to the caprice of his own fancy. They were delivered to public officers, who initiated them early in the manners, the maxims, the exercises, the toils; in a word, in all the mental and bodily acquirements and habits which corresponded with the genius of the state. Family connections had no place. The first and leading object of their affection was the general welfare. This tuition was carefully continued till they were enrolled in the list of men."

With respect to the Athenian government, he says, page 62, "The first and ruling defect in the institution of this republic seems to have been the total want of an established education, suitable to the genius of the state. There appears not to have been any public, regular, or prescribed appointment of this kind, beyond what custom had accidentally introduced."

He says, page 70, "There were three fatal circumstances admitted into the very essence of the Roman republic, which contained the seeds of certain ruin; the first of which was, the neglect of instituting public laws, by which the education of their children might have been ascertained."

He complains, page 83, "that the British system of policy and religion is not upheld in its native power like that of Sparta, by correspondent and effectual rules of education; that it is in the power of every private man to educate his child, not only without a reverence for these, but in absolute contempt of them; that, at the revolution, p. 90, the education of youth was still left in an imperfect state; this great revolution having confined itself to the reform of public institutions, without ascending to the great fountain of political security, the private and effectual formation of the infant mind; and, p. 107, that education was afterwards left still more and more imperfect."

Lastly, he asserts, p. 156, "that the chief and essential remedy of licentiousness and faction, the fundamental means of the lasting and secure establishment of civil liberty, can only be in a general and prescribed improvement of the laws of education, to which all the members of the community should legally submit; and that for want of a prescribed code of education, the manners and principles, on which alone the state can rest, are ineffectually instilled, are vague, fluctuating and self contradictory. Nothing," he says, "is more evident, than that some reform in this great point is necessary for the security of public freedom; and that though it is an incurable defect of our political state, that it has not a correspondent and adequate code of education inwrought into its first essence; we may yet hope, that, in a secondary and inferior degree, something of this kind may still be inlaid; that, though it cannot have that perfect efficacy, as if it had been originally of the piece, yet, if well conducted, it may strengthen the weak parts, and alleviate defects, if not completely remove them."

In conducting my examination of these sentiments, I shall make no remarks upon any particular passages in the book, but consider only the author's general scheme, and the proper and professed object of it. And as the doctor has proposed no particular plan of public education, I shall be as general as he has been, and only shew the inconvenience of establishing, by law, any plan of education whatever.

This writer pleads for a plan of education established by the legislature, as the only effectual method of preventing faction in the state, and securing the perpetuity of our excellent constitution, ecclesiastical and civil. I agree with him, in acknowledging the importance of education, as influencing the manners and the conduct of men. I also acknowledge, that an uniform plan of education, agreeable to the principles of any particular form of government, civil or ecclesiastical, would tend to establish and perpetuate that form of government, and prevent civil dissentions and factions in the state. But I should object to the interference of the legislature in this business of education, as prejudicial to the proper design of education, and also to the great ends of civil societies with respect to their present utility. I shall moreover show, that it would be absolutely inconsistent with the true principles of the English government, and could not be carried into execution, to any purpose, without the ruin of our present constitution. I beg the candour of the public, while I endeavour to explain, in as few words as possible, in what manner, I apprehend, this interference of the civil magistrate would operate to obstruct these great ends; and I shall consider these articles separately.

I observed in the first place, that a legal code of education might interfere with the proper design of it. I do not mean what this writer seems to consider as the only object of education, the tranquility of the state, but the forming of wise and virtuous men; which is certainly an object of the greatest importance in every state. If the constitution of a state be a good one, such men will be the greatest bulwarks of it; if it be a bad one, they will be the most able and ready to contribute to its reformation; in either of which cases they will render it the greatest service.

Education is as much an art (founded, as all arts are, upon science) as husbandry, as architecture, or as ship-building. In all these cases we have a practical problem proposed to us, which must be performed by the help of data with which experience and observation furnish us. The end of ship-building is to make the best ships, of architecture the best houses, and of education, the best men. Now, of all arts, those stand the fairest chance of being brought to perfection, in which there is opportunity of making the most experiments and trials, and in which there are the greatest number and variety of persons employed in making them. History and experience show, that, cæteris paribus, those arts have always, in fact, been brought the soonest, or the nearest to perfection, which have been placed in those favourable circumstances. The reason is, that the operations of the human mind are slow; a number of false hypotheses and conclusions always precede the right one; and in every art, manual or liberal, a number of awkward attempts are made, before we are able to execute any thing which will bear to be shown as a master-piece in its kind; so that to establish the methods and processes of any art, before it has arrived to a state of perfection (of which no man can be a judge) is to fix it in its infancy, to perpetuate every thing that is inconvenient and awkward in it, and to cut off its future growth and improvement. And to establish the methods and processes of any art when it has arrived to perfection is superfluous. It will then recommend and establish itself.

Now I appeal to any person whether any plan of education, which has yet been put in execution in this kingdom, be so perfect as that the establishing of it by authority would not obstruct the great ends of education; or even whether the united genius of man could, at present, form so perfect a plan. Every man who is experienced in the business of education well knows, that the art is in its infancy; but advancing, it is hoped, apace to a state of manhood. In this condition, it requires the aid of every circumstance favourable to its natural growth, and dreads nothing so much as being confined and cramped by the unseasonable hand of power. To put it (in its present imperfect state) into the hands of the civil magistrate, in order to fix the mode of it, would be like fixing the dress of a child, and forbidding its cloaths ever to be made wider or larger.

Manufacturers and artists of several kinds already complain of the obstruction which is thrown in the way of their arts, by the injudicious acts of former parliaments; and it is the object of our wisest statesmen to get these obstructions removed, by the repeal of those acts. I wish it could not be said, that the business of education is already under too many legal restraints. Let these be removed, and a few more fair experiments made of the different methods of conducting it, before the legislature think proper to interfere any more with it; and by that time, it is hoped, they will see no reason to interfere at all. The business would be conducted to much better purpose, even in favour of their own views, if those views were just and honourable, than it would be under any arbitrary regulations whatever.

To shew this scheme of an established method of education in a clearer point of light, let us imagine that what is now proposed had been carried into execution some centuries before this time. For no reason can be assigned for fixing any mode of education at present, which might not have been made use of, with the same appearance of reason, for fixing another approved method a thousand years ago. Suppose Alfred, when he founded the university of Oxford, had made it impossible, that the method of instruction used in his time should ever have been altered. Excellent as that method might have been, for the time in which it was instituted, it would now have been the worst method that is practised in the world. Suppose the number of the arts and sciences, with the manner of teaching them, had been fixed in this kingdom, before the revival of letters and of the arts, it is plain they could never have arrived at their present advanced state among us. We should not have had the honour to lead the way in the most noble discoveries, in the mathematics, philosophy, astronomy, and, I may add, divinity too. And for the same reason, were such an establishment to take place in the present age, it would prevent all great improvements in futurity.

I may add, in this place, that, if we argue from the analogy of education to other arts which are most similar to it, we can never expect to see human nature, about which it is employed, brought to perfection, but in consequence of indulging unbounded liberty, and even caprice in conducting it. The power of nature in producing plants cannot be shown to advantage, but in all possible circumstances of culture. The richest colours, the most fragrant scents, and the most exquisite flavours, which our present gardens and orchards exhibit, would never have been known, if florists and gardeners had been confined in the processes of cultivation; nay if they had not been allowed the utmost licentiousness of fancy in the exercise of their arts. Many of the finest productions of modern gardening have been the result of casual experiment, perhaps of undesigned deviation from established rules.

Observations of a similar nature may be made on the methods of breeding cattle, and training animals of all kinds. And why should the rational part of the creation be deprived of that opportunity of diversifying and improving itself, which the vegetable and animal world enjoy?

From new, and seemingly irregular methods of education, perhaps something extraordinary and uncommonly great may spring. At least there would be a fair chance for such productions; and if something odd and eccentric should, now and then, arise from this unbounded liberty of education, the various business of human life may afford proper spheres for such eccentric geniuses.

Education, taken in its most extensive sense, is properly that which makes the man. One method of education, therefore, would only produce one kind of men; but the great excellence of human nature consists in the variety of which it is capable. Instead, then, of endeavouring, by uniform and fixed systems of education, to keep mankind always the same, let us give free scope to every thing which may bid fair for introducing more variety among us. The various character of the Athenians was certainly preferable to the uniform character of the Spartans, or to any uniform national character whatever. Is it not universally considered as an advantage to England, that it contains so great a variety of original characters? And is it not, on this account, preferred to France, Spain, or Italy?

Uniformity is the characteristic of the brute creation. Among them every species of birds build their nests with the same materials, and in the same form; the genius and disposition of one individual is that of all; and it is only the education which men give them that raises any of them much above others. But it is the glory of human nature, that the operations of reason, though variable, and by no means infallible, are capable of infinite improvement. We come into the world worse provided than any of the brutes, and for a year or two of our lives, many of them go far beyond us in intellectual accomplishments. But when their faculties are at a full stand, and their enjoyments incapable of variety, or increase, our intellectual powers are growing apace; we are perpetually deriving happiness from new sources, and even before we leave this world are capable of tasting the felicity of angels.

Have we, then, so little sense of the proper excellence of our natures, and of the views of divine providence in our formation, as to catch at a poor advantage adapted to the lower nature of brutes. Rather, let us hold on in the course in which the divine being himself has put us, by giving reason its full play, and throwing off the fetters which short-sighted and ill-judging men have hung upon it. Though, in this course, we be liable to more extravagancies than brutes, governed by blind but unerring instinct, or than men whom mistaken systems of policy have made as uniform in their sentiments and conduct as the brutes, we shall be in the way to attain a degree of perfection and happiness of which they can have no idea.

However, as men are first animals before they can be properly termed rational creatures, and the analogies of individuals extend to societies, a principle something resembling the instinct of animals may, perhaps, suit mankind in their infant state; but then, as we advance in the arts of life, let us, as far as we are able, assert the native freedom of our souls; and, after having been servilely governed like brutes, aspire to the noble privilege of governing ourselves like men.

If it may have been necessary to establish something by law concerning education, that necessity grows less every day, and encourages us to relax the bonds of authority, rather than bind them faster.

Secondly, this scheme of an established mode of education would be prejudicial to the great ends of civil society. The great object of civil society is the happiness of the members of it, in the perfect and undisturbed enjoyment of the more important of our natural rights, for the sake of which, we voluntarily give up others of less consequence to us. But whatever be the blessings of civil society, they may be bought too dear. It is certainly possible to sacrifice too much, at least more than is necessary to be sacrificed for them, in order to produce the greatest sum of happiness in the community. Else why do we complain of tyrannical and oppressive governments? Is it not the meaning of all complaints of this kind, that, in such governments, the subjects are deprived of their most important natural rights, without an equivalent recompense; that all the valuable ends of civil government might be effectually secured, and the members of particular states be much happier upon the whole, if they did not lie under those restrictions.

Now, of all the sources of happiness and enjoyment in human life, the domestic relations are the most constant and copious. With our wives and children we necessarily pass the greatest part of our lives. The connections of friendship are slight in comparison of this intimate domestic union. Views of interest or ambition may divide the nearest friends, but our wives and children are, in general, inseparably connected with us and attached to us. With them all our joys are doubled, and in their affection and assiduity we find consolation under all the troubles and disquietudes of life. For the enjoyments which result from this most delightful intercourse, all mankind, in all ages, have been ready to sacrifice every thing; and for the interruption of this intercourse no compensation whatever can be made by man. What then can be more justly alarming, to a man who has a true taste for happiness, than, either that the choice of his wife, or the education of his children should be under the direction of persons who have no particular knowledge of him, or particular affection for him, and whose views and maxims he might utterly dislike? What prospect of happiness could a man have with such a wife, or such children?

It is possible indeed, that the preservation of some civil societies, such as that of Sparta, may require this sacrifice; but those civil societies must be wretchedly constituted to stand in need of it, and had better be utterly dissolved. Were I a member of such a state, thankful should I be to its governors, if they would permit me peaceably to retire to any other country, where so great a sacrifice was not required. Indeed, it is hardly possible that a state should require any sacrifice, which I should think of so much importance. And, I doubt not, so many others would be of the same mind, that there would soon be very little reason to complain of the too great increase of commerce in such a country. This, however, would render very necessary another part of our author's scheme; viz. putting a restraint upon travelling abroad, lest too many persons should be willing to leave such a country, and have no inclination to return.

If there be any natural rights which ought not to be sacrificed to the ends of civil society, and no politicians or moralists deny but that there are some (the obligations of religion, for instance, being certainly of a superior nature) it is even more natural to look for these rights among those which respect a man's children, than among those which respect himself; because nature has generally made them dearer to him than himself.

If any trust can be said to be of God, and such as ought not to be relinquished at the command of man, it is that which we have of the education of our children, whom the divine being seems to have put under our immediate care; that we may instruct them in such principles, form them to such manners, and give them such habits of thinking and acting, as we shall judge to be of the greatest importance to their present and future well being.

I believe there is no father in the world (who, to a sense of religion, joins a strong sense of parental affection) who would think his own liberty above half indulged to him, when abridged in so tender a point, as that of providing, to his own satisfaction, for the good conduct and happiness of his offspring. Nature seems to have established such a strong connexion between a parent and his children, at least during the first period of their lives, that to drag them from the asylum of their natural guardians, to force them to public places of education, and to instill into them religious sentiments contrary to the judgment and choice of their parents, would be as cruel, as obliging a man to make the greatest personal sacrifice, even that of his conscience, to the civil magistrate.

What part of the persecution which the protestants in France underwent did they complain of more feelingly, and with more justice, than that of their children being forced from them, and carried to be educated in public monasteries? God forbid that the parental affections of free born Britons should ever be put to so severe a trial! or to that which the poor Jews in Portugal suffered; many of whom cut the throats of their children, or threw them into wells, and down precipices, rather than suffer them to be dragged away to be educated under the direction of a popish inquisition; thinking the lives of their children a less sacrifice than that of their principles.

It was a measure similar to that which Dr. Brown recommends, at which the whole christian world took the greatest alarm that was ever given to it, in the reign of that great man, but inveterate enemy of christianity, the emperor Julian; who would have shut up the schools of christians, and have forbidden them to teach rhetoric and philosophy. Similar to this scheme, in its nature and tendency, was the most odious measure of the most odious ministry that ever sat at the helm of the British government, and which was providentially defeated the very day that it was to have been carried into execution; I mean the schism bill, patronized by the Tory ministers in the latter end of the reign of queen Ann. Should these measures be resumed, and pursued, Farewell, a long farewell to England's greatness! Nor would this be said in a hasty fit of unreasonable despair. For, besides that such a measure as this could not but have many extensive consequences; it is not to be doubted, but that whoever they be who do thus much, they both can and will do more. Such a scheme as this will never be pushed for its own sake only.

In examining the present operation and utility of any scheme of policy, we ought to take into consideration the ease or the difficulty of carrying it into execution. For if the disturbance, which would be occasioned by bringing it into execution, would be so great an inconvenience, as to overbalance the good to be effected by it, it were better never to attempt it. Now, though the doctor hath laid down no particular scheme of public and established education, and therefore we cannot judge of the particular difficulties which would attend the establishing of it; yet, if it be such as would answer the end proposed by him, this difficulty would appear to me absolutely insuperable, in such a country as England.

Whatever be the religious, moral, and political principles, which are thought conducive to the good of the society, if they must be effectually instilled into the infant and growing minds of the community, it can never be done without taking the children very early from their parents, and cutting off all communication with them, till they be arrived to maturity, and their judgments be absolutely fixed. And if this author judged, that the reason why a scheme of this nature did not take place in Athens, was the difficulty of establishing it, after the people were tolerably civilized; he must certainly judge it to be infinitely more difficult, among a people so much farther advanced in the arts of life than the Athenians.

He well observes, p. 53, that, "to give children a public education where no education had taken place, was natural and practicable;" but he seems to be aware, that an attempt to carry any such plan into execution, in the most flourishing period of a free and civilized state, would be highly unnatural, without the least probable hope of success, and dangerous to such as took it in hand. For he says, p. 52, that, "to effect a change of government only is a work sufficient for the abilities of the greatest legislator; but to overturn all the preestablished habits of the head and heart, to destroy or reverse all the fixed associations, maxims, manners, and principles, were a labour which might well be ranked among the most extravagant legends of fabulous Greece."

What might be expected from the business of education being lodged by the state in the hands of any one set of men, may be imagined from the alarm which the Newtonian system gave to all philosophers at the time of its first publication; and from what passed at Oxford with respect to Locke's Essay on the human understanding, which hath done so much honour to the English nation in the eyes of all the learned world. We are told by the authors of Biographia Britannica, in the life of Mr. Locke, that "there was a meeting of the heads of houses at Oxford, where it was proposed to censure, and discourage the reading of this Essay; and that, after various debates, it was concluded, that, without any public censure, each head of a house shall endeavour to prevent its being read in his own college." This passed but a little before Mr. Locke's death, and about fourteen years after the first publication of the Essay.

Hitherto I have argued against established modes of education upon general principles, shewing how unfavourable they are to the great ends of civil society, with only occasional references to the English constitution; and in these arguments I have, likewise, supposed these methods of education, whatever they be, actually established, and to have operated to their full extent. I shall now add, that, before these methods can be established, and produce their full effect, they must occasion a very considerable alteration in the English constitution, and almost inevitably destroy the freedom of it; so that the thing which would, in fact, be perpetuated, would not be the present constitution of England, but something very different from it, and more despotic. An alteration of so great importance, which tends to defeat one of the principal objects of this government, cannot but give just cause of alarm to every friend of the present happy constitution and liberties of this country. In support of this assertion, I desire no other argument than that with which Dr. Brown himself furnishes me, from the influence he allows to education, operating, likewise, in the very manner which he describes, and to the very end for which he advises the establishing of its mode.

Education is considered by the doctor only in a political view, as useful to instill into the minds of youth particular maxims of policy, and to give them an attachment to particular forms of it; or as tending to superinduce such habits of mind, and to give such a general turn of thinking, as would correspond with the genius of a particular state. This education he would have to be universal and uniform; and indeed, if it were not so, it could not possibly answer the end proposed. It must, therefore, be conducted by one set of men. But it is impossible to find any set of men, who shall have an equal regard to all the parts of our constitution; and whatever part is neglected in such a system of education, it cannot fail to be a sufferer.

The English government is a mixture of regal, aristocratical, and democratical power; and if the public education should be more favourable to any one of these than to another, or more than its present importance in the constitution requires, the balance of the whole would necessarily be lost. Too much weight would be thrown into some of the scales, and the constitution be overturned. If the Commons, representing the body of the people, had the choice of these public instructors, which is almost impossible, we should see a republic rise out of the ruins of our present government; if the Lords, which is highly improbable, we should, in the end, have an aristocracy; and if the court had this nomination, which it may be taken for granted would be the case (as all the executive power of the state is already lodged in the hands of the sovereign) it could not but occasion a very dangerous accession of power to the crown; and we might justly expect a system of education, principles, and manners favourable to despotism. Every man would be educated with principles, which would lead him to concur with the views of the court. All that opposition from the country, which is so salutary in this nation, and so essential to the liberties of England, would be at an end. And when once the spirit of despotism was thus established, and had triumphed over all opposition, we might soon expect to see the forms of it established too, and thereby the very doors shut against old English liberty, and effectually guarded against the possibility of its return, except by violence; which would then be the only method of its re-entrance.

It is evident to common understanding, that the true spirit and maxims of a mixed government can not otherwise be continued, than by every man's educating his children in his own way; and that if any one part provided for the education of the whole, that part would soon gain the ascendancy; and, if it were capable of it, would become the whole. Were a state, for instance, to consist of papists and protestants, and the papists to have the sole power of education, protestantism would expire with that generation: whereas, if the papists and protestants educated each their own children, the same proportion would continue to subsist between them, and the balance of power would remain the same. For the same reason the only method of preserving the balance, which at present subsists among the several political and religious parties in Great-Britain, is for each to provide for the education of their own children.

In this way, there will be a fair prospect of things continuing nearly upon their present footing, for a considerable time; but subject to those gradual alterations which, it may be hoped, will prove favourable to the best interests of the society upon the whole. Whereas, were the direction of the whole business of education thrown into the hands of the court, it would be such an accession of power to the regal part of our constitution, as could not fail to alarm all the friends of civil liberty; as all the friends of religious liberty would be justly alarmed, if it should devolve upon the established clergy. And it were the greatest injustice to the good sense of free born Britons, to suppose the noble spirit of religious liberty, and a zeal for the rights of free inquiry confined within the narrow circle of Protestant Dissenters.

Considering the whole of what hath been advanced in this section, I think it sufficiently appears, that education is a branch of civil liberty, which ought by no means to be surrendered into the hands of the magistrate; and that the best interests of society require, that the right of conducting it should be inviolably preserved to individuals.

2

"Of National Education"

William Godwin

An Enquiry Concerning Political Justice (1793), Vol. II, Chapter VIII

William Godwin (1756–1836) came from a long line of Dissenters (or Nonconformists). He received his higher education at Hoxton Academy, one of the many Dissenting Academies in England that emerged in the early eighteenth century as free-market alternatives to Oxford and Cambridge, from which Dissenters were barred for refusing to subscribe to the Thirty-Nine Articles of the established Anglican Church. Dissenters had suffered severe legal disabilities since the Restoration of the Stuart dynasty in 1660. For example, the Act of Uniformity decreed that "every Schoolmaster keeping any public or private school, and every person instructing or teaching any youth in any house or private family as a tutor or school-master" must conform to the liturgy of the Church of England.

As a consequence of repression, Dissenters established their own educational institutions, which quickly became, in the words of one historian, "the greatest schools of their day." Even when political conditions became more favorable for Nonconformists, most still preferred the vastly superior educational opportunities of Dissenting Academies over the torpid and regressive education provided at Oxford and Cambridge, and this preference was shared by many Anglicans as well. Teachers in the Dissenting Academies were some of the best minds of the English Enlightenment, such as Joseph Priestley, who taught at the Warrington Academy. As Priestley noted, the academies were "exceedingly favourable to free inquiry." They were also celebrated for teaching the latest developments in science.

After graduating Hoxton Academy, Godwin set his sights on becoming a minister. After failing miserably in several venues, however, he decided to pursue a career as a writer. Shortly thereafter Godwin abandoned his religious beliefs for deism, and he later became an avowed atheist.

Godwin was also a Tory when he left Hoxton—an unusual political position for a student at Hoxton, given that most teachers and students were radical whigs (the libertarians of their day, in effect). But after extensive reading and countless discussions with acquaintances Godwin converted to republicanism of the sort defended by Thomas Paine (whom he greatly admired), and from there Godwin moved on to anarchism.

Godwin did not call himself an "anarchist," nor did he endorse "anarchy"—a term which carried the same negative connotations in the eighteenth century that it does today. (P. J. Proudhon, in 1840, was the first person to call himself an "anarchist.) Godwin contrasted anarchy "as it is commonly understood" with a "well-conceived form of society without government," and he looked forward to the "euthanasia of government" that would eventually come about with the progress of knowledge. The "true supporters of government are the weak and uninformed, and not the wise. In proportion as weakness and ignorance shall diminish, the basis of government will also decay." Thus Godwin's masterpiece, *Enquiry Concerning Political Justice* (1793), has become known as the first defense of philosophic anarchism ever written.

Given his personal experience with voluntary education and his dislike of state power, it is not surprising that Godwin was a severe critic of state education, which he predicted would be used to strengthen the power of government. Essential to Godwin's case was his belief in the supreme value of independent judgment. There are three types of authority, according to Godwin. First is the authority of one's own reason, as manifested in independent judgment. Second is the authority of a person whom we respect for his wisdom and whose advice we choose to follow voluntarily. This type of authority is completely different from the third type of authority— the authority claimed by government, which issues not advice but commands backed by brute force. We may obey a government as a practical matter because we fear the sanction imposed for disobedience, but we should never attribute to government any inherent *moral* authority. To confound these two kinds of authority will lead to "a debasement of the human character." Godwin expressed this point vividly in the *Enquiry,* in the chapter titled "Of Obedience."

The greatest mischief that can arise in the progress of obedience, is, where it shall lead us, in any degree, to depart from the independence of our understanding, a departure which general and unlimited confidence necessarily includes. In this view, the best advice that could be given to a person in a state of subjection, is, "Comply, where the necessity of the case demands it; but criticize while you comply. Obey the unjust mandates of your governors; for this prudence and a consideration of the common safety may require; but treat them with no false lenity, regard them with no indulgence. Obey; this may be right; but beware of reverence. Reverence nothing but wisdom and skill: government may be vested in the fittest persons; then they are entitled to reverence, because they are wise, and not because they are governors: and it may be vested in the worst. Obedience will occasionally be right in both cases: you may run south, to avoid a wild beast advancing in that direction, though you want to go north. But be upon your guard against confounding things, so totally unconnected with each other, as a purely political obedience, and respect. Government is nothing but regulated force; force is its appropriate claim upon your attention."

The right of independent judgment was the basis for Godwin's political theory, and it explains his stress on the importance of education. Education should teach children the importance of independent judgment rather than indoctrinate them with the beliefs that their government may wish them to accept. The essentials of a good education are quite simple: "Speak the language of reason and truth to your child, and be under no apprehension for the result. Show him that what you recommend is valuable and desirable, and fear not but he will desire it. Convince his understanding, and you enlist all his powers animal and intellectual in your service."

———————

A mode in which government has been accustomed to interfere for the purpose of influencing opinion, is by the superintendence it has in a greater or less degree exerted in the article of education. It is worthy of observation that the idea of this superintendence has obtained the countenance of several of the most zealous advocates of political reform. The question relative to its propriety or impropriety is entitled on that account to the more deliberate examination.

The arguments in its favour have been already anticipated. "Can it be justifiable in those persons, who are appointed to the functions of magistracy, and whose duty it is to consult for the public welfare, to neglect the cultivation of the infant mind, and to suffer its future excellence or depravity to be at the disposal of fortune? Is it possible for patriotism and the love of the public to be made the characteristic of a whole people in any other way so successfully, as by rendering the early communication of these virtues a national concern? If the education of our youth be entirely confided to the prudence of their parents or the accidental benevolence of private individuals, will it not be a necessary consequence, that some will be educated to virtue, others to vice, and others again entirely neglected?" To these considerations it has been added, "That the maxim which has prevailed in the majority of civilised countries, that ignorance of the law is no apology for the breach of it, is in the highest degree iniquitous; and that government cannot justly punish us for our crimes when committed, unless it have forewarned us against their commission, which cannot be adequately done without something of the nature of public education."

The propriety or impropriety of any project for this purpose must be determined by the general consideration of its beneficial or injurious tendency. If the exertions of the magistrate in behalf of any system of instruction will stand the test as conducive to the public service, undoubtedly he cannot be justified in neglecting them. If on the contrary they conduce to injury, it is wrong and unjustifiable that they should be made.

The injuries that result from a system of national education are, in the first place, that all public establishments include in them the idea of permanence. They endeavour it may be to secure and to diffuse whatever of advantageous to society is already known, but they forget that more remains to be known. If they realised the most substantial benefits at the time of their introduction, they must inevitably become less and less useful as they increased in duration. But to describe them as useless is a very feeble expression of their demerits. They actively restrain the flights of mind, and fix it in the belief of exploded errors. It has commonly been observed of universities and extensive establishments for the purpose of education, that the knowledge taught there, is a century behind the knowledge which exists among the unshackled and unprejudiced members of the same political community. The moment any scheme of proceeding gains a permanent establishment, it becomes impressed as one of its characteristic features with an aversion to change. Some violent concussion may oblige its conductors to change an old system of philosophy for a system less obsolete; and they are then as pertinaciously attached to this second doctrine as they were to the first. Real intellectual improvement demands that mind should as speedily as possible be advanced to the height of knowledge already existing among the enlightened members of the community, and start from thence in the pursuit of farther acquisitions. But public education has always expended its energies in the support of prejudice; it teaches its pupils, not the fortitude that shall bring every proposition to the test of examination, but the art of vindicating such tenets as may chance to be previously established. We study Aristotle or Thomas Aquinas or Bellarmine or chief justice Coke, not that we may detect their errors, but that our minds may be fully impregnated with their absurdities. This feature runs through every species of public establishment; and even in the petty institution of Sunday schools, the chief lessons that are taught, are a superstitious veneration for the church of England, and to bow to every man in a handsome coat. All this is directly contrary to the true interest of mind. All this must be unlearned, before we can begin to be wise.

It is the characteristic of mind to be capable of improvement. An individual surrenders the best attribute of man, the moment he resolves to adhere to certain fixed principles, for reasons not now present to his mind, but which formerly were. The instant in which he shuts upon himself the career of enquiry, is the instant of his intellectual decease. He is no longer a man; he is the ghost of departed man. There can be no scheme more egregiously stamped with folly, than that of separating a tenet from the evidence upon which its validity depends. If I cease from the habit of being able to recall this evidence, my belief is no longer a perception, but a prejudice: it may influence me like a prejudice; but cannot animate me like a real apprehension of truth. The difference between the man thus guided, and the man that keeps his mind perpetually alive, is the difference between cowardice and fortitude. The man who is in the best sense an intellectual being, delights to recollect the reasons that have convinced him, to repeat them to others, that they may produce conviction in them, and stand more distinct and explicit in his own mind; and he adds to this a willingness to examine objections, because he takes no pride in consistent error. The man who is not capable of this salutary exercise, to what valuable purpose can he be employed? Hence it appears that no vice can be more destructive than that which teaches us to regard any judgment as final, and not open to review. The same principle that applies to individuals applies to communities. There is no proposition, at present apprehended to be true, so valuable as to justify the introduction of an establishment for the purpose of inculcating it on mankind. Refer them to reading, to conversation, to meditation; but teach them neither creeds nor catechisms, neither moral nor political.

Secondly, the idea of national education is founded in an inattention to the nature of mind. Whatever each man does for himself is done well; whatever his neighbours or his country undertake to do for him is done ill. It is our wisdom to incite men to act for themselves, not to retain them in a state of perpetual pupillage. He that learns because he desires to learn, will listen to the instructions he receives, and apprehend their meaning. He that teaches because he desires to teach, will discharge his occupation with enthusiasm and energy. But the moment political institution undertakes to assign to every man his place, the functions of all will be discharged with supineness and indifference. Universities and expensive establishments have long been remarked for formal dullness. Civil policy has given me the power to appropriate my estate to certain theoretical purposes; but it is an idle presumption to think I can entail my views, as I can entail my fortune. Remove all those obstacles which prevent men from seeing and restrain them from pursuing their real advantage, but do not absurdly undertake to relieve them from the activity which this pursuit requires. What I earn, what I acquire only because I desire to acquire it, I estimate at its true value; but what is thrust upon me may make me indolent, but cannot make me respectable. It is extreme folly to endeavour to secure to others, independently of exertion on their part, the means of being happy.—This whole proposition of a national education, is founded upon a supposition which has been repeatedly refuted in this work, but which has recurred upon us in a thousand forms, that unpatronised truth is inadequate to the purpose of enlightening mankind.

Thirdly, the project of a national education ought uniformly to be discouraged on account of its obvious alliance with national government. This is an alliance of a more formidable nature, than the old and much contested alliance of church and state. Before we put so powerful a machine under the direction of so ambiguous an agent, it behooves us to consider well what it is that we do.

Government will not fail to employ it to strengthen its hands, and perpetuate its institutions. If we could even suppose the agents of government not to propose to themselves an object, which will be apt to appear in their eyes, not merely innocent, but meritorious; the evil would not the less happen. Their views as institutors of a system of education, will not fail to be analogous to their views in their political capacity: the data upon which their conduct as statesmen is vindicated, will be the data upon which their instructions are founded. It is not true that our youth ought to be instructed to venerate the constitution, however excellent; they should be instructed to venerate truth; and the constitution only so far as it corresponded with their independent deductions of truth. Had the scheme of a national education been adopted when despotism was most triumphant, it is not to be believed that it could have for ever stifled the voice of truth. But it would have been the most formidable and profound contrivance for that purpose that imagination can suggest. Still, in the countries where liberty chiefly prevails, it is reasonably to be assumed that there are important errors, and a national education has the most direct tendency to perpetuate those errors, and to form all minds upon one model.

It is not easy to say whether the remark, "that government cannot justly punish offenders, unless it have previously informed them what is virtue and what is offence," be entitled to a separate answer. It is to be hoped that mankind will never have to learn so important a lesson through so corrupt a channel. Government may reasonably and equitably presume that men who live in society know that enormous crimes are injurious to the public weal, without its being necessary to announce them as such, by laws to be proclaimed by heralds, or expounded by curates. It has been alleged that "mere reason may teach me not to strike my neighbour; but will never forbid my sending a sack of wool from England, or printing the French constitution in Spain." This objection leads to the true distinction upon the subject. All real crimes are capable of being discerned without the teaching of law. All supposed crimes, not capable of being so discerned, are truly and unalterably innocent. It is true that my own understanding would never have told me that the exportation of wool was a vice: neither do I believe it is a vice now that a law has been made affirming it. It is a feeble and contemptible remedy for iniquitous punishments, to signify to mankind beforehand that you intend to inflict them. Nay, the remedy is worse than the evil: destroy me if you please; but do not endeavour by a national education to destroy in my understanding the discernment of justice and injustice. The idea of such an education, or even perhaps of the necessity of a written law, would never have occurred, if government and jurisprudence had never attempted the arbitrary conversion of innocence into guilt.

From The Sphere and Duties of Government

Wilhelm von Humboldt

Chapter 6 of *The Sphere and Duties of Government*, trans. Joseph Coulthard (London: John Chapman, 1859)

Wilhelm von Humboldt (1767–1835) gave us one of the most compelling defenses of limited-government libertarianism ever written. According to Humboldt, "Any State interference in private affairs, where there is no immediate reference to violence done to individual rights, should be absolutely condemned."

After a young Humboldt finished his book in 1792, at age 25, some chapters were printed in two German periodicals. A complete German edition did not appear until 1852, long after Humboldt's death, and this was followed by Joseph Coulthard's English translation two years later under the title *The Sphere and Duties of Government*. This was published by the English libertarian and freethinker John Chapman, who also published Herbert Spencer's *Social Statics*. A later translation by J. W. Burrow, which was based on Coulthard's version, was published in 1969 by Cambridge University Press as *The Limits of State Action*, and reprinted (with corrections) in 1993 by Liberty Fund. The following excerpt is from Coulthard's translation.

In later life Humboldt retreated from his opposition to state education, as he drifted toward Prussian nationalism. Indeed, in 1809 Humboldt accepted the position of chief of education in the Prussian Ministry of the Interior, and over the next two years he instituted a free and universal system of state education. He also founded the University of Berlin (now known as the Humboldt University of Berlin) in 1810. In addition to his educational activities, Humboldt was a pioneer in linguistics and semiotics. His theories influenced Noam Chomsky, among many others.

Many English readers first learned of Humboldt's early libertarian book from J. S. Mill's *On Liberty* (1859). Mill quoted Humboldt in the epigraph and mentioned this "excellent essay" several times in his text. Humboldt's influence is especially evident in Chapter 3 ("On individuality as one of the elements of well-being"), in which Mill wrote:

> Few persons, out of Germany, even comprehend the meaning of the doctrine which Wilhelm von Humboldt, so eminent both as a savant and as a politician, made the text of a treatise—that 'the end of man, or that which is prescribed by eternal or immutable dictates of reason, and not suggested by vague and transient desires, is the

highest and most harmonious development of his powers to a complete and consistent whole'; that therefore,
the object 'towards which every human being must cease-
lessly direct his efforts, and on which especially those
who design to influence their fellow-men must ever keep
their eyes is the individuality of power and development';
that for this there are two requisites, 'freedom and variety of situations'; and that from the union of these arise
'individual vigour and manifold diversity', which combine themselves in 'originality'.

By "freedom," Humboldt meant the external freedom to act
without coercive interference by others, so long as individual rights
are respected. Humboldt regarded such freedom as an essential
precondition of personal growth, fulfillment, and happiness—or
what he called the culture of the individual. The word "culture,"
as used by Humboldt, pertains primarily to the individual, not to
society. He meant it in the sense of "cultivation." We need to cultivate ourselves, especially our inner selves, if we are to approach
or achieve the highest stage of development of which human
nature is capable.

Humboldt therefore sees the good life as a continuous process
of self-perfection, whereby a person achieves the harmonious
exercise and integration of his or her faculties and abilities. This
process of self-cultivation is for Humboldt the essence of individuality. The more we develop our particular talents and combine them into a harmonious whole, the more we become unique
individuals.

Humboldt identifies two primary benefits from this ongoing process of self-cultivation. First, we become more valuable to ourselves because we are able to lead a rich and fulfilling life. Second, we become more valuable to others, and to society as a whole, because others will benefit, through voluntary social interaction, from the unique features of our individuality.

Humboldt identifies, in addition to freedom, another social condition that is necessary for self-cultivation, namely, a variety of situations. We may have political freedom, we may be free to make choices according to our own judgment; but if our range of alternatives is excessively narrow, owing to social customs and norms, then our freedom cannot be put to its most productive use. Cultural diversity is essential both to the development of the individual and to the cultural progress of a society.

This theory of a spontaneous cultural order was the foundation of Humboldt's opposition to state education. Progress in education requires the freedom and diversity found in market competition. State education, in contrast, will impose a dulling uniformity that will stifle individuality and freeze educational progress.

Having seen in a preceding chapter that it is not only a justifiable but necessary end of Government to provide for the mutual security of the citizens, it here becomes our duty to enter on a more profound and explicit investigation into the nature of such a solicitude, and the means through which it acts. For it does not seem enough merely to commit the care for security to the political power as a general and unconditional duty, but it further becomes us to define the especial limits of its activity in this respect; or, at least, should this general definition be difficult or wholly impossible, to exhibit the reasons for that impossibility, and discover the characteristics by which these limits may, in given cases, be recognized.

Even a very limited range of observation is sufficient to convince us that this care for preservation may either restrict its efforts to a very narrow sphere, or launch into bolder measures, and embrace wide and indefinite means of influence to reach its design. Confined sometimes to the reparation of irregularities actually committed and the infliction of appropriate punishment, it may embrace, at others, precautions for preventing their occurrence, or even suggest the policy of moulding the mind and character of the citizen after the fashion most suitable to its preconceived scheme of social order. This very extension even of the governmental plans, admits, so to speak, of different degrees. The violation of personal rights, for example, and any encroachment on the immediate rights of the State, may be carefully investigated and duly reproved, or—by regarding the citizen as accountable to the State for the application of his powers, and therefore as one who robs it, as it were, of its rightful property when he does aught calculated to enfeeble them or disturb their harmonious action—a watchful surveillance may be exercised over those actions even which affect none but the agent himself. I have therefore found it expedient at present to comprise under one head all these varied manifestations of political solicitude, and must therefore be understood to speak of all State-institutions collectively which are dictated by the general design of promoting public security. Meanwhile, it is only necessary to add, that although the very nature of the subject precludes the possibility of any just and accurate division, all those institutions which refer to the moral welfare of the citizen will naturally present themselves in the order of this inquiry; for if they do not, in all cases, aim at security and tranquillity exclusively, these are in general the prominent objects of such institutions. In my manner of discussing the merits and demerits of these, I shall therefore adhere to the system I have hitherto adopted. It will be seen, from the preceding chapters, that I have set out with supposing the utmost extension of State agency conceivable, and then endeavoured, step by step, to ascertain the different provinces from which it should properly be withdrawn, until at length the concern for security is all that has remained to its appropriation. And now it becomes us to adopt, with regard to this general object of security, the same method of procedure; I will therefore begin by supposing the widest acceptation in which the efficient discharge of such a trust can be viewed, in order to arrive, by successive limitations, at those fundamental principles which enable us to determine its true extent. Should such a systematic investigation be regarded as somewhat lengthy and tedious, I am ready to admit that a dogmatic exposition would require a method of treatment exactly the reverse. But, by confining ourselves strictly to inquiry, we can at least be sure of having fully and honestly grappled with the essential subject, and of having omitted nothing of real importance, while unfolding its principles in their natural and consecutive order.

It has, of late, been usual to insist on the expediency and propriety of preventing illegal actions, and of calling in the aid of moral means to accomplish such a purpose; but I will not disguise that, when I hear such exhortations, I am satisfied to think such encroachments on freedom are becoming more rare among us, and in almost all modern constitutions daily less possible.

It is not uncommon to appeal to the history of Greece and Rome in support of such a policy; but a clearer insight into the nature of the constitutions of those ancient nations would at once betray the inconclusiveness of such comparisons. Those States were essentially republics, and such kindred institutions as we find in them were pillars of the free constitution, and were regarded by the citizens with an enthusiasm which rendered their hurtful restrictions on private freedom less deeply felt, and their energetic character less pernicious. They enjoyed, moreover, a much wider range of freedom than is usual among modern States, and anything that was sacrificed was only given up to another form of activity, viz. participation in the affairs of government. Now, on our States, which are in general monarchical, all this is necessarily changed; and whatever moral means the ancients might employ, as national education, religion, moral laws, would under present systems be less fruitful of good results, and productive of far greater injury. We ought not to forget, moreover, in our admiration of antiquity, that what we are so apt to consider the results of wisdom in the ancient legislators, was mostly nothing more than the effect of popular custom, which, only when decaying, required the authority and support of legal sanction. The remarkable correspondency that exists between the laws of Lycurgus and the manners and habits of most uncultivated nations, has already been clearly and forcibly illustrated by Ferguson; and when we are led to trace the national growth in culture and refinement, we only discern the faint shadow of such early popular institutions. Lastly, I would observe, that men have now arrived at a far higher pitch of civilization, beyond which it seems they cannot aspire to still loftier heights save through the development of individuals, and hence it is to be inferred that all institutions which act in any way to obstruct or thwart this development, and compress men together into vast uniform masses, are now far more hurtful than in earlier ages of the world.

When we regard the working of those moral means which admit of more large and indefinite application, it seems to follow, even from these few and general reflections, that national education— or that which is organized or enforced by the State—is at least in many respects very questionable. The grand, leading principle, towards which every argument hitherto unfolded in these pages directly converges, is the absolute and essential importance of human development in its richest diversity; but national education, since at least it presupposes the selection and appointment of some one instructor, must always promote a definite form of development, however careful to avoid such an error. And hence it is attended with all those disadvantages which we before observed to flow from such a positive policy; and it only remains to be added, that every restriction becomes more directly fatal, when it operates on the moral part of our nature,—that if there is one thing more than another which absolutely requires free activity on the part of the individual, it is precisely education, whose object it is to develop the individual. It cannot be denied that the happiest results, both as regards the State and the individual, flow from this relation between them,—that the citizen becomes spontaneously active in the State itself, in the form assigned him by his peculiar lot and circumstances, and that by the very contrast or antagonism between the position pointed out to him by the State, and that which he has spontaneously chosen, he is not only himself modified, but the State constitution also is subject to a reciprocal influence; and although the extent and operation of such influences are not of course immediately evident, they are still distinctly traceable in the history of all States, when we keep in view the modifications to which they are subject from the difference of national character. Now this salutary interaction always diminishes in proportion to the efforts made to fashion the citizen's character beforehand, and to train him up from childhood with the express view of becoming a citizen. The happiest result must follow, it is true, when the relations of man and citizen coincide as far as possible; but this coincidence is only to be realized when those of the citizen pre-suppose so few distinct peculiarities that the man may preserve his natural form without any sacrifice; and it is to the expediency of securing this perfect harmony between the requirements of man and citizen that all the ideas I have in view in this inquiry directly converge. For, although the immediately hurtful consequences of such a misrelation as that to which we have referred would be removed when the citizens of a State were expressly trained up with a view to their political character, still the very object would be sacrificed which the association of human beings in a community was designed to secure. Whence I conclude, that the freest development of human nature, directed as little as possible to ulterior civil relations, should always be regarded as paramount in importance with respect to the culture of man in society. He who has been thus freely developed should then attach himself to the State; and the State should test and compare itself, as it were, in him. It is only with such a contrast and conflict of relations, that I could confidently anticipate a real improvement of the national constitution, and banish all apprehension with regard to the injurious influence of the civil institutions on human nature. For even although these were very imperfect, we could imagine how the force of human energies, struggling against the opposing barriers, and asserting, in spite of them, its own inherent greatness, would ultimately prove superior in the conflict. Still, such a result could only be expected when those energies had been allowed to unfold themselves in all their natural freedom. For how extraordinary must those efforts be which were adequate to maintain and exalt those energies, when even from the period of youth they were bound down and enfeebled by such oppressive fetters! Now all systems of national education, inasmuch as they afford room for the manifestation of a governmental spirit, tend to impose a definite form on civic development, and therefore to repress those vital energies of the nation.

When such a prevailing form of development is definite in itself, and still beautiful, although one-sided, as we find it to be in the ancient constitutions and even yet observe it perhaps in many a republic, there is not only more facility in its actual working, but it is attended with far less hurtful consequences. But in our monarchical constitutions, happily enough for human development, such a definite form as that which we describe does not at all exist. It clearly belongs to their advantages, however numerous may be the concomitant evils, that inasmuch as the State union is strictly regarded as the means requisite for the desired end, individual power is not necessarily sacrificed to its accomplishment, as is the case with republics. So long as the citizen conducts himself in conformity with the laws, and maintains himself and those dependent on him in comfort, without doing anything calculated to prejudice the interests of the State, the latter does not trouble itself about the particular manner of his existence. Here therefore national education,—which, as such, still keeps in view, however imperceptibly, the culture of the citizen in his capacity of subject, and not, as is the case in private education, the development of the individual man,—would not be directed to the encouragement of any particular virtue or disposition; it would, on the contrary, be designed to realize a balance of all opposing impulses, since nothing tends so much as this to produce and maintain tranquillity, which is precisely the object most ardently desired by States so constituted. But such an artificial equilibrium, as I have before taken occasion to observe, leads at once to utter torpidity and stagnation, or a depression and deficiency of energy; while, on the other hand, the greater regard for single objects which is peculiarly characteristic of private education, operates to produce that equipoise more surely and effectually, by a life of different relations and combinations, and that without any attendant sacrifice of energy.

But even though we were to deny to national education all positive furtherance of particular systems of culture—if we were to represent it as an essential duty that it should simply encourage the spontaneous development of faculties, this would still prove impracticable, since whatever is pervaded by a unity of organization, invariably begets a corresponding uniformity in the actual result, and thus, even when based on such liberal principles, the utility of national education is still inconceivable. If it is only designed to prevent the possibility of children remaining uninstructed, it is much more expedient and less hurtful to appoint guardians where parents are remiss, and extend assistance where they are in indigent circumstances. Further, it is not to be forgotten, that national education fails in accomplishing the object proposed by it, viz. the reformation of morals according to the model which the State considers most conducive to its designs. However great the influence of education may be, and however it may extend to the whole course of a man's actions, still, the circumstances which surround him throughout his whole life are yet far more important. And hence, if all these do not harmonize with its influences, education cannot succeed in effecting its object.

In fine, if education is only to develop a man's faculties, without regard to any definite civil forms to be collaterally imparted to his nature, there is no need of the State's interference. Among men who are really free, every form of industry becomes more rapidly improved,—all the arts flourish more gracefully,—all sciences become more largely enriched and expanded. In such a community, too, domestic bonds become closer and sweeter; the parents are more eagerly devoted to the care of their children, and, in a higher state of welfare, are better able to follow out their desires with regard to them. Among such men emulation naturally arises; and tutors better befit themselves, when their fortunes depend upon their own efforts, than when their chances of promotion rest on what they are led to expect from the State. There would, therefore, be no want of careful family training, nor of those common educational establishments which are so useful and indispensable. But if national education is to impose some definite form on human nature, it is perfectly certain that there is actually nothing done towards preventing transgressions of law, or establishing and maintaining security. For virtue and vice do not depend on any particular form of being, nor are necessarily connected with any particular aspect of character; in regard to these, much more depends on the harmony or discordancy of all the different features of a man's character—on the proportion that exists between power and the sum of inclinations, etc. Every distinct development of character is capable of its peculiar excess, and to this it constantly tends to degenerate. If then an entire nation has adhered to some certain variety of development, it comes in time to lose all power of resisting the preponderant bias to this one peculiarity, and along with it all power of regaining its equilibrium. Perhaps it is in this that we discover the reason of such frequent changes in the constitution of ancient States. Every fresh constitution exercised an undue influence on the national character, and this, definitely developed, degenerated in turn and necessitated a new one.

Lastly, even if we admit that national education may succeed in the accomplishment of all that it proposes, it effects too much. For in order to maintain the security it contemplates, the reformation of the national morals themselves is not at all necessary. But as my reasons for this position refer to the whole solicitude for morality on the part of the State, I reserve them for the after part of this inquiry, and proceed meanwhile to consider some single means which are often suggested by that solicitude. I have only to conclude from what has been argued here, that national education seems to me to lie wholly beyond the limits within which political agency should properly be confined.

4

"Shall the State Educate the People?"

Thomas Hodgskin

The Economist, April 3, 1847

The Englishman Thomas Hodgskin (1787–1869) was one of the best libertarian theoreticians of the nineteenth century. Although not as well known as his younger contemporary Herbert Spencer, Hodgskin's approach to libertarianism was more consistent. His best known (if least satisfactory) work, *Labour Defended Against the Claims of Capital* (1825), has led to a common misconception that Hodgskin was a "Ricardian Socialist," whereas he was in fact an individualist libertarian who staunchly defended laissez-faire and the rights of private property. He was also highly critical of Ricardo's theory of economics, preferring the approach of Adam Smith instead.

Hodgskin was born December 12, 1787. His spendthrift father, despite making decent money as a storekeeper at the Chatham naval stockyard, managed to keep his family in dire financial straits, so he sent Thomas (who was barely twelve) to serve as a cadet aboard a British warship.

Although he served with distinction during the Copenhagen expedition and rose to the rank of lieutenant, Hodgskin detested his twelve years as a sailor. For one thing, it deprived him of an education. His access to books was limited, so he could do little more than "reflect in the midnight watch, on the solitary deck, on the wide ocean, amidst the wildest or the most peaceable scenes of nature . . . before I had acquired a sufficient stock of material."

Hodgkin's independent spirit, his intense dislike of unjust authority, and his determination "to make a powerful resistance to oppression every time I was its victim" were not well suited to the rigors and harsh discipline of naval life. Thus, when it became clear that he would be passed over for promotion, Hodgskin complained "of the injury done to me, by a commander-in-chief, to himself, in the language that I thought it merited." This of course only made matters worse. Hodgskin, at age twenty-five, was forced into retirement at half-pay, after which he wrote *An Essay on Naval Discipline* (1813), a scathing indictment of conscription and the brutal conditions endured by British sailors.

Hodgskin's experience with the horrific punishments inflicted on British sailors for even minor offenses caused him to question both the justice and utility of the supposed "right" to punish. British sailors, who typically hailed from lower-class backgrounds, were frequently pressed into service against their wills, and their officers tended to view them as brutes who could be controlled only by the lash.

Hodgskin, who by this time had read John Locke, William Paley, and other moral philosophers, had a different opinion. Humans, created by God with "similar passions," are "everywhere made alike." Many individual differences are caused by different social and political environments. If the English tended to be happier and more virtuous than people from other nations, this was largely because they were less governed than other nations. And if English sailors appeared more brutish than other Englishmen, this was owing not to any inherent defects in their natures but to the barbarous conditions of naval life.

In short, if you treat men like brutes, they will behave like brutes. Press gangs and conscription, according to Hodgskin, should be abolished and replaced by voluntary, short-term enlistments; pay should be increased so that sailors can afford a decent standard of living; and the draconian penal laws of the navy—which were applied arbitrarily, without recourse to due process—should be eliminated. If there must be punishment, then the navy should follow the example of the civilian courts in England, which "do not punish the innocent" and which are administered according to impartial laws, not by the whims of superiors.

When peace returned to Europe in 1815, Hodgskin decided to take the grand tour and write a book based on his experiences. The result was his first major work, *Travels in the North of Germany*, published in two volumes in 1820. These volumes combined interesting observations with political commentary on "the much governed countries of Germany." Hodgskin emphasized the inefficiency and waste of government projects. For example, he commented on the inferior quality of state-financed roads in

Germany, contrasting them with the privately financed roads in England, and he even suggested that police functions should be placed in private hands. As Hodgskin put it, "the real business of men, what promotes their prosperity, is always better done by themselves than by any few separate and distinct individuals, acting as a government in the name of the whole." The belief that government intervention is necessary for economic prosperity "is one of those general prejudices which men have inherited from an ignorant and barbarous age, and which more extensive knowledge and greater civilization will show to be an error full of evil." Government intervention retards both material and intellectual progress: "Undoubtedly the abolition of all restrictions of whatever kind is the great point to be aimed at. We want a destroying legislature whose great business would be to do away with the enactments of their predecessors." All governmental laws are designed by ruling oligarchies to further their own private interests, and these laws conflict with those natural laws of society that serve the general interests of the people. This recurring theme in Hodgskin's writing would later receive an extensive treatment in Hodgskin's most important book, *The Natural and Artificial Right of Property Contrasted* (1832).

In 1823, Thomas Hodgskin co-founded, with his friend Joseph C. Robertson, the *Mechanics' Magazine*, which addressed the problems of working-class artisans. With the Baconian maxim "Knowledge is power" on its masthead, the *Mechanics' Magazine* stressed the crucial role of knowledge and innovation in improving the productive powers of labor. Inventors and creative engineers, such as James Watt (inventor of the steam engine), were praised as exemplars that all workers should seek to emulate. The thesis that the progress of knowledge is essential to the betterment of the working classes was a recurring theme in the writings of Thomas Hodgskin, one that he would elaborate upon in considerable detail in his book on economics, *Popular Political Economy* (1827).

In various articles published in the *Mechanics Magazine*, Hodgskin argued that government was no friend of the working classes and that the individual freedom of *laissez-faire* was the best policy. An ardent Voluntaryist, Hodgskin opposed all state interference in education. He wrote in the *Mechanics' Magazine* (Oct. 11, 1823):

> The education of a free people, like their property, will always be directed more beneficially for them when it is in their own hands. When government interferes, it directs its efforts more to make people obedient and docile than wise and happy. It devises to control the thoughts, and fashion even the minds of its subjects; and to give into its hands the power of educating the people is the widest possible extension of that most pernicious practice which has so long desolated society, of allowing one or a few men to direct the actions, and control the conduct of millions. Men had better be without education—properly so called, for nature of herself teaches us many valuable truths—than be educated by their rulers; for then education is but the mere breaking in of the steer to the yoke; the mere discipline of a hunting dog, which, by dint of severity, is made to forego the strongest impulse of nature, and instead of devouring his prey, to hasten with it to the feet of his master.

Hodgskin became senior editor of *The Economist* in 1846—a position he would hold for eleven years. Hodgkin's many articles for *The Economist* made it one of the most interesting and provocative libertarian periodicals of its time. In addition to supporting *laissez-faire*, voluntary education, and other (classical) liberal causes, Hodgskin also opposed capital punishment and questioned the traditional wisdom about the efficacy of punishment as a deterrent to crime.

In the following article from *The Economist*, published a year after repeal of the Corn Laws in 1846, Hodgskin argues that the same natural laws that make free trade in commerce beneficial also apply to education. "The State certainly has the art of contaminating that which it touches."

There are two questions, on which there is a universal concurrence of opinion: one is, that our present parochial and common schools are as bad as can be; the other is, education ought to be extended and improved. Our present schools are universally denounced; and whatever might have been the case twenty years ago, almost every man now demands improved education. We fully share these opinions. We have visited many schools on the continent, and are sensible of the great inferiority of English schools. We have, in our sphere, too, contributed to promote education, and desire as ardently as any of our contemporaries, that the whole people should be well-informed, virtuous, and happy. We differ, however, from our contemporaries, and several valuable correspondents—some of whose communications we have inserted—as to the best means of educating the people; and our present purpose is to explain our reasons for objecting to that being undertaken by the State.

In the United States is to be found the most persuasive and influential example of the State providing education that we are acquainted with; but the government there is so strictly a government of the people—it is so municipal, so parochial, so domestic—it embraces, particularly, in the Northern and Eastern States, where education is the best, so entirely the bulk of the community, that it is like the fathers of the hamlet meeting in council and settling their own affairs. There the people, strictly speaking, provide for their own education. Here the people, to be educated as the rule, have no voice whatever in the matter. Education is to be provided for them—not by them; and the classes to be educated are distinct in feelings, sympathies, and rank, from the classes providing and regulating the education. On this distinction, we think that the example of the United States does not apply to England, nor to any of the nations of Europe; and we cannot conclude, from the success of their parochial and municipal education, that the upper classes, the Parliament, and Ministry, should provide here for the education of the lower classes.

To form a correct opinion, we must look at what the State has already effected. That the protectionist policy, irreclaimably given up to the delusion that the State can regulate wages, settle profits, and increase production, still smarting from their overthrow in one of their strongest positions, and threatened in others, should seek to extend their principles in another direction and, essay to controul, by education, that knowledge which is so adverse to their doctrines, seems quite natural. We give them credit for much sagacity in the undertaking. We have long seen that their present devotion to social improvement is the offspring mainly of apprehension. The case is different with the free trade party. They have just practically established the great doctrine that the State cannot beneficially controul wages, profits, or production, and invariably does mischief by meddling with them. That those who embrace the principles of free trade should all at once, as to education, adopt the protectionist principle, and claim the interference of the State with education, does not convert us to their creed, but makes us infer that they do not fully appreciate the principles on which they have been induced to act. Before they can with propriety ask the State to extend its interference with education, they ought to prove that its interference with trade has been beneficial. But they know, and therefore it is not necessary for us to illustrate the point at great length, that the State never has interfered with trade but to derange, paralyse, and destroy it.

The State has, for example, at various times undertaken, with the best intentions, to promote the manufacture of linen, the catching and curing of fish, the increase of shipping, the extension of agriculture, and it has, to attain these ends, given bounties, established monopolies, and devised elaborate schemes of navigation and corn laws. But every one of these schemes has in the end turned out failures. No man can point out, either in this or any other country, a single branch of trade or industry, born of state regulations, and nourished by them into healthy, profitable and vigorous existence. Not only has the State everywhere failed to promote, by its regulations, the material wealth of the people—failed to encourage fisheries by bounties, and trade by monopolies—failed to beget abundance of ships and corn, but it has been continually compelled, in order to make room for the advancing wealth of society, and not further to damage the public welfare, to put down bounties, abolish monopolies, gradually to relax, and finally to suspend, because they could not be sustained, the navigation and corn laws. The natural progress of population, carrying with it extended knowledge, new arts, a further and further division of labour, and more and more rapid communication, has obliged our Legislature, after withstanding the progress, after shirking its demands and stopping it or shoving it aside by one pretext and one inquiry after another, as long as possible, to give up as erroneous, a great part of its most elaborate and best devised schemes for increasing the national wealth. If ever we could deduce a law of nature from many successive facts, the necessary and continual abolition, in modern times, under all parties, before as well as since Parliament was reformed, of the most highly prized regulations for the encouragement of trade have clearly established the existence of a law of nature which is hostile to the State regulating the trade and the industry of the people. That law of nature is the law of free trade, and, being thorough free traders, we believe that the law is applicable to education as to the manufacture of cotton cloth or the supply of corn.

If the State, meaning well, has been unable to advance, by its regulations, the material wealth of the people, is it likely that it can advance their mental power or immaterial wealth? The mode of increasing the quantity of corn is far better known than the mode of increasing useful knowledge. It is easier successfully to cultivate the ground than the mind. All the means of increasing material wealth are tangible; they almost fall with common arithmetic. The means of increasing knowledge, exciting proper motives, and regulating the mind, are not visible nor tangible; and, at the very least, the State is more likely to mistake the means of advancing the moral than the material improvement of the people. From the failure of the State, therefore, in its attempts to augment wealth, we infer the certain failure of its present schemes to improve education, and therefore we object to its attempting to educate the people.

We regard its past exertions in that direction as failures. By its means and its power the two universities are endowed and maintained; and there is no doubt that their revenues might be much more beneficially applied to the promotion of useful education than at present. Were those revenues, and the other funds set apart by the piety of our ancestors for the religious and moral education of the people, now properly applied, no further calls for this purpose would be requisite on the public purse. But the State sanctions and ordains the improper application of those funds, and what reason have we to suppose that it will not also, after a short time, sanction some improper applications of the funds now proposed to be applied to education? The application of the funds for education for purposes hostile to useful education leads to the erection of an erroneous standard of scholastic acquirements. Education is neglected or perverted throughout the country, and generally ill understood, because it has long been misapplied and perverted at Oxford and Cambridge. To the men educated there who have long been the general teachers, the present condition of education in England is mainly to be attributed. They have fastened upon us forms of substance—false grammar for good sense—and heathen ignorance upon modern science. The funds intended for education, too, having been appropriated in princely incomes to the teachers of Latin, Greek, and Theology, a completely false appreciation has got abroad of the money-value of scholastic acquirements; while schoolmasters on the Continent are at once highly respectable zealous teachers (at least in Germany of which we speak from much personal acquaintance), and very moderately paid, here they are, in the main, greedy after great emoluments, comparatively uninformed, and zealous chiefly to rival in outward splendour the Master of Westminster, the Provost of Eton, or the Heads of Houses.

Our contemporaries justly condemn our common schools. The *Times* of Monday, echoing the *Chronicle* of weeks before, said—

> We will confess that as far as regards the most numerous, and therefore the most important class of our country,— as far as concerns those whom we ought to be thinking of when we speak of 'the English' as a whole,—we believe the education of this country to be a miserable, make believe, superficial, illusory system. It is one great quackery from beginning to end. It does not stand the test of half a year's trial on any one subject, sacred or secular. It is all the same with both parties. There is only a difference in name between the National 'humbug' and the British and Foreign 'humbug.' The children come out pretty nearly as incapable, as giftless, as mere children, as mere parrots, as they went in.

That is only one of many testimonies to the inefficiency of our present education. But surely there is no nation in Europe where the State has devoted larger funds for the education of the people. Most carefully has it preserved all the old institutions to that end. Very much, too, has it increased their endowments. During the last thirty years it has never ceased to foster education, and the result is, according to the *Times*, that "The children come out of school as incapable, as giftless, as mere parrots as they went in." The bulk of this system of education has been in the hands, and under the control of men educated at the two national universities, which are preserved in all their rich endowments by the State. The State has meddled with them only to protect them from needful reform. The people are now, in fact, State educated; and what the *Times* describes is State education; and from that we conclude that the State is quite as incapable of promoting good education as profitable trade. If these be not conclusive arguments against the State meddling further with education, at least they inculcate great caution, and warrant great mistrust.

One of our correspondents asks us, whether the State should not educate the people in order to prevent the crimes which it is obliged to punish. That leads us to reply, that the State has been equally unsuccessful in preventing crime and in promoting trade. Within a short time it has had to avow that its scheme of transportation is a failure. The other schemes of silent and solitary punishments, its hulks, its gaols, have all been failures. The gibbet, in spite of the State, has almost been abolished, because it was a failure. From these facts, and many similar facts we cannot do otherwise than suspect that the State is quite as incapable by its acts—except as it may protect property and person, its proper and its only functions—of promoting the mental as the material improvement of the people. At the same time, every one of its acts involves considerable cost—some restriction—some additional paid officers—some mere visits of the tax-gatherer; and being the zealous advocates of laissez-faire, of trusting to the people, we object to every system of which the good, like that of the State education, is doubtful, while the cost is certain.

We have another objection on principle, and we state our opinions freely, because we know that they are extensively canvassed, and not very greatly criticized. Whether for good or for evil, they do not fall on barren ground. Education is of less importance to the community than subsistence. Without subsistence there will be no people to educate. Vain, too, will be the best education to prevent or repress crime unless subsistence be abundant. If it be the duty of the State, as proposed by the minute of the Privy Council, to rear good schoolmasters and pension them, it must *a fortiori* be its duty to perform the important part of rearing good cultivators of the soil, and securing them a proper payment. It has attempted that, but egregiously failed. If it undertake to pay schoolmasters, it must undertake to pay farmers and all other useful labourers. It must, as it is now by some persons required to do, feed the people, and it must, in spite of the laws of nature, in seasons of dearth or famine like the present, secure, as well as at every other time, to every man in the community, as well as to the schoolmaster, a fair day's wages for his work. But, as all reasonable men admit the utter impossibility of the State undertaking the major and more important duties which are implied in its undertaking the minor, we conclude, on principle, contrary we know to the present set of the popular current, that it ought not to undertake to teach the people, and has no business to rear, and pension, and reward schoolmasters.

We are at the same time perfectly convinced that our present system of school education is as bad as possible. But we are also convinced that our system of cookery is far from good in England. It is extremely wasteful. The people generally speaking are ignorant of the chemical properties of food, and ignorant of the art of making it at once tasteful and nutritive. We are of opinion, too, in common we believe with many other persons, that the means of subsistence are unfairly distributed. While some of the population are fed in the most scanty manner, others waste great quantities of food in riot and extravagance. We are sensible of the existence of many evils in other parts of society as in education, but we do not conclude that the Government should equalize the means of subsistence, and reform the national cookery; neither can we agree with those who affirm that it should provide education for the people. We reprobate its interference with education, because we do not see how it can then object to equalizing the means of subsistence and reforming our cookery. Nay, we are convinced, that from calling on the State to educate the people, to calling on it to equalize property, the stages are few and short.

We value education too highly not to be anxious that it should not be brought into discredit. The State certainly has the art of contaminating that which it touches. The numerous prohibitions against importing and exporting various commodities, carry with them a conviction that the thing prohibited is essentially advantageous, and smuggling is stimulated both by that and the desire to profit. The converse of the rule equally holds good; and when the

State undertakes to promote any object, by bounties or encouragements, it implies that there are difficulties to be overcome or pain to be endured. Its schemes of education involve compulsory taxation. Our Government, from administering and controlling which a large part of the people is excluded, is necessarily unpopular, and for the State to meddle in education, is to bring education somewhat into discredit. In many cases it now happens that the people, instead of regarding school education as beneficial to them, regard it as the contrary, and reluctantly send their children to school, as a favour to their masters and employers.

We are not surprised at such a result. Education is, with much parade, provided by one class for another; after many years of schooling, the children have learnt little more than their catechism, and, perhaps, some little contempt for their less-instructed parents. After leaving school, it is a chance whether they ever find any use or advantage from what they have been taught. Were education left untouched by the State, its own beauties and inherent advantages are so great that the people would be as naturally attracted to it as they are to high wages, and would be as eager to obtain it as they are to get plenty of fine clothing and wholesome food. We advocate *laissez-faire*, therefore, as in trade, because our firm conviction is, that it is the best, and, indeed, the only means of ensuring that improved and extended education which we all desire.

We must take leave to say, that we doubt the frankness and sincerity of many of those who now advocate State education. Individuals of both parties appear to us to entertain an ulterior and unavowed purpose. The hidden thought of the lower classes is, "Let us get knowledge, and we shall know how to use it. Let the Government, or the State, or the middle classes, teach us and our children—let us get from them all we can—and then we shall be able to help ourselves in opposition to them." The unavowed thought of the State, or the upper classes is, "The people are getting intelligence for themselves—they are becoming powerful through their acquirements as well as by their numbers—and if we do not direct their progress, they will escape altogether from our control." Some promote education, then, with a view to preserve power; others, in towns at least, willingly accept it as the means of destroying the superiority of the class which promotes education. These appear to us—we say it with deference, but conviction—to be something like the hidden objects of many of both classes, and, apart from our confidence in perfect frankness—our belief that no good can ever come of any attempt at deceit—we see clearly that this mode of proceeding must increase the expectations and power of both parties to do mischief, till it ends not in the gradual subversion of what is false, but in a hostile collision. Were the people left to educate themselves, real knowledge—not theories and systematized errors—would eventually be evolved in both classes, and both would gradually learn to get rid of false expectations, and abate reciprocal pretensions. That great differences profoundly agitate these classes is known to every observer, however calm at times the surface may be. Capital and labour make conflicting claims, *laissez-faire* and government-control are daily at issue, the Church and the Voluntary system can never be reconciled, and the system of education that sharpens the powers and encourages the false expectations of each of these opponents, aiming covertly to obtain superiority by its means, seems to us pregnant with future disaster. These conflicts are daily going on. By the natural and gradual progress of society they may be brought to a quiet conclusion; but a system that at once glazes over and strengthens the elements of discord, cannot fail, we think, to promote convulsion.

5

From The Proper Sphere of Government

Herbert Spencer

Nonconformist (1842–43), Letters VII and VIII

In later life Herbert Spencer (1820–1903) remarked that he had been raised in "an essentially *dissenting* family; and dissent is an expression of antagonism to arbitrary control." A "wish to limit State-action is a natural concomitant" of this perspective.

In 1833, at age thirteen, Herbert Spencer was sent by his parents to live with his uncle and aunt. Herbert's uncle, Rev. Thomas Spencer (1796–1853), assumed responsibility for his education over the next three years. Herbert described his uncle (a Cambridge graduate) as a leader of the evangelical movement within the Anglican Church, a movement that shared the "asceticism" of "the Wesleyan movement outside of it." Despite some occasional tension between nephew and uncle—the former had rebelled against authority for as long as anyone in his family could remember, and this future "agnostic" never showed much interest in religion—Herbert admired his uncle for his "philanthropy" and for his political views. Thomas Spencer had evolved from a typical Anglican Tory early in his career to a radical (classical) liberal who worked with the Anti-Corn Law League on behalf of free trade, who championed universal suffrage and the separation of church and state, and who spoke out against state education, militarism, war, and British imperialism. As Thomas Spencer wrote in his booklet *The People's Rights: and How to Get Them*:

> The expenses . . . of a just government are very small; and the rights of property require that the least possible amount that is consistent with security, and a sense of security, shall be taken away. Taxation becomes unjust, when those to whom the power of taxing is entrusted use it for other purposes than for the preservation of order. Taxes raised for the teaching of religion, for the building of places of worship, for the undertaking for the people the education of their children, for the dispensing of their alms, for granting of pensions, for extending the boundaries of empire, for interfering with the affairs of other nations, for controlling commerce, and for standing armies and useless wars, are so many infringements of this right. Taxes for these purposes involve a principle of injustice. . . .

A 22-year-old Herbert Spencer, whose political views at this time were the same as Thomas Spencer's, published his first extended discussion of his libertarian views in 1842 in a series of twelve Letters "The Proper Sphere of Government" that appeared in Edward Miall's *Nonconformist*—a leading periodical in the movement to disestablish the Church of England. Spencer quickly reprinted, at his own expense, these Letters as a pamphlet in the hope that it would serve as a sample of his writing and ideas that would get him get additional work. This strategy paid off in 1848, when James Wilson, proprietor of *The Economist*, read the pamphlet and hired Spencer as a sub-editor, a position he held for several years. During his time with *The Economist*, Spencer worked closely with the senior editor, Thomas Hodgskin, a fellow libertarian and Voluntaryist.

Two of Spencer's Letters, which are reprinted here in their entirety, are devoted to a critique of state education. It is possible that Spencer's arguments for Voluntaryism influenced the views of other Radical Dissenters, given that their organized campaign against state education took off in 1843. Spencer indicated that Edward Miall was so impressed with his Letters that "if the *Nonconformist* had had a more extensive circulation he should have been happy to have offered me a share in the editorship." Miall recommended Spencer to Thomas Price as a possible con-tributor to the *Eclectic Review*—another major outlet for Radical Dissenters. Spencer then submitted an article on education to Price. This was accepted but never published.

Spencer published another critique of state education in his first book, *Social Statics* (1851). As late as 1903, the chapter "National Education" was reprinted by The Society for the Liberation of Education from State Control. Spencer's ideas on education were presented in his influential book *Education: Intellectual, Moral and*

Physical (1861), a collection of four articles previously published in British Reviews. This book solidified Spencer's reputation as a pioneer in progressive education.

Letter VII

The question of state interference has been hitherto examined, only in those departments of its application, in which its existing effects are visible—viz., in commerce, religion, charity, war, and colonisation. In all of them that interference has been deprecated. It now remains to consider those social institutions which, though at present prospering in their original unfettered simplicity, are threatened by schemes for legislative supervision. Of these the first in importance stands—education.

It is clear that a system of national instruction is excluded by our definition. It cannot be comprehended under the administration of justice. A man can no more call upon the community to educate his children, than he can demand that it shall feed and clothe them. And he may just as fairly claim a continual supply of material food, for the satisfaction of their bodily wants, as of intellectual food, for the satisfaction of their mental ones. It will be the aim of the succeeding arguments to show the advantages of this exclusion.

Mankind are apt to decide upon the means to be employed in the attainment of an end, without sufficient examination into their fitness. Some great object in contemplation, the most obvious mode of securing it is chosen, without duly considering the extreme importance of discovering whether it is the best mode—

without ever inquiring whether its ultimate effects may be as good as its immediate ones—without asking what corruptions the machinery of their institution may be liable to—never putting to themselves the question: Is there any other way of arriving at the desideratum?—and neglecting a host of other considerations of like character. Such is the treatment of the question before us. The education of the people is the end in view; an end fraught with results the most momentous—results more intimately connected with the prosperity and happiness of posterity, than, perhaps, any others that may flow from our conduct—results which may accelerate or retard the advancement of mankind for hundreds, perhaps thousands, of years. Yet are there objections, to the method by which this end is to be compassed, of the utmost consequence, that have been entirely overlooked by its advocates—objections fundamentally affecting the principles upon which it rests; and which, if they be admitted as valid, must completely overthrow the whole scheme.

In the first place, national education assumes that a uniform system of instruction is desirable. A general similitude in the kinds of knowledge taught, and the mode of teaching it, must be necessary features in a state-training establishment. The question therefore presents itself—Would a universal fixed plan of intellectual culture be beneficial? After due consideration, I think the general answer will be—No. Almost all men of enlightened views agree that man is essentially a progressive being—that he was intended to be so by the Creator—and that there are implanted in him, desires for improvement, and aspirations after perfection, ultimately tending to produce a higher moral and intellectual condition of the world. The grand facts of history, both sacred and profane—the great principles and promises of revealed religion—the deductions of abstract reasoning—all go to prove that, notwithstanding the oft-repeated falling back, in spite of every difficulty that may be thrown in the way, and in defiance of all apparently adverse circumstances, still, that the grand and irresistible law of human existence, is progressive improvement. The very obstacles themselves ultimately serve as stepping stones to a higher condition—the tyranny of an aristocracy is working out the liberties of the people—the corruption of an established church has helped to raise the standard of religious purity—the blindfolding doctrines of priestcraft produce the more perfect discovery, and the still deeper appreciation of the great principles of Christianity—and, as of old, so in our day, the opposition to truth, still tends to accelerate its final triumph. If, then, the belief set forth at the commencement of this essay—that as there are laws for the guidance of the inorganic world—laws for the government of the animate creation—laws for the development of individual mind—so there are laws for the social governance of man—if, I say, this belief be received, it may be fairly assumed, that, in accordance with the great design of human progression, the Almighty has given laws to the general mind, which are ever working together for its advancement. It may be fairly assumed that, in this case as in the more tangible ones, the apparently untoward circumstances are, in reality, eminently conducive to the attainment of the object sought after. That all the prejudices, the mental idiosyncrasies, the love of opposition, the tendencies to peculiar views, and a host of other qualities, in their infinitely varied proportions and combinations, are all conspiring to bring about the intellectual, moral, and social perfection of the human race. If it be granted that man was created a progressive being, it must be granted, also, that the constitution, given to him by his Creator, was the one most perfectly adapted to secure his progression. It may be presumed that, if a uniform construction of mind had been best calculated to attain this end, it would have been adopted; but, as the opposite law has been given—so that, instead of finding minds similar, we find no two alike—unlimited variety, instead of uniformity, being the existing order of things—we must infer that this is the arrangement tending, in the greatest degree, to produce perfection. This conclusion may be supported, not only by abstract reasoning, but by experience. Varied mental constitution produces variety of opinion; different minds take different views of the same subject; hence, every question gets examined in all its bearings; and, out of the general mass of argument, urged forward by antagonist parties, may sound principle be elicited. Truth has ever originated from the conflict of mind with mind; it is the bright spark that emanates from the collision of opposing ideas; like a spiritual Venus, the impersonation of moral beauty, it is born from the foam of the clashing waves of public opinion. Discussion and agitation are the necessary agents of its discovery; and, without a universal dissimilitude in the minds of society, discussion and agitation could never exist.

If, then, it be admitted, that infinite variety in the mental conformation of individuals is essential to the advancement of the general human mind, what shall we say to a system which would train the feelings and intellects of a whole nation after one pattern—which hopes to correct all the irregularities implanted by the Creator, and proposes to take the plastic characters of our youth, and press them, as nearly as possible, into one common mould? And yet this must be the manifest tendency of any uniform routine of education. Natures differently constituted must be gradually brought, by its action, into a condition of similarity. The same influences, working upon successive generations, would presently produce an approximation to a national model. All men would begin to think in the same direction—to form similar opinions upon every subject. One universal bias would affect the mind of society; and, instead of a continual approach to the truth, there would be a gradual divergence from it. Under our present condition, the eccentricities and prejudices induced by one course of education, are neutralised by the opposing tendencies implanted by others; and the growth of the great and truthful features only of the national mind ensues. If, on the other hand, an established system were adopted, however judicious its arrangements might be—notwithstanding it might endeavour to promote liberality and independence of thought, it must eventually produce a general one-sidedness and similarity of character; and inasmuch as it did this, it would dry up the grand source of that spirit of agitation and inquiry, so essential as a stimulus to the improvement of the moral and intellectual man. It matters not what provisions might be made to guard against this evil—what varieties in the mode of instruction might be instituted; such is the general longing after uniformity, and such would be the ignorance of its evils, that we may rest assured no national system would long continue without merging into it.

Nor would this be the only disadvantage arising from a sameness of instruction. It must be remembered, that differently constituted as are the minds of men, each possessing its peculiar perfections and defects, the same mode of culture cannot with any propriety be pursued in all cases. Every character requires a course of treatment somewhat modified to suit its particular circumstances, and no such modifications are ever likely to be made under a national system. It is to be hoped that the time will come, when the wisdom of the teacher will be shown, in adapting his instructions, to the peculiarities of each of his pupils: when it will be his aim to correct this feeling, and to develop the other faculty, and so to train and prune the mind of every scholar, as to send him forth into the world, as perfect a being as possible. Under our present natural arrangement we may one day expect to see this. While the master is amenable to public opinion—while his interests require that he should adopt the most efficient modes of education, we may presume that he will be always zealously endeavouring to improve his methods—ever investigating the principles of his profession, and daily applying the results of those investigations to practice. But no one would ever expect the salaried state-teacher, answerable only to some superior officer, and having no public reputation at stake to stimulate him—no one would expect that he should study the character of each of his scholars, and vary his ordinary routine to suit each case; no one would expect that he should be continually improving, and ever endeavouring to perfect his moral machinery. We may rest assured, that in education as in everything else, the principle of honourable competition, is the only one that can give present satisfaction, or hold out promise of future perfection.

Probably, the existing educational institutions of Prussia and Germany will be appealed to in evidence of the fallacy of these arguments. It may be urged that the plan has been there many years in operation—that no such evils have arisen—that the people are in a comparatively enlightened condition—and that these results, when contrasted with our own, show that we have not made such great advances under the natural system, as they have under the artificial. Strong as this argument may appear, it will be found when closely considered, to be wholly superficial. The foundations of a palace may be hardly above ground, when an ordinary house is nearly complete; but we do not thence infer that the palace will not ultimately be the most magnificent building. It is not argued that because the hot-house plant outstrips its out-door contemporaries, that it will therefore make the most perfect tree; experience teaches the contrary. We do not conclude that the precocious child will make a better man than his less forward companion; we know that the reverse is generally the case. In the same manner, it must be remembered, that although an established education, may, for a time, stimulate the national mind into a rapid growth, we must not therefore presume, that its results will not be ultimately far surpassed by those of the natural system. It is one of the grand laws of creation, that the more perfect the being, the longer must be the time occupied in its development; and analogy would lead us to suppose, that the same may be true of the general mind of man—that the more noble the standard to which it is to attain, the more gradual must be its advancement—the more distant must be the day when it shall arrive at its climax; that the power which is to lead to its highest

pinnacle of perfection, must have a broad and deep foundation—
must root itself in some fundamental, and unchangeable attributes of human nature; and that as its results are to be great, so
must its action be slow.

Letter VIII

An overwhelming prejudice in favour of ancient and existing
usages has ever been, and probably will long continue to be, one of
the most prominent characteristics of humanity. No matter how
totally inconsistent with the existing condition of society—no
matter how utterly unreasonable, both in principle and practice—
no matter how eminently absurd, in every respect, such institutions or customs may be—still, if they have but the countenance
of fashion or antiquity—if they have but been patronised and
handed down to us by our forefathers—their glaring inconsisten-
cies, defects, and puerilities, are so completely hidden by the radiant halo wherewith a blind veneration has invested them, that it
is almost impossible to open the dazzled eyes of the world, to an
unprejudiced view of them. They are reverenced as relics of the
so-called "good old times"—reason and philosophy are laid pros-
trate before them—and the attempt to introduce amendment is
akin to sacrilege. Classical education affords a suitable illustration
of this. During those dreary times of rampant Roman catholi-
cism, when ecclesiastical dominion had attained its full growth,
and all Europe, under its deadly shade, slumbered in dark and
debasing ignorance, it became the practice amongst the more
enlightened, to make themselves acquainted with the ancient

languages, for the purpose of gaining access to the knowledge that was written in them; writings in their own tongue they had none—learning had fallen into neglect, and their only path to a condition above that of the common herd, was through the study of Latin and Greek. In process of time, however, great changes were effected. Man was not doomed to remain for ever in a state of spiritual bondage—the social mind awoke with new vigour from its long sleep—ignorance and bigotry were swept away by the returning tide of intelligence—science and philosophy soared far above the height to which they had before attained—and the knowledge of the ancients dwindled into insignificance, when compared with that of the moderns. It might have been presumed that, under these circumstances, the dead languages would gradually have sunk into disuse. But, no! such is the extreme veneration for precedent—such is the determined adherence to the practices of our ancestors, that, notwithstanding the conditions of the case are entirely altered—although the original necessities no longer exist, still is the same custom persevered in. It boots not to tell them that words are but the signs of ideas, and not the ideas themselves—that language is but a channel for the communication of knowledge—a means to an end; and that it is valuable only in so far as it serves that end. It matters not how clearly it may be shown that he who learns a language for its own sake, is like a workman who constructs a set of tools at immense cost of time and labour, and never afterwards uses them; or like a man who spends the best years of his life in making a ladder, for the purpose of gathering a scanty supply of indifferent fruit from the top of a high tree, when other fruit, of superior quality, is hanging in abundance within reach on a neighbouring one. No matter, I say, how clearly this may be shown, so great is the influence of ancient prescription, and so strong the desire to "do as the world does," that even in this enlightened age, men neglect the rich stores of real knowledge within their grasp, to follow fashion over the barren waste of grammars and lexicons.

Here then stands an example of a system, which, in spite of its many and manifest absurdities, has for centuries bid defiance to the general flood of improvement; and stands in the midst of our progressing social institutions, its main features unaltered from their original condition. What may we infer from this? Does it not warn us of the dangerous consequences that may ensue, from the erection of any lasting scheme of education? If a system, not nationally established, but rooted only in the prejudices, and sheltered by the bias of society, has been able thus to withstand for ages, the assaults of reason and common sense, how much more difficult would it be to reform one, which, in addition to these supporting influences, should receive the protection of the law? It may indeed be provided that the power of remodelling such an establishment be placed in the hands of the people, but practically this would amount to nothing. We have abundant evidence of the almost insuperable difficulties attending the modification of existing institutions, even when the people have theoretically the means of altering them; and we have no right to assume, that these difficulties would not, to a great degree, exist in time to come. Take, for instance, the church. The national body of dissenters are of opinion, that many of its ordinances, services, and ceremonies, require amendment; the great mass of its own communicants think the same; its founders themselves contemplated such a revision; there are no class interests at stake; the amendments alluded to would entail no loss upon the ecclesiastical body; yet, with all these circumstances in favour of a re-arrangement, things remain as they were. How much greater, then, would be the obstacles in reforming an institution, where any extensive change, would probably incapacitate many of its officers?

Even allowing, for a moment, that there would be no great difficulty in introducing improvements into a system of national education; the important question yet remains—Would the people see the necessity for those improvements? Analogy would lead us to answer—No. The blinding effects of prejudice in favour of existing modes of instruction has already been pointed out, and every day presents us with cases illustrative of the same influence. Ask the classical scholar his opinion of mathematics; or the mathematician what he thinks of geology, chemistry, or physiology, and both their answers will imply a bias in favour of their own kind of education.

It is argued, therefore, that men would never appreciate the imperfections of a mode of teaching, under which they had been brought up; and that even if they did, it would be extremely difficult for them to make any amendments. Should the truth of these conclusions be admitted, there remains but one ground upon which a state education can be defended; namely, the assumption, that it would never require any reform; which is the same thing as saying, that we of the present day, have attained to the pinnacle of mental elevation—that we have duly determined the relative merits of the various kinds of information, and are prepared to point out the most complete scheme of intellectual training—that we are fully competent to decide, not only for ourselves, but for future generations, what are the most valuable branches of knowledge, and what are the best modes of instruction; and that, being perfect masters of the philosophy of mind, we are quite justified in dictating to our successors. Truly a most sensible supposition!

Presuming that all other considerations were favourable, it still behoves us seriously to inquire—What guarantee have we that the beneficial results intended to be secured would, in future ages, be realised? How do we know that the evils and perversions that have never yet been kept out of social institutions by the most perfect human arrangements, would not creep in here also, to the ultimate destruction of the proposed advantages? No satisfactory answer can be given to these questions. We may feel fully convinced, that corruptions and abuses would gradually make their appearance, in defiance of the most carefully regulated provisions for their exclusion—despite of all our endeavours to ensure good management. Again may we turn to the church for an example. Little did our protestant reformers suspect, that the machinery they were about to employ for the support of their religion, was destined to become a tool for political party—an instrument for extortion—a genteel means of gaining a comfortable living—a thing of outside purity and inward depravity—a mere heap of worldliness. True, they had before their eyes the glaring abominations of the church which they had over-turned; but they intended to provide against the recurrence of such calamities. And how have they succeeded? As with them, so with us. We may depend upon it that, were the scheme of state instruction carried out, ere a century was expired, we should have educational sinecures, pluralities, non-resident tutors, highly-paid master, and half-starved teachers, wealthy inspectors, lay patrons, purchasable livings, and numberless other perversions analogous to those of our national church; whilst the whole institution would resolve itself, like its representative, into a field for aristocratic patronage. Surely, if Christianity, the most powerful of all moral antiseptics, has been unable to keep pure, the apparatus devoted to its own ministration; much less can we anticipate freedom from corruption, where the same temptations would exist unopposed by the like preserving influences. It is of no use saying that the people would never again allow such iniquities to be practised. So, in all probability, thought the founders of our state church. But the people *have* allowed them—they *have* had the power to prevent abuses, and have never used it; and we have no right to assume that they would not be equally negligent in time to come.

Another objection, stronger perhaps than any of the foregoing, still remains. The advocates of national education, if they be men who uphold freedom of conscience—if they do not desire one man to pay towards the support of privileges enjoyed only by others— in a word, if they are friends to civil and religious liberty, must necessarily assume that all members of the community, whether churchmen or dissenters, catholics or jews, tories, whigs, radicals, or republicans, will agree, one and all, to support whatever system may be finally adopted. For, if their education is to be truly a national one, it must be managed by the government, and sustained by state funds; those funds must form part of the revenue; that revenue is raised by taxation; that taxation falls upon every individual—upon him that has no children as well as upon him that has; and the result must be, that all would pay towards the maintenance of such an institution, whether they had need of it or not—whether they approved of it or otherwise. Many would, on principle, dissent from a state education, as they would from a state church. Some men would disapprove of the species of instruction—others of the mode of teaching. This man would dislike the moral training—that the intellectual. Here they would disagree upon details—and there protest against the entire system. Would it then be just, would it be reasonable, to let these men bear the burden of an institution from which they derived no benefit? Surely not. Every argument used by religious nonconformists to show the unfairness of calling upon them to uphold doctrines that they cannot countenance, or subscribe towards a ministration which they do not attend, is equally effective in proving the injustice of compelling men to assist in the maintenance of a plan of instruction inconsistent with their principles; and forcing them to pay for teaching, from which neither they nor their children derive any benefit. In the one case, the spread of religious knowledge is the object aimed at—in the other the spread of secular knowledge; and how this difference could affect the right of dissent it would be difficult to discover.

Before dismissing the subject, it may be as well to remark that, rather than see the people educated by means over which they have no control, our government would, no doubt, be very happy to take the task of instruction into their own hands; and we may pretty accurately anticipate what the tendencies of that instruction would be. Bold and independent reasoning, originality of thought, firmness in defence of principles, and all characteristics of that class, we need little expect to be encouraged. Great veneration for authority, a high respect for superiors, and implicit faith in the opinions of the great and learned, would no doubt be studiously inculcated. As for their religious education, we may predict that such virtues as meekness and humility would occupy so much attention as to leave no time for the rest; and we may be sure that the teachers would take especial care to instil into the minds of their pupils all those important and fundamental principles of our religion, such as—"Let every soul be subject to the higher powers"—"Servants be obedient to your masters"—"Learn to be content in that station of life to which it has pleased God to call you"; and other such appropriate selections. An apt illustration of the species of mental training our rulers would patronise, is afforded by the late parliamentary grant for teaching singing. Truly, it would be a lucky thing for the aristocracy, if the people could be persuaded to cultivate their voices instead of their understandings. The nation asks for cheap bread. Their rulers reply—No, we cannot give you cheap bread, because we should lose part of our rents; but, never mind, we will put aside part of your own money to give you lessons in music! We will not give you back your food, but we will teach you to sing! O generous legislators!

The objections to national education are:

1. That it necessarily involves a uniform system of moral and intellectual training, from which the destruction of that variety of character, so essential to a national activity of mind, would inevitably result.

2. That it takes away the grand stimulus to exertion and improvement on the part of the teacher, that must ever exist under the natural arrangement.

3. That, considering the improbability of amendments being introduced in future ages, it practically assumes that we are capable of pointing out to our descendants, what kinds of knowledge are the most valuable, and what are the best modes of acquiring them—an assumption which is anything but true.

4. That it would be liable to the same perversions as a national religion, and would, in all probability, become ultimately as corrupt.

5. That, if it is intended to be an equitable institution, it must be necessarily presumed that all men will agree to adopt it—a presumption which can never be borne out.

6. That it would be used by government as a means of blinding the people—of repressing all aspirations after better things—and of keeping them in a state of subserviency.

From abstract reasoning, and from the evident analogy with existing institutions, it is, therefore, concluded, that national education would, in the end, be a curse, rather than a blessing.

6

"The Principle of State Education"

Edward Baines, Jr.

Letter II of *Letters to the Right Hon. Lord John Russell, First Lord of the Treasury, on State Education* (London: Ward & Co; and Simkin, Marshall, & Co., 1847)

Edward Baines, Jr. (1800–1890), was the leading Voluntaryist in Victorian England. Baines followed in the journalistic footsteps of his father, Edward Baines, Sr., proprietor and editor of the *Leeds Mercury*—the most influential provincial newspaper of its day with the largest circulation outside of London. Baines junior joined the staff of the *Mercury* at age 15, became co-editor in his twenties, and became the sole editor after his father was elected MP for Leeds in 1834. The *Leeds Mercury*, under the supervision of both father and son, was a strong voice for radical liberalism. It advocated free trade across the board and called for abolition of the Corn Laws (import tariffs on grain) long before the formation of the Anti-Corn Law League in 1838; it advocated retrenchment of the English government and sounded alarms about the growth and dangers of bureaucracy; it supported parliamentary reform and extension of the franchise; and it crusaded for the abolition of church rates and for the complete disestablishment of the Church of England. (The term "Voluntaryist" was first used as a label for the British Nonconformists who called for the complete separation of church and state; only later was it applied to those who also advocated the separation of school and state. The arguments for both positions were quite similar.) Beginning in 1843, Baines became the leading Congregationalist in the crusade against state education, writing many articles in the *Leeds Mercury* that combined principled arguments against state education with detailed statistics that purportedly showed the satisfactory progress of voluntary schools in Britain. Many of these articles were later reprinted as booklets. Baines was elected to the House of Commons in 1859 and served until 1874. He was knighted in 1880.

The following excerpt is from Letter II of *Letters to the Right Hon. Lord John Russell, on State Education.* Originally published in the *Leeds Mercury* and later reprinted as a short book (1847) of 147 pages, the twelve letters in this book illustrate a recurring problem that frustrated Edward Baines and other Voluntaryists. Lord John Russell, like Baines, was a Whig and a reform-minded liberal who advocated free trade. But Russell, though he had praised the success of voluntary schools, also defended state education. This was a flagrant inconsistency, in the eyes of Baines and other Voluntaryists. How could someone who understands the detrimental effects of government intervention in industry and trade fail to understand that government intervention in education will result in the same kind of harmful, if unintended, consequences? As Baines wrote to Russell in Letter I:

> You have, in common with other enlightened men . . . seen reason decisively to condemn and wholly to abandon the principle of State Protection to Industry. Now there is a great analogy between Government Protection to *Industry* and Government Protection to *Mind.* They are attempted in great part from the same motives; they indicate the same distrust of individual exertion and prudence; they are supported by similar arguments. . . . In each case, the Government undertakes to do for the people what they are able to do better for themselves. In each case, the effect of that Government protection is to impair the exertions of individuals and classes. In each case, the habit of leaning on the Government entails other unforeseen evils. . . . In one case, as your Lordship has said, Protection has been *"the bane of agriculture,"*—in the other, I believe it would be the *bane of education."*

Russell had supported repeal of the Corn Laws in 1846, just a year before he delivered a speech calling for state education. Baines wryly commented: "To begin your interference with Education just where you end your interference with Industry, would, in my humble judgment, show that Governments are slow to learn from experience."

In the following excerpt, Baines repeatedly emphasizes the importance of establishing and maintaining clear principles when determining the proper limits of governmental power. If those principles are violated by the selfsame liberals who should be defending them, then all theoretical arguments against the indefinite expansion of state power will have been effectively nullified. This stress on the crucial importance of defending liberal principles recurs in many of Baines's writings against state education.

———————

My Lord,—It is a truth perhaps never denied, but too often forgot, that all legislation should be founded on correct *principles*. If it is not so founded, but consists merely of a series of temporary expedients, it will necessarily become a mass of inconsistency and confusion. Principles will be introduced unawares, which, being afterwards carried out, will be productive of the utmost practical inconveniences, mischief, and injustice.

There are many disorders and evils in a community which Government could not correct, without stepping beyond its province, and violating an important *principle*. There are also many things in themselves desirable, which Government, even though it had the power, ought not to attempt to do or to enforce, because it would in so doing go beyond its province, and violate *principle*.

For example, the introduction of new and improved machinery often causes distress among the classes who have worked with the old and inferior machinery: but Government could not in any case prohibit the use of the new machines without admitting a *principle* that would put a stop to all invention and improvement.

In the case of the Hand-loom Weavers, whose distress and whose numbers were so great as to lead to the appointment of a Government Commission of Inquiry, the Legislature, acting on the correct *principle*, most properly refused to prohibit or to tax the Power-looms.

Many other illustrations might be given, such as the sale of spirituous liquors, by which thousands of lives are sacrificed yearly,—the neglect of public worship and of religious duties,—the publication of false principles in politics, morals, and religion,— the pursuit of occupations dangerous to life or destructive to health,—and indeed innumerable other cases, where there might appear a good *prima facie* case for interference, but in which nevertheless Parliament could not interfere, without violating the *principles* of personal, commercial, or religious liberty, or liberty of the press.

If, in any of these cases, a Bill should be brought into Parliament to accomplish the object, you would think it your duty to resist it,—admitting, as you would, the excellence of the proposers' motive, but contending that Parliament could not interfere without sanctioning a false *principle*, from which, in other matters, disastrous consequences might result.

Principles, like the mustard seed of the parable, are "the least of all seeds, but when they are grown, they are the greatest among herbs, and become a tree," whose branches spread through the earth. Look at a recent notable example, which I quote not to express any opinion upon it, but simply as an illustration. In 1796 the Irish Parliament passed *sub silentio* a grant of several thousand pounds, to aid in building a college at Maynooth for the education of the Roman Catholic Clergy: the grant became annual: from the Irish it was transmitted to the Imperial Parliament: when the college was built, it had to be maintained: the last year the grant was raised from £9,000 a-year to £30,000 a-year, and it was made perpetual. Now observe; Mr. Macaulay has argued, with irresistible logic, that the *principle* was involved in the very first grant, and that it was no new principle at all, but simply a consistent and effective acting out of that principle, to treble the grant and make it perpetual. But your Lordship, infinitely more bold and not less logical than Mr. Macaulay, declared last year that your predecessors ought, on the self-same *principle, to endow the whole of the Roman Catholic Clergy of Ireland!* And with precisely the same reason it might be proposed to pay the ministers of *every* religion throughout the British Empire, not excepting the Brahmin priests of India, or even the dancing girls of the Hindoo temples. Such mighty consequences would naturally and justly flow from a *principle* introduced silently and unobserved in a grant of the Irish Parliament!

Nor is there any limit in the point of *time* to the fruitfulness of a *principle*. Half a century had this principle lain dormant in the Maynooth grant, when lo! It suddenly takes root, and shoots forth in this prodigious growth. *Principles* are like the grains of wheat found in the wrappings of the Egyptian mummy, which, after three thousand years, have proved the vital seed of new harvests. They are immortal.

I have dwelt upon this point, my Lord, because it is of incalculable importance in the question of State Education. I shall not shrink from a discussion of the question as one of *practice* and *experience.* But it is of far greater importance to ascertain the *principle* on which it is proposed to act. If the principle is good, it is your duty to carry it out consistently to the utmost extent. But if the principle is bad, it is your duty to decline acting upon it in any form or degree. No wise legislature, and no wise people, will suffer their laws to be *founded on false principles.*

Let us inquire, then, upon what *principle* State Education is founded.

Is it not upon this—that *it is the duty of a Government to train the MIND of the people?*

Probably the advocates of State Education would, as a matter of *policy*, decline to put the principle thus broadly. They might limit it in various ways. They would perhaps only maintain it to be the duty of Government to educate *the young*: some of them would draw a distinction between *secular* and *religious* education, and would say it is the duty of Government to give the *former*, but not to give the *latter*: some of them would limit the principle to the education of the children of *the poor*: and some would say that it is the duty of the government to offer education, but not to make it *compulsory.*

But these limitations seem to me purely arbitrary, and adopted from motives of policy and expediency. The fundamental principle, I conceive, must be, that *it is the duty of a Government to train the MIND of the people.*

I infer this from the arguments by which State Education is recommended. Those arguments are, first, that mental cultivation and good moral and religious principles in the people are necessary to the public welfare, (which I admit); and second, that

Government, being bound to care for the public welfare, is consequently bound to give the cultivation and the principles which are essential to it (which I *deny*).

I infer it also from the consistency of things. If it is the duty of Government to give the lower and elementary branches of education, it must *à fortiori* be its duty to give the higher branches, which go to the formation of the moral and religious character, . . . infinitely more than by school learning, that the interests of society are affected. If, from any cause, be it what it may, elementary and secular instruction cannot safely be left to the people themselves, still less could moral and religious instruction be safely left to them. If Government is bound to see that the poorer classes receive a sound and efficient education, it is bound to see that the middle and higher classes receive an education not less sound and efficient, though it may not be absolutely bound to provide it. If Government is called upon to provide education, and to tax the people for that purpose, it would be no great stretch to make the education universal and compulsory. Nay, still further, if the education of children ought to be in the hands of the State, who shall say that the continued training of the youth and the adult in religious knowledge, upon which private virtue and the public welfare so mainly depend, ought not equally to be in the hands of the State? And where, acting on these principles, could you consistently stop? Would not the same paternal care which is exerted to provide schools, schoolmasters, and school-books, be justly extended to provide mental food for the adult, and to guard against his food being poisoned? In short, would not the principle clearly justify *the appointment of the Ministers of Religion, and a Censorship of the Press?*

I declare my conviction that all these things hang together,—that they all flow naturally and necessarily from the same principles,—and that, however your Lordship or other statesmen or writers of the present day might deprecate such an application of the principles, they might consistently be pushed to that extent. There is no *tenable* ground short of it.

Nor is this a matter of mere speculation. Several of the Governments which have taken the education of the young into their own hands, do, in point of fact, extend their superintendence and control to every class of society, to every age of life, to the means of religious instruction, and to the organs of political intelligence and speculation. The pulpit and the press are as much under their control as the schoolmaster's desk or the professor's chair. Nor is the domestic circle sacred from the intrusion of their police-spies; no house is a castle, no home a sanctuary, from their all-searching despotism.

Whether, therefore, we look at the arguments by which State Education is recommended, at the consistency of things, or at the practice of the Governments which have taken education into their own hands, we find that the only intelligible principle on which State Education can be based is that already expressed, namely, that *it is the duty of a Government to train the MIND of the People.*

The principle of the ancient Greek philosophers, put forth with apparent acquiescence in some modern publications, is, that the State is bound to superintend the education of all the youth, because, unless they are trained up in attachment to the particular form of government and institutions of the country, the State itself must perish. This principle would obviously require a *universal* and *compulsory* education, not only in general knowledge, but also *in political and religious opinions!* And however absurd such a principle may appear to most readers, it is gravely recommended by an able writer of our own day; and it is thoroughly acted upon in the systems of State Education of the German States. It serves to illustrate how far the theory and practice of State Education may be pushed; and to show that I have not exaggerated the importance of looking well to principles in this question. I need not say that such a practice as that recommended by the Greek philosophers, however congenial to the despotic governments of Germany, is in total opposition to the liberty and mental independence of the English people. Our history proves the theory to be a vain speculation, inasmuch as the freely-educated people of England are equally attached to their institutions with other nations, though their minds are not all cast in one Government mould by State schoolmasters.

I am quite aware that most Members of Parliament and many other practical politicians will think my jealousy as to principles excessive. They will say—'These are visionary fears; there is no danger of Government in this country adopting measures unfavourable to liberty; public opinion would prevent it; here is a great evil to be remedied—popular ignorance; voluntary liberality cannot cope with it; no power but that of the State is strong enough; let us do practical good, and not be deterred by the fear of possible and distant evils.'

I intend to discuss the question as a practical one, but I cannot allow such a mode of treating the subject to pass without my strong protest. The practical legislation which is careless as to principles, is likely to produce abundant practical mischief. I have learnt, as a political economist, in regard to commercial legislation, to be very jealous in watching over principles. We have seen bad principles, though in the best-intentioned laws, hearing their appropriate fruit in a long course of vicious legislation, which has entailed a series of mischiefs upon industry, not to be corrected without extreme difficulty, some constitutional danger, and hardship to numerous classes. As a Protestant and a Dissenter, too, I have learnt the importance of adhering closely to principle. I believe that the well-meant interference of the civil power under imperial Rome, in support of Christianity, was the source of the manifold evils which have resulted to mankind from Papal tyranny, and from every form of compulsory and State religion. The motive to that interference was pious; the inducement was strong; practical men would have scoffed at the scruples which should have opposed it. But such deviations from the straight course, out of regard to expediency, are like By-path Meadow in Bunyan's inimitable allegory, smooth, green, and pleasant to the feet of weary pilgrims, and appearing to run exactly alongside of the king's highway, but imperceptibly leading off from it, till the traveller finds himself involved in manifest transgression and danger. I would take the part of Hopeful, and warn my Christian friends to resist the soft seduction, to stand fast in the way of truth, though it be sometimes hard and stony, and to be assured that it is the path of wisdom, as well as of duty.

I object, then, my Lord, to the interference of Government with the Education of the people, because of the false and dangerous principle on which I conceive it to rest. If I have correctly explained the nature and scope of that principle, its viciousness will be self-evident. But I may say, in more express terms, that, in my judgment, *it is not the duty or province of the Government to train the mind of the people.* It is true, Government has often gone beyond its province. In the innumerable laws for the protection of various branches of industry, it did so. In establishing and endowing a particular form of Religion, it did so. In attaching civil disabilities to religious opinions, it did so. And in this matter of Education it is doing so. Of course I mean that such is my opinion; I do not wish to speak dogmatically.

In all countries Government has gone beyond its province, and especially in the matters I have referred to. This is very natural in unenlightened times. Much of the business of civilization is to undo the follies of former ages. Legislation is a power so mighty, and men are naturally so fond of the use of power, that there has always been a tendency to *over-legislate*. The temptation is irresistible. An imprudent legislature is like a boy with his first knife, who, in his impatience to use it, notches his mother's tables and chairs. The hardest lesson for Government or urchin to learn is what it ought *not* do. It is perhaps the highest attainment of a constitutional Government, *to confide in the People*.

I have said that I think it is not the province of the Government to train the mind of the people. What are the duties of Government? Generally speaking, to maintain the frame of society; and for this end to restrain violence and crime,—to protect person and property,—to enact and administer the laws needful for the maintenance of peace, order, and justice,—to sanction public works called for by the general convenience, as docks, harbours, canals, railways, &c.—to conduct the relations of society with other communities,—to provide for the public safety against external attack,—to appoint the officers, raise the taxes, pass the laws, construct the buildings, &c., requisite for these purposes.

On the other hand, it is *not*, I conceive, the duty of Government to interfere with the free action of the subject beyond what is necessary for these protective and defensive objects. It is *not* the duty of the Government to feed the people, to clothe them, to build houses for them, to direct their industry or their commerce, to superintend their families, to cultivate their minds, to shape their opinions, or to supply them with religious teachers, physicians, schoolmasters, books, or newspapers.

These are things which the people can and ought to do for themselves, and which it is not the province of Government to do for them. In all these things Governments have interfered, and I believe in all with mischievous effect. The natural faculties, instincts, and reason of men, together with the powerful stimulus of self-interest, the sense of individual responsibility to God, and the revelation of truth and love given by our Divine Lawgiver and Saviour, are sufficient to stimulate and to guide them in these matters.

Not that there may not be ten thousand errors committed every day in these very things. To err is human. But still it is not the province of Government to correct those errors; no Government is competent to correct them; and it could not even attempt it without acting upon false principles, violating liberty, and doing infinitely more harm than good.

Authors, philosophers, and divines, of high name, have advocated the interference of Governments with the religion, as well as with the education, of subjects. This was, indeed, the very system enforced by Rome for many centuries throughout Christendom, and inherited by Reformed countries. I have endeavoured to show that, to act out the principle and to accomplish the object it is necessary to carry the interference very far; and it has practically been carried to the extent, in many countries and for many centuries, of appointing the ministers of religion, controlling the press, and coercing opinion even by the prison and the stake.

I am aware that there are questions of nicety as to the limits of the duties of Government. One has reference to a national provision for the poor. Partly to protect society from the evils of mendicancy and crime, and partly out of humanity, a legal provision is made for the destitute. Admitting that there seems a paramount necessity for such a provision, it must be observed that this is found in practice to be one of the most difficult and delicate duties a Government has to discharge. Only within a few years, abuses existed in the administration of the Poor Law which seemed to be eating like a cancer into society, cutting the sinews of industry, and pauperizing the labouring class. When a system was adopted to reform these abuses, it became odious from the centralized and arbitrary power created. The liability to abuse in any poor-law system, local or central, is extreme.

It is doubtless a fair question, whether Government is not called upon to provide *education* for the children of the pauper class, as it provides them with food. Some advocate a state provision for education on this ground, to operate as a kind of *preventive-police*.

Let me, then, point out, that the analogy would justify nothing whatever beyond a provision for the education of the *pauper class*. It would justify no scheme of State Education for the working classes generally, still less for the whole country. It would be strictly limited by the necessity of the case, and would be an exception to the great rule. This, therefore, would not countenance in the slightest degree the extensive projects propounded by Dr. Hook, and supposed to be contemplated by yourself; which clearly go on the principle that Government ought to provide for and superintend the education of *the country at large*. It would not countenance any kind of interference with schools, but would rather look to a weekly parochial allowance to pauper families for the payment of school pence, leaving the parents at liberty to choose the schools. This would be a totally different thing from any proposal hitherto made. It would be excessively open to fraud and abuse. The changing residences of the pauper population, and the very uncertain continuance of their dependence on the parish, would make such a plan difficult to administer. And it would require the most cautious examination whether the plan would tend to encourage pauperism or to prolong its duration.

My opinion is decidedly *against* the attempt of Government to provide education for the children of *out-doors* paupers. The existing educational societies—possibly with some addition to their plans—would do it better than the Government. It is in entire accordance with their principles and with their present operations. "Ragged schools," for this purpose, are already multiplying.

There can be no difference of opinion as to the propriety of educating the children in the workhouses. They are for the most part orphans, thrown absolutely on public support, and shut up in the parochial building. The parish is to them in the relation of parents, and it is its duty to supply them with education, as it does with food, clothing, and lodging,—though this ought to be done on the most liberal plan, and not on the principle on which Dr. Hook has acted in the Leeds Workhouse in regard to religious instruction, where he has contrived to exclude all the Dissenting and Wesleyan Ministers, the Town Missionaries, and Sunday School Teachers, who had given religious instruction there with great regularity for years, and has monopolised the place for himself and his clerical coadjutors.

But I repeat, there is nothing in the circumstances of the pauper class to justify a plan of State Education.

Such, my Lord, are my views as to the *principles* which any plan of State Education must involve, and which forbid Government from undertaking the education of the people. If these views are correct, *State Education is wrong in principle.*

7

"On the Progress and Efficiency of Voluntary Education in England"

Edward Baines, Jr.

Crosby-Hall Lectures on Education (London: John Snow, 1848)

This selection is from what is probably the most remarkable collection of articles against state education ever published. Bearing the bland and uninformative title, *Crosby-Hall Lectures on Education*, this book is virtually unknown today, even among scholars of classical liberalism in Britain. It is a difficult book to find, and none of the articles has ever been reprinted. We are pleased to fill this unfortunate lacuna, at least partially, by reprinting selections from three lectures.

The *Crosby-Hall Lectures on Education* came about in the following way: At an 1848 meeting of the Congregational Board of Education in Derby, England, it was decided that the multifaceted case against state education should be made available to a general audience. A convention was therefore held at Crosby Hall in London, one that featured some of the brightest stars in the Voluntaryist movement: Edward Baines, Jr., Algernon Wells, Richard Winter Hamilton, Andrew Reed, Edward Miall, Henry Richard, and Robert Ainslie. A number of these men were Congregationalist ministers who had worked for years as administrators and teachers in voluntary schools, whereas others (such as Baines and Miall) made their most important contributions to Voluntaryism as writers. The written Crosby-Hall lectures were published separately in the *British Banner* in 1848, and then collected into an anthology in the same year.

In this selection, Edward Baines, Jr., summarizes the Voluntaryist case against state education, and he compares freedom of education and schooling to freedom of the press and other civil liberties. Baines points out that every free institution has faults and deficiencies, but these problems do not warrant state interference to remedy such problems. No one would claim, for example, that a free press results in nothing but good literature—on the contrary, much of it is junk—but this does not mean that a government should control the press in the vain hope of producing better products. The same reasoning, Baines insists, applies to voluntary education. Not every voluntary school is a good school, but the overall quality of voluntary schools had been improving; and the quality will continue to improve over time, as competition in educational methods generates a better product, and provided the government refrains from imposing rigid requirements that will freeze all progress. "The fact is, that *freedom* and *willingness* infinitely surpass Governments in invention, enterprise, and of adaptation to circumstances." Governments lack the "heart and soul" needed for innovation and progress. The "natural and normal state" of government institutions, including government schools, "is to be at rest."

Among the many controversies of the age, it is cheering to find some great truth which receives general assent. Few persons, for example, would question the proposition, that Religion, Knowledge, and Liberty conduce to the highest prosperity of nations. There would be great diversity of opinion as to the practical application of the truth,—as to the kind of religion, the method of promoting knowledge, and the best form of liberty. But it is an advantage, and one which England has not very long enjoyed, that the general principle is admitted. No English writer, now-a-days, commends Ignorance as the mother of devotion, or advocates the despotic preference to the representative form of government.

Religion, knowledge, liberty, then, may be regarded as forming the golden tripod on which the genius of Britain sits, dispensing truth and happiness to the world. Each stem of the tripod should have the strength of the rock, and all should lean towards and support each other. The religion should be that divine principle which not merely restrains, but animates and ennobles,—which shuts out no ray of light, and sanctions no species of injustice. The knowledge should be pure truth, free from all superstition and servility, illustrating at once the claims of God and the rights of man among his fellow-men. The liberty should be according to knowledge, and consistent with the peace and order inculcated in the Gospel.

I shall not be understood by this figure to imply that I elevate any right or interest of man into rivalry with the claims of his Maker. No. But I deem knowledge and liberty to be heaven-born,—to belong to religion itself,—to be embraced with it in the same radiant circle—even the girdle of righteousness and love with which the Almighty encompasses his decrees.

If this view be correct, it is the sacred duty of Englishmen to protect and advance religion, knowledge, and liberty, in their alliance with each other, and never to promote one at the expense of the rest. The facts to be brought out in this Lecture seem to me to illustrate the connection of which I have spoken, as natural and worthy of being perpetuated. Venerating religion and loving liberty, it will be my object to show that knowledge ought to be promoted among the youth of England with a due regard to both.

It is humbling but salutary to remember, that the influential classes of this country have not long admitted the duty, or even the safety, of encouraging the bulk of the people, that is, the labouring classes, to acquire knowledge. Popular education in England may be said to bear date from the commencement of the present century. Before that period, knowledge, like liberty, had been slowly though surely making way; but it very rarely extended beyond the upper and middle classes. It was thought unsuitable for the labouring class, or beyond their reach. The aristocracy, and even the clergy, regarded ignorance as the safeguard of order, and knowledge as incompatible with subordination.

In the middle of the nineteenth century, when education is more extended, and more rapidly extending and improving, than at any former period, our rulers have taken up the belief, that it is not safe to leave education to the people themselves, but that, in order to make it general and efficient, it must be aided and controlled by the Government. It is my firm and sorrowful conviction, that this is one of those aberrations in the progress of truth, of which history contains so many examples. How often have we seen error, when defeated on one side, unexpectedly making head on another, and threatening to recover all ground it had lost! It has been so in the history of religion, of government, and in many of the departments of knowledge. Imperfect reformations, half conquests, and balanced advantages characterise the march of truth through this erring world. The eagle gaze of Luther did not receive every ray of solar light. The Protestant Reformation of Germany, Switzerland, and England did not quite destroy the shackles of prejudice. The almost blameless Revolution of America left the monster form of Slavery to rear itself beside the largest growth of Freedom. The great Reform of the English House of Commons was neither complete nor unblemished. In Germany and France we have seen philosophy debased by infidelity. The revival of spiritual religion in our own emancipated industry from Government control, under the name of "protection," when the same control, under nearly the same misnomer, lays its grasp on the more sacred interests of education.

It seems very remarkable that Government, which in all former ages held aloof from the education of the people, should now, for the first time, claim its superintendence as a right and duty, when the people have made such extraordinary advances in educating themselves. If it be indeed the duty of Government to promote the education of the people, it is a duty which has been so entirely neglected through all the periods of our history, that we could not safely rely upon the Government for its discharge in future. Of this newly-claimed right and newly-discovered duty we may say, that no claim could be made with a worse grace, and that the duty is undertaken precisely when it is least needed.

It will hardly be denied, within the limits of England, that *the people* have a *right* to educate their own children, and that it is their *duty* to educate them; that this right and duty belong first, by the law of nature, to *parents*, and next, by the law of Christianity, to those whom Providence enables to assist their poorer neighbours.

I shall not further discuss this question, because it will be undertaken by an abler hand in the future Lecture. I will only remind you of the general rule, that the more responsibility is divided, the less efficiently is the duty performed.

Whilst I believe that education is the duty of the people themselves, I am equally persuaded that it does not come within the province of Government, according to just views of what that province is, under a system of political and civil liberty. But I am, if possible, still more strongly of opinions, that wherever the duty lies, it is eminently the *interest* of the people to discharge it themselves; and for these, amongst other reasons:—1st. That a duty is likely to be best discharged by the parties on whom it most directly rests, and who have the strongest motives for its performance. 2nd. That our duties are the discipline ordained by Heaven for our moral improvement, and that to relieve men of their duties is to deprive them of their virtues. 3$^{rd.}$ That the virtues especially cultivated by Voluntary education are those which most conduce to the interests of liberty and religion, namely, self-reliance, the great safeguard of freedom,—and active Christian benevolence, our only hope for the evangelization of the world. 4$^{th.}$ That education conducted by a people themselves, is likely to have a more vigorous and healthful character, than it could have if the school-masters were continually looking with hope and fear to Government officers. 5$^{th.}$ That new and improved methods of instruction are more likely to be introduced under the free competition of a Voluntary system, than under the uniformity and *vis inertiæ* which usually characterize a Government system. 6$^{th.}$ That with whatever zeal a Government agency might be worked at first, it would be likely to be perverted to purposes of Ministerial *patronage.* 7$^{th.}$ That though at present a wish is professed only to *aid* Voluntary effort, yet the natural tendency of the system is to deaden the Voluntary spirit, and to bring schools more and more into dependence upon the Government. 8$^{th.}$ That the question of education is implicated with that of *religion*, and therefore the serious objections which apply to Government interference with religion apply also to Government interference with education. 9$^{th.}$ That in the state of things which exists now, and is likely still to continue, a Government Education Board must be under the influence of the Church and the Aristocracy; and from this and other causes, the Church of England is sure to obtain the lion's share of every education grant,—the only alternative being, the still worse evil of subsidizing the schools of all sects, which amounts to the subsidizing of all forms of religion.

I am aware that some of these reasons will not have their due weight with the friends of Church Establishments. It is evident that many have been prejudiced against the Voluntary system in religion. Nor can I deny—on the contrary, I am fully convinced—that both rest substantially on the same principles, and must be opposed or defended by the same arguments. Whatever weakens the cause of Voluntary education, weakens that of Voluntary religion; and whatever strengthens the one, strengthens the other.

Two great and influential classes among our public men are jealous of the Voluntary Principle,—first, the partizans of the Church, because they regard that principle as hostile to the existing Establishment; and, secondly, the disciples of the Continental policy, of endowing all education and all religion, because, I believe, they really do not understand the Voluntary Principle, but connect it with over-earnestness, or fanaticism, in religion— an error with which they themselves are certainly not chargeable. Some object to the Voluntary Principle as *inefficient;* but others object to it, though they do not say so, because it is *too efficient.* Most think it not trustworthy, on account of its alleged want of steadiness and uniformity: and, with all my admiration for the Voluntary Principle, I must admit that it has the same defects as—*Nature* and *Freedom;*—that it does not always move in straight lines, or array its forces in regimental order, or obey pedantic rules, or make the succeeding century a copy of the preceding, or flatter statesmen by limiting improvement within Acts of Parliament; but still I believe that, like Nature and Freedom, it has a magnificent rule and range—the rule of a living spirit, and the range of whatever achievement God has made possible to man.

I speak here of the Voluntary Principle in an enlarged sense, not confining myself to its operation in providing the means of religious instruction. Of course I do not ask for it, throughout the scope of my whole argument, that New Testament sanction and authority, which rests the support of religion on voluntary liberality, to the exclusion of the compulsory interference of the magistrate. We must, indeed, extend that New Testament principle to religious education; for, if we once receive public money for religious instruction in our schools, we should very soon receive it for religious instruction in our chapels. On that point there can be no dispute, except with men whose views are exceedingly confused. Nonconformists, giving religious education, are precluded by their religious principles from receiving Government money.

But I do not confine my views, in defending "Voluntary education," to merely religious education: I apply the terms to the cultivation of the human mind in all its extent—to literature, science, art, and politics—to colleges, newspapers, magazines, books, and literary and scientific institutions—to the life-long training of the adult, as well as the elementary instruction of the child. Concerning all these I am ready to declare my opinion, that the Voluntary Principle is adequate, is the most consistent with liberty, is conducive to the highest improvement; and, on the other hand, that these things do not come within the province of Government, whilst Governmental interference often retards advancement and shackles freedom. In support of my views, I appeal to the free press, the free literature, the free science, and the free education of England, in opposition to countries where all these things are taken under the care of Government.

If my argument should fail to vindicate the freedom of our schools, it must equally fail to protect the freedom of our periodical press and our general literature. The press is quite as important an educator as the school: the case for placing the former under Government help and superintendence, is as strong as for placing the latter,—nay, stronger as any one will be convinced who reflects on the manifold defects and abuses of a free press, and on the unspeakable importance of that great engine, which so principally moulds the mind and will of England. Nearly all the Continental Governments which pay and direct the school, pay and direct also the pulpit and the press. They do it consistently. And our Government educationists at home would only be consistent, should they recommend Government grants and inspection to all our ministers, our editors, and our authors.

To prevent misconception, I may say, that I do not deny the power of an enlightened despot to erect a vast and complete machinery of education, and by a large expenditure of his people's money on colleges, museums, galleries, and theatres, to force the growth of learning, art, and taste among them, especially when they are precluded from the nobler duties and more practical enterprises of a free people. I look at the whole question, and at the whole man; and, regarding man in all the capacity of his moral and intellectual nature, and communities in all their interests, I reject the petty advantages of despotism, and claim the more generous, though perhaps looser, regimen of freedom.

It may be well also to explain, that the Voluntary Principle does not exclude, or affect to be independent of, the aid which men of wealth, power, and station can give to public objects. It even asks, that "kings should be nursing fathers and queens nursing mothers" to religion. It invites the largest donations of princes and nobles towards the erection of the temple, the college, or the school, when "they offer *willingly* of *their own proper goods*"—acknowledging that "all things come of God, and that of his own they have given him." It accords praise to our Alfreds, our Henrys, and our Edwards, and to a long train of nobles, prelates, ladies, gentry, and merchants, whose munificence founded, out of their own estates and incomes, most of our ancient schools of learning. The only conditions of accepting help which the Voluntary Principle requires are these— first, that the gift be truly Voluntary, not the produce of exaction, or the appropriation of what does not belong to the donor himself; and secondly, that it in no way interferes with the absolute self-government of the Church. Thus the Voluntary Principle is independent, without pride,—willing to accept, without covetousness or subserviency,—jealous for the purity of the Church and the interests of liberty,—not anxious for endowments, because of their liability to abuse,—more willing to give than to receive,—ever appealing to, and thereby cultivating and strengthening, the highest motives, love and duty to God, and love and duty to our fellow-men.

But we are told, by a thousand tongues and pens,—"The Voluntary Principle is a failure; however plausible it may appear in argument, experience proves its inefficiency."

I accept the appeal to experience; and boldly maintain that the Voluntary Principle, so far from having failed, has triumphantly succeeded . . . But I may be told that a retrospect of the centuries we have glanced at is not satisfactory for the Voluntary Principle,—that it shows the people did not do much to educate themselves. I reply, if the people did little, what did the Government do? Nothing. Worse than nothing. During part of the time, it placed the Press under censorship, and often punished the free and fair use of it with cruel severity. The ruling and influential classes habitually, with few exceptions, frowned on the instruction of the working people. Whatever schools there were, whether superior schools, common schools, or charity schools, were provided on the Voluntary Principle. The means of education kept pace with the public sense of its desirableness, and even with the amount of intellectual food that proceeded from the Press. During the whole period we have reviewed, I apprehend that the improvements realized in our laws, institutions, literature, industry, and national character, originated mainly with the people, and in very few cases with the Government.

Our civil freedom, the main source of our present greatness, was undoubtedly won from reluctant governors, by the pressure from beneath. It is readily admitted that the Voluntary Principle in its action follows public opinion, and does not precede it. But Government, though in some rare cases it may precede public opinion, in the immense majority of cases refuses even to follow—until it is compelled. The grand question, after all, is, *which is the natural and usual source of popular improvement,—the Government or the people?* If it is the Government, I give up my cause as lost. But if it is the people, then the interests of education, like those of liberty, are most safely committed to their keeping. . . . I remark, then, on this great institution—first, that it is purely *Voluntary*,—and, secondly, that it is distinctively *religious*. It is the fruit of the zeal of religious bodies for the religious education of the poor. I must claim it as a magnificent effect of the *Voluntary Principle*, combined with the *religious spirit*. It is unprecedented in the history of the world. An army—a vast army—numbering a quarter of a million, of teachers, organised and disciplined for a work of pure religious benevolence, and continuing at their duty year by year, without fee or reward,—devoting themselves affectionately and prayerfully to the moral and spiritual improvement of no less than two millions of our rising youth, distributed among them in little companies of six or eight, so that nearly all the children of the working class, in their turns, receive the truest kindness and the most valuable example from those somewhat above them in society;—it is a spectacle beyond measure noble and delightful! England ought to be more proud of its Raikes than even of its Newton.

Imagine, for one moment, that all these two million children could be educated on the Sabbath by paid teachers under Government support and inspection. Would the result be as valuable? Not by one half. It is not the receivers only of the good, but the *doers* of it that are benefited; and, for our congregations to lose these fields of sweet and profitable employment for their young men and women,—and for society to lose this precious cement of its different classes,—would be a calamity of the greatest magnitude. But would any Government have ever conceived such a project, or attempted to execute it? The idea is ridiculous. The fact is, that *freedom* and *willingness* infinitely surpass Governments in invention, enterprise, and power of adaptation to circumstances. Governments have neither heart nor soul; and, so far from being disposed to self-denying activity, their natural and normal state is to be at rest. . . .

Looking at the mighty progress that has been made, at the velocity with which the great engine of education is now travelling on its magnificent way, at the unexhausted force of the motives which are impelling it, at the momentum which even the brute mass of society has acquired, I no more expect to see it brought to a stand, than to see our planet halt in its revolution round the source of light. But I could as soon believe this, as I could believe that the substitution of the Compulsory for the Voluntary Principle would mend its speed. To my judgment, the change is as wise as it would be, in dissatisfaction with the unseen forces and noiseless movements of the orbs of light, to hang each planet to its sun in visible chains. I think there never was a more vulgar piece of narrow statesmanship than that of Lord John Russell, in adopting the project of Mr. Kay Shuttleworth.

But we are told that the justification of that measure is in the inefficient character of the education now given. Two years ago, it was the fashion to say, that we had not half as many schools as were wanted. That delusion having been dispelled, we are now told that the education given in the schools is worthless. I frankly admit that we have still many wretched schools. I have been told by the *Morning Chronicle*, that I am the advocate-general of bad schools. In one sense I am. I maintain that we have as much right to have wretched schools as to have wretched newspapers, wretched preachers, wretched books, wretched institutions, wretched political economists, wretched Members of Parliament, and wretched Ministers. You cannot proscribe all these things without proscribing Liberty. The man is a simpleton who says, that to advocate Liberty is to advocate badness. The man is a quack and *doctrinaire* of the worst German breed, who would attempt to force all mind, whether individual or national, into a mould of ideal perfection,—to stretch it out or to lop it down to his own Procrustean standard. I maintain that Liberty is the chief cause of excellence; but it would cease to be Liberty if you proscribed everything inferior. Cultivate giants if you please; but do not stifle dwarfs. The servants were well-intentioned, but not wise, who proposed to pluck up the tares; for there was danger that they should root up the wheat with them. Yet this is the very spirit in which many Members of Parliament and leading journalists,— calling themselves Liberal, too—are now proposing to remodel society by Act of Parliament, and to govern mind and morals by Boards of Commissioners. . . .

The methods of tuition, the school apparatus, the school-books, the plans of constructing and ventilating school-buildings, the combination of moral and religious with secular instruction, and every other branch of this great practical question, have been illustrated and improved to a most gratifying extent, by Pestalozzi, Oberlin, Bell, Lancaster, Fellenberg, Wilderspin, Arnold, Stow, and many others,—by the Normal-schools of Yverdun, the Borough-road, Battersea, Chelsea, Gray's Inn-road, Edinburgh, Glasgow, and Dublin. The Central Society of Education, the Society for the Diffusion of Useful Knowledge, and many other voluntary associations, have at least circulated the improvements of others, if they have not made discoveries themselves. The science of education has made far greater progress in our own day than that of medicine, jurisprudence, or political economy.

Now, inasmuch as our Normal-schools at present contain about 1,000 schoolmasters and schoolmistresses, which number is renewed every year, or every two or three years, and as fresh Normal-schools are constantly rising up, it is absolutely certain that the country will soon be pervaded with well-trained teachers; and by the natural and necessary competition among teachers, in the presence of a critical public—and perhaps few portions of the public more critical than the parents among the working classes, or I may even say the children themselves, who are ever comparing notes with each other—the improved methods of tuition must inevitably be forced into general adoption.

If it be said, that private schoolmasters will not adopt these improvements, I reply, that they are far more interested in adopting them than the teachers of public schools. Their livelihood absolutely depends on their success. And if Parliament can discover stronger motives than *self-interest* and *necessity* for the rapid and sure adoption of improvements, it is the most remarkable discovery of the day. I am by no means sure, that large public schools will in the long run prove the most efficient instruments of education. The discovery of Dr. Bell was long supposed to be invaluable; but the monitorial system is now condemned by many able educators, especially on the Continent. Let every system have an open field, and in the end the best will win the day. Let private schoolmasters receive fair-play from the Government, and not be unjustly discouraged by grants of public money to public schools which compete with them. Every interference of Government tends to increase the necessity for that interference and the habit of it; the more Government interferes, the more likely shall we be to have a practical *Act of Uniformity* in regard to schools; and in my judgment that uniformity, so far from being an advantage, as many *doctrinaires* suppose, would be the greatest obstruction to improvement.

The private schoolmasters have just adopted an institution which promises to be of great utility, if it should keep clear of Government, and avoid the evils of a monopolising corporation, namely, the *"College of Preceptors."* If wisely and popularly conducted, the College will acquire public confidence; and its examinations and certificates will be quite as valuable as those of any learned body. This is another proof of the unlimited inventiveness of freedom.

It would be just as hopeless to continue bad modes of education when better become generally known, as it would have been to retain the old weapons of war after the discovery of gunpowder,—to spin with the one-thread wheel after Arkwright and Hargreaves had perfected their spinning-frames, and Watt the steam-engine,—or to travel by pack-horses and stage-wagons, after the construction of railways.

Even the strongest of all the Educational Societies is subject to the law of competition. In the year 1826, Dr. Bell, finding that the National Schools were falling off, wrote as follows:

"Our schools are not attended as they might be, because neither parents nor children find they are worth attending; and other schools, inferior in almost every respect, but where something is taught, however badly, have attractions for scholars which ours have not, because superior attention is paid to their modes of instruction, however inferior in themselves, and to superintendence."

The National Society, then, was under the same necessity as any other Society,—of improving its schools, or losing its scholars. And so it ought. I am aware that Government wish to promote good education. The first effect of their interference may be to produce some improvement; but unless all experience is valueless, the ultimate effect will be *to stereotype the methods of teaching, to bolster up old systems, and to prevent improvement.*

One of the grand arguments of our State Educationists is, that the Voluntary Principle will not, and cannot, sustain the annual expense of well-conducted schools. This argument is strongly pressed both by Professor Hoppus and Dr. Vaughan; and my respected friend, the Professor, in a recent letter in the *Morning Chronicle*, after making a calculation of what he supposed would be the annual cost of public schools, appealed to me whether it was possible for the Voluntary Principle to sustain it. My reply is brief, but I think conclusive. First, That the Voluntary Principle, by its two modes of operation, namely, the payments of those who are benefited, and the contributions of the benevolent, can sustain, amply sustain, every needful cost, both of education and of religion. And, secondly, That if the people cannot sustain it, the Government cannot; for the Government has neither strength nor money but what it derives from the people.

It may be responded—"We know that the people have the power, if they are disposed to use it, but they are not; and therefore, it is necessary to compel them." Oh, then, it is not a pecuniary or a physical ability that is wanting, but a *moral* ability; and for *that* you leave the people and fly to the Government!—you abandon the Voluntary for the Compulsory Principle! For shame!—Where have you been living, that you know so little, and think so meanly, of the people of England? Have you been shut up within the walls of colleges, poring over German philosophy? Yet even those colleges should have spoken to you of the power of English liberality and public spirit; for every stone of them was laid by the Voluntary Principle. Have you never heard that the Nonconformists of England and Wales, who are the poorer sections of the community, have built about 13,000 places of worship, and are sustaining their own ministers and services; which, at an average of only 120 £ a year for each place, implies an aggregate Voluntary expenditure of more than a million and a half yearly? Are you not aware that the Church of England have, within our own generation, built or rebuilt several thousands of churches, and that for most of them new funds have been provided? Do you forget the millions that must have been expended in building and supporting Sunday-schools and Day-schools; and the still more extraordinary fact of the moral and spiritual agency employed in the Sunday-schools? . . .

For myself, when I survey the recent history of my country, my heart swells with exultation. I am proud to be an Englishman, and still more proud to be a Voluntary. But if I am proud of the past, I can trust the future advancement of my country to the same principle which has achieved such great moral triumphs. I should neither think it honourable nor wise to change our policy in the full tide of our success. And if a Continental policy should be creeping in among us,—a policy whose spirit is materialism, and whose grand resource is functionarism,—a policy which would impair the noble self-reliance of the people, and bring religion itself into bondage,—I call upon you to give it your utmost resistance, and to rally but the closer around that standard of *virtuous Willinghood*, which our fathers reared in worse times, which we will never desert, and which, I confidently believe, will wave over a regenerated world.

8

"A Letter to the Most Noble the Marquis of Lansdowne"

Edward Baines, Jr.

Sixth Edition (London: Ward & Co.; and Simpkin, Marshall, & Co., 1847)

This selection by Edward Baines, Jr., was precipitated by the support given by Lord Lansdowne (a peer in the House of Lords) to a series of educational proposals drafted by a special committee in the House of Lords in December 1846. Titled "Minutes of the Committee of Council on Education" and described in the subtitle as "Regulations Respecting the Education of Pupil Teachers and Stipendiary Monitors," this was an effort to distribute government funds to schools in a nonpartisan manner and thereby avoid the sectarian controversies that had plagued previous proposals. Many of the provisions appear innocent enough, but the Voluntaryists suspected, with good reason, that the Minutes were an attempt by the English government to get its foot farther in the door of education with the ultimate goal of controlling the school system.

In this excerpt we see Baines's polemical skills in full flower. He accused many supporters of the Minutes of loving "Government *surveillance* for its own sake." Many of the champions of state education wished England to adopt the comprehensive and compulsory system of state education found in Prussia and other "Continental despotisms"—systems characterized by "the *police spirit*" of "universal *espionage*,— a system of inspection, dictation, and control by public functionaries, or regimental uniformity, and of dependence on public funds." Moreover, given the standard justifications for state education, there is no reason why government could not justify control of "the *pulpit* and the *press*" by invoking the same principles. Government control of education, like government control of religion and the press, contradicts the "national freedom" prized by Englishmen.

. . . At a time when Education is far more extensive than in any other former period in our history, when it is every day advancing with giant strides, when enlightened zeal and liberality are improving the quality, extending the range, and adapting the modes of instruction, so as to reach the very lowest classes of the community,—at such a time it is that your Government brings forward a plan, involving a prodigal expenditure of public money, and a dangerous increase of Government patronage, for the sake of transferring to its own hands the superintendence and the virtual and ultimate direction of the Education of the country!

Until within the last few months I should have supposed that Parliament and people would with one voice have assented to this proposition, namely, that if the nation could and would educate itself, without interference on the part of Government, it were infinitely better that it should do so; not merely because perfect freedom of education has been the practice in England, but because it is in itself most desirable,—as being congenial with civil liberty, favourable to the most vigorous growth and action of the public mind, and conducive to that inestimable quality in individuals or communities—self-reliance. I myself, in my profound sense of the value of liberty, should have gone much further, and have maintained, that even though education were less extensive than was to be desired, and theoretically less perfect than under a great Government system, yet that freedom of education was to be guarded as a sacred thing, because forming an essential branch of civil freedom. But I had at least believed that every man in England would have assented to the former proposition, and have regarded a self-educated people as occupying the highest ground among free and civilized nations.

It was a great mistake. There are, it now appears, many Members of Parliament and many writers who love Government *surveillance* for its own sake; or at least who have got so much of the *police spirit* that characterizes the statesmen of Germany, as not to be satisfied without something like a universal *espionage*,—a system of inspection, dictation, and control by public functionaries, of regimental uniformity, and of dependence on public funds, characteristics of the Continental despotisms. These persons, many of them able and distinguished men, but forgetting, in the zeal for mechanical completeness, that much higher value of a living spirit, demand that we should imitate the Prussian or some similar system, and place the education of the whole people under the care and control of the Government. It is true that there are not many writers who as yet avowedly go this length; but there are many who manifestly admire compulsory and State education, and who only shrink from recommending its immediate adoption, because they believe the nation is not prepared for and would not endure it.

Nay, my Lord, I am compelled to conclude, that you yourself and most of your colleagues in office, would decidedly approve of such a system. Nothing else is to be inferred from the declaration at the beginning of your speech last Friday, which is thus reported:

He (Lord Lansdowne) confessed that *it would have been a source of the greatest pleasure and satisfaction to him*, if he had been enabled to state that Her Majesty's Government were prepared with *a plan for public education in this country so large and comprehensive* in its character *as to put the population of this country, with respect to education, in that condition in which the populations of some parts of Europe were placed*, where an uneducated child was an almost solitary exception, and where among the great mass of the people education was universal.

Your Lordship must of course allude to states where the whole machinery of education is under Government direction: and I can infer nothing else than this, that you would, if you could, introduce the same system in England.

I differ from your Lordship as strongly as is possible, consistently with personal respect. I regard your declaration with unfeigned alarm. And I am compelled to take it as a key to explain whatever may be obscure and undeveloped in your plan. No man can fail to see, that your plan is constructed in harmony with your principles and wishes. It is a part of your ideal whole. It is a step towards your perfect system. Nay, it is a step so formed that you cannot possibly stop there but must move onward in the same course.

It would be superfluous, but for your declaration quoted above, to remind your Lordship, that there are many things which Governments cannot do as well as the people themselves, and many things which they ought not to do, even if they could do them better. It was surely no improper reflection on Governments, when a Noble Lord said, the other day, in the House of Peers—

> "It is universally admitted that Governments are the *worst of cultivators,* the *worst of manufacturers,* and the *worst of traders.*"

Your Lordship at least will not find fault with this plain-speaking, as it proceeded from your own lips. And yet, my Lord, there is hardly a Government in the world that has not directly or indirectly acted in defiance of this principle, and legislated as though the direct reverse of your axiom were true. There is nothing for which a more plausible argument might be constructed than for *Government interference with industry,*—except, perhaps, that a more persuasive case still might be made out for *perfect despotism.* Take any of the Inspectors or masters from the Prussian schools, and they would write a capital defence of the all-pervading despotism of that country,—a despotism not mitigated in its practical details by the nominal constitution just proclaimed. *And that defence would pass over precisely the same ground as the arguments in favour of State Education in England.* Yet would it be true, in spite of the sophists, that liberty deserves to be "prized above all price," and that despotism is an accursed invasion of man's right and oppression of man's energies.

If Governments, notwithstanding their power, their command of money, and their command of talent, are "the worst of cultivators, the worst of manufacturers, and the worst of traders," is it not contrary to all probability that they should be the best of educators? The same qualities and circumstances which prevent their success in the former capacities, are likely to prevent their success in the latter. But if any one should prove that Governments are well qualified to conduct our schools, he would be able with equal ease to prove that they are well qualified to conduct those other educators, the *pulpit* and the *press*! And when such reasoning shall be reduced to practice, the destruction of our liberties will be complete.

Liberty is not the most faultless, though it is the best state of human communities. There is not one of the bulwarks of English freedom, which might not as reasonably be impugned and dispensed with as the freedom of education. *Trial by jury* has led to a thousand absurd verdicts, and let a thousand rogues go free. The *freedom of the press* leads to the publication of folly and falsehood that is often most mischievous. The *representative system*, besides all the corruption incident to it, gave us at the very last election a House of Commons for the express purpose of upholding the monopolies it has since destroyed. But no man of sober judgment would on these accounts undervalue the great safeguards of our national freedom. Neither ought we, because free education is not a faultless system, to discard it for the coercive machinery of State education.

9

"On the Non-Interference of the Government with Popular Education"

Edward Miall

Crosby-Hall Lectures on Education (London: John Snow, 1848)

Edward Miall (1809–1881) was a leader in the movement to disestablish the Church of England. An uncompromising defender of the separation of church and state, he later argued along similar lines for the separation of school and state. Miall and Edward Baines, Jr., were the most prominent defenders of educational Voluntaryism in England. (It should be remembered that the label "Voluntaryist" was originally embraced by advocates of church-state separation; only later, beginning in 1843, was this label used by those Dissenters who also called for the separation of school and state.)

After graduating Wymondley Theological Institution in Stevenage (in the county of Hertfordshire), Miall was ordained an Independent (i.e., Congregational) minister in 1831. He briefly held the pastorate of the congregation in Ware before moving, in 1834, to the Bond Street Chapel in Leicester. As a youth Baines had rejoiced at the repeal of the Test and Corporation Acts—laws that barred Nonconformists from holding any civil or political offices; he later called this development "the commencement of a new era for the advancement of religious liberty." And shortly after becoming a minister in Leicester, Miall was heartened by a declaration by some Nottingham Dissenters that called for the separation of church and state, and by the quick endorsement of this call for "religious liberty" by other Nonconformist groups in towns throughout England and Scotland. Around this time, according to his son, Miall's mind was "burning" with ideas about the violation of conscience entailed by a state church. In 1838, in a village near Leicester, Baines delivered a speech, "The Two Portraits, or Christianity and the Compulsory System Contrasted." In this speech we see Miall's utter contempt for any state interference in matters of conscience—an argument that he later developed, in considerable detail, against any state interference in education.

> Ignorant of the rights of conscience, [a state church] profanely tramples them into the dust. Its appeals are made, not to the sympathies of men, but to the arm of magistracy. Its power ultimately resides, not in its own intrinsic charms, but in those darkest dens of bigotry and oppression, Ecclesiastical Courts. It drowns the sweet voice of

heavenly truth in the din of its own vociferous clamour for support. Its apparatus is all grinding and destructive. Its means and appliances all smell of the earth, earthy. Backed by this obtrusive and scowling champion, Christianity is compelled to bear the curse of the oppressed and the jeer of the infidel; is taunted as the child of priestcraft, and the deceiving mistress only of fools. Such are, have been, and ever will be the lamentable results of legislative intermeddling with religion.

In 1839, the Dissenter John Thorogood was arrested and jailed for refusing to pay church rates. Then in the following year and closer to home, a member of Miall's congregation and a close friend, William Baines, was jailed for the same offense. The latter event generated an uproar among Leicester Nonconformists, who responded by forming the "Leicester Voluntary Church Society." At a speech before the first meeting of this group, Miall chided many of his fellow Dissenters for their timidity in advocating the complete separation of church and state. He asked, "What have you gained by your silence and inactivity?" He answered that Dissenters had been treated with contempt by even petty officials, and that their modest entreaties to parliament had been treated with "haughty and supercilious derision." To those Dissenters who had refused to condemn the imprisonment of Thorogood in unequivocal moral terms, Miall warned: "You have made one error, beware you make another."

Here we see Miall's insistence that Nonconformists should ground their efforts to secure religious and civil liberty in the foundational principle of the complete separation of church and state. Halfway measures were ineffective and only bred contempt in their adversaries. Members of the Leicester Voluntary Church Society agreed. Edward Miall's son, Arthur, described the outcome: "Aggressive action in some form they were determined upon, and it became clear to them, as they considered the lamentable indifference and narrowness of view that characterized the principal organs of Dissent in the press, that nothing could be achieved in the direction of securing intelligent and coherent action, until the foundation principles of Nonconformity were consistently advocated through the newspaper press."

Spurred by the need for a radical and principled journal to spearhead the cause of religious freedom, Miall left his pastorate in 1841 to found and edit the *Nonconformist,* which one historian has described as "the journalistic mainstay of Victorian militant Dissent." The first issue (April 14, 1841) advised Dissenters to battle religious intolerance by uniting on the principle of the "ENTIRE SEPARATION OF CHURCH AND STATE." The *Nonconformist* vigorously supported other causes of radical liberalism, including the Anti-Corn Law League and its struggle for free trade, opposition to Sabbatarian laws, and the Complete Suffrage Union led by the Quaker Joseph Sturge, another champion of both religious and educational voluntaryism. After Dissenting opposition to state education crystalized in 1843, the *Nonconformist* became a powerful voice in that movement as well. Moreover, in 1842 Miall published the first political articles by a young Herbert Spencer. A significant portion of these twelve letters on "The Proper Sphere of Government" criticized state education, and Spencer's articles in the *Nonconformist* probably influenced the birth of organized educational Voluntaryism in the following year.

The following selection is excerpted from Miall's speech at a Voluntaryist conference held in 1848 at Crosby Hall, in London. The lectures by seven notable Voluntaryists were attended by around 500 people, according to one observer. After being published in the columns of a Dissenter paper, the *British Banner,* the Congregational Union arranged for the lectures to be included in a book, *Crosby-Hall Lectures on Education.*

In Miall's lecture we see a theme that he emphasized more than any other Voluntaryist (with the possible exception of Herbert Spencer), namely, the moral superiority of voluntary over coercive methods when attempting to achieve desirable social goals. Advocates of state education typically focused on short-term goals while ignoring the detrimental long-term consequences of involving the state in matters of education.

The subject assigned to me for exposition by the [Congregational] Committee who arranged for the present series of Lectures was described by them in the following words:—"The Non-interference of the Government with Popular Education." If, guided by a reference to the other topics selected by them for treatment, and in the absence of a more exact specification of their plans, I have correctly caught their meaning; it is this—That it is neither the duty of Civil Government, nor would it be for the interest of its subjects, to make legal provision for the education of the people. This, at any rate, is the conclusion to which it will be my aim to conduct you. . . .

Let me not, however, be misunderstood. Painfully alive as I am to the deficiencies under which I labour, in this attempt to make good the position assigned me to defend, I have not the smallest misgiving as to the soundness of the position itself. With all my consciousness of the fallibility of human judgment, and with the readiest and heartiest recognition of the authority, learning, and talent arrayed against me, I feel myself entitled to declare, that my convictions on the subject are settled, and, I think, unchangeable. This profession, I am aware, savours somewhat of presumption; but unless a modest estimate of our own powers binds us to surrender at discretion any or all knowledge which we hold to be morally certain, at the biding of superior intellect, or it may be, pre-eminent virtue, I think I may retain my humility without letting go my confidence. A child upon a hill-top may see the relative bearings of the objects outspread before him more clearly than a philosopher at its base. That the advocates of a compulsory provision for the education of the people are wrong, I have no more doubt than I have that some of their premises are right; but the whole strain of their argument convinces me that they look at the question from a low position. I impugn not their motives—I am far from underrating their ability—but I do say, in no faltering accents, that from the ground of immediate and temporary expediency, they cannot command a view of the whole subject before them. How the means of elementary education may most speedily overtake the wants of the people, however important an inquiry, is not one the answer to which could be held to decide the propriety of Government interference. And here, as it seems to me, is the radical error of our opponents. Their benevolence is in a hurry. The eyes of their judgment are bedimmed with the tears of their sympathy. Themselves rejoicing in the abundance of pleasure and profit resulting from education, and feeling acutely for the privations of the ignorant, they burn to impart to others what they value for themselves with all the haste which human possibilities will admit of. Like over-fond parents, they wish to stimulate the mind of their country into precocious development, forgetting, in the excess of their affectionate concern, that by a general law, admitting of but few exceptions, precocity of all kinds is followed by an early death.

I must protest, therefore, at the very outset of this discussion, against the claim of any conclusion to be regarded as final, which covers nothing more than the proof of a clear want, and a plan adapted to supply that want. I protest against the wrong done to my reason, when I am told, here is a terrible evil, and here are means by which it may be removed, and am bidden at the same moment to overleap all the considerations which lie between the want and the proposed method of removal. . . . My business, as I conceive, is this—I have to consider whether, taking for granted the worst of these representations which have been made to us of popular ignorance, and assuming virtue in the specific recommended, a wise people should consent to remove the one by the application of the other—whether there are not some great laws of mind and of Providential government which, in doing this, we should violate, and the violation of which will entail penalties more to be dreaded than those which past neglect have brought upon us,—whether, in a word, we should do well to listen to the advice of men who propose to alleviate present misery, without paying any very solicitous regard to prospective and remote consequences. Our opponents may be considered as counsel for the present generation. I stand here as counsel for posterity. They call for an instant suppression of a crying grievance. I ask for a wise suppression of it. They appeal to the specialties of the case. I appeal to broad, general, indefeasible principles. . . .

It may be as well, at the outset, to state, that I shall have no occasion to put this audience to the trouble of drawing a distinction between secular and religious education—a distinction so easily laid down on paper, and so impossible to be preserved in practice. It will content me, so far as the present question is concerned, to understand by the term "education" the communication of desirable knowledge, and the formation of praiseworthy habits. This, I imagine, to be a fair statement of the good sought to be imparted, whether by the Government, or by any other organized agency. Neither do I intend to push my opponents to a strict definition of what is meant by popular education. It is quite certain, that to the eye of a statesman attempting to reduce theory to practice, and words to things, a grave difficulty might be seen to lurk under the term. Is he to give education to the people, irrespectively of their worldly circumstances, to rich and poor alike; or is he to select the poor only, and if so, where is he to draw the line of demarcation? I repeat it, I will dispense with the advantage which common sense might wrest from our opponents, by these and similar demands for further and more precise information. I will suppose this information to have been furnished—I will suppose the word "popular," or "national," when employed to designate the precise range within which a compulsory provision of the means of instruction is expected to bear fruit, to exclude all who can afford to educate their own children, and to include those only who are absolutely dependent upon help from without. Further, I will allow the advocates of Government interference—and herein I shall be far more liberal to them than the Legislature, whose aid they invoke—to choose their own plan, to construct their own machinery, to appoint their own officers, schoolmasters, and monitors, and to preside in every parish or district over their own schools. So far as I can avoid it, I will give them no opportunity of setting aside all my reasoning—the good, the bad, and the indifferent alike—by telling me that it is directed against the theory of a State system of education, whereas they contend merely for a National system. Government interference I will assume to mean nothing more than a legal provision of the means of desirable instruction for those who cannot secure them for themselves. And now I come to the point to be determined. A certain, and in accordance with my concessions, a clearly defined portion of the community are wholly destitute of the means of suitable instruction. On what principle is that destitution to be met?—on the principle of moral and religious obligation, or on the principle of legal authority? Granting, not as a fact, but simply as an argument, that the force of "you ought" has not sufficed as yet to remove the evil, is it wise, is it just, is it, in the long run, kind to resort, for that purpose, to the force of "you shall?" With all the emphasis which strong conviction can give to expressive language, I answer "No!" . . .

The first thought which beckons me in the direction of my final decision, is suggested by the spontaneous concession of our opponents. I find them forward to admit, that the education of the young devolves originally upon the parent, and that any lack of power in the parent to discharge his trust would be more fitly supplied, supposing it to be supplied at all, by benevolence, than by authority. They say, that if the force of "you ought" were but adequate to do the whole work of education, it were unquestionably to be preferred to the force of "you shall." True, some who have conceded this in terms, recall it in their argument, and claim for the poor man the luxury of demanding the education of his offspring as a right rather than a boon. I will not stay to test the validity of this claim, further than to ask from what source a man with nine shillings a week, and who may be taken, for argument sake, to come just within the line of destitution, derives his right to require from his neighbour, with ten shillings a week, who stands on the other side of the line, to contribute in taxation to the instruction of his children? Setting aside, then, this novel and over-stretched claim as empty flourish, I ask, whether the admission generally made, that Voluntary benevolence, if it were but up to the mark, is superior as a moving power to magisterial authority, does not imply something worth consideration? Either there is a virtue in this agency which cannot be discovered in that, or there is a defect or danger in that which does not attach itself to this. Whether a sense of moral and religious obligation works the machinery of popular education more kindly,—whether it elicits and exercises more nobleness of soul, or gives freer scope to the play of generous affections,—whether its movements are less clumsy, and are capable of readier adaptation to changing circumstances,—or whether legislative intervention imports some elements of danger, deadens some laudable sensibilities, or drains its vitality from a spirit of self-reliance, it is not necessary for me to decide in the present state of the argument. My immediate business is with the concession itself,—with the recognised superiority in kind of "ought" over "shall," as a moving force in the matter of national education. It occurs to me, as I should presume it will occur to every thoughtful mind, to inquire what is the exigency which dictates a resort from the one to the other. The Voluntary principle, it is said, cannot overtake the evil calling for removal. Now, what does this mean? That it cannot overtake the evil this year, or next, or within twenty years, or within fifty? What are the broad features of its past history? Until a very recent date, it did whatever work was done, single-handed and alone,—did it, too, when fashion and authority opposed its influence, and sneered at it for its pains and perseverance. Well, has education advanced under its auspices,—and is it still advancing? Instances, no doubt, may be adduced, of efforts here and there given up, or of periods of exhaustion after particular outbreaks of spasmodic excitement and exertion. But draw not your inferences from the wavelets that ripple at your feet. The tide may be steadily rising, though the pebble you saw covered but just since is not left dry. Calculate by some surer marks. Cast your eye back some twenty years. Are the means of education fewer, in proportion to the population, now than they were then? Are the working classes, on the whole, more brutal in their tastes, or less intelligent and enlightened than they were? Or, comparing the last five years of the twenty with the first, can it be averred, that sense of moral obligation in this particular matter is less general, less powerful, or less active than it was? I am not afraid of the answer. The pen of history has written it, and the world has yet to witness the effrontery which would tear out the leaf. Mark now the demand that is made upon us! Two generations have scarcely passed away since England awoke to the importance of educating the poorer classes. Spontaneous benevolence commenced the work,—carried it on, spite of numerous difficulties and powerful opposition,—is still active, energetic, and, I may add, augmenting, both in power and in skill. Do you really believe, in the face of all this evidence, that what yet remains to be done can never be accomplished by this same system of agency,—a system which you admit to be preferable in kind to that of magisterial or legal compulsion? Let *your* faith, however, be what it may, *ours* roots itself in a knowledge and experience of the past. We cling to the confessedly superior system, and doubt whether "ought," which is prospering in its work, can be prudently thrust aside by "shall," simply because it has not yet completed it; because, although advancing by rapid strides, it is not "as swift as meditation or the thoughts of love." You point us to much yet remaining to be done,—to much more than Government itself can do in a trice; but we will take leave to question whether the ulterior and less difficult stages of the enterprise ought to be handed over for achievement to a totally opposite principle of agency to that which accomplished the earlier and the more arduous. We do not say that out of the concessions of our opponents we can fairly extract a justification of our refusal to admit compulsory aid; but we say that, viewed in juxta-position with the history of popular education in this country, they may well make us pause, and think further before we finally commit ourselves.

And here a second and still graver thought forces itself upon our consideration. The advocates of a legal provision for the education of the poor call for the adoption of a change so entire, so vast, so fraught with new elements of influence and contingencies of peril, that we must be excused for asking them if they really know and appreciate what they are about. Let us look at it first in miniature. Is it too much to assert, that individual character is largely, is incalculably affected, for good or for evil, by the kind of force which is brought to bear upon it, in order to the determination of conduct? Is not every one aware, that when the moving power is from within, the wheels, if I may so express it, which it sets agoing, and which direct and regulate, whilst they transmit it to its chosen end, are the main elements of virtue? and that, when the moving power is from without, the whole mechanism of mind is superseded as useless? Why, what is the essential distinction between a freeman and a slave, but simply this, that the personal conduct of the one is prompted by his will, that of the other dictated by authority? The two states differ most materially, not merely in the class of enjoyments each will yield, but in the kind of virtues which they admit of. *No* moral change can happen to a man calculated more extensively to affect his destiny, than that which removes him from the sphere of "you ought" to that of "you shall." It brings the growth of his character under subjection to an entirely opposite set of conditions. Most of the impulses which before moved him become useless. All the exercises of thought, desire, prudence, judgment, self-command, and the like, are thrown out of gear. To the whole extent to which he is under external pressure and constraint, he ceases to be a living soul—he is nothing more than a structure of complex animal mechanism.

Now, we take the liberty to ask our opponents when, in relation to one great department of social responsibility and duty, they aim to transfer a whole nation from the dominion of the one force to that of the other—from the self-moving power of moral obligation to the external power of legal authority—whether they possess any certain means of measuring the extent of the moral change they are seeking to effect? Few of them, we suspect, have seriously taken this into account. They talk loudly of the impolicy, the cruelty, the danger of leaving so large a section of the community as are now devoid of the means of instruction in their present state of helpless ignorance; but have they, in that spirit of manliness which dares to look on both sides of the question, pondered the result upon, not a fragment of society, however large, but society itself—of placing it under what may be called a new dispensation? Why, in reach and duration of influence over national character, I cannot conceive of any merely political revolution that might bear comparison with it. How far it would ultimately reverse the current of thought—the seeds of what novel habits it would sow— what modifying power it would exert upon the sympathies—or what sort of effect it might have upon sense of obligation—are problems of solemn moment where a great nation is concerned; of far more solemn moment, though, perhaps, not generally so felt, than any change in the form of civil government. I do not determine, at this stage of the discussion, whether the alteration would be for weal or woe. My purpose, just now, is simply to draw attention to its magnitude. Men have talked so glibly, and even jestingly, about it, that we are in danger of contracting the notion, that nothing more serious is involved than more or fewer schoolmasters—a better or worse provision for the instruction of the poor. The truth, however, is that the proposal put before us is nothing less than that, to an immense extent, we should shift the axis of social morality, and that, whereas, so far as care of the mind and morals of our neighbour is concerned, it once turned upon sense of responsibility, it shall turn, for the future, upon legal compulsion. Without deciding whether this be right or wrong, we say the change recommended is so vast, so incapable of accurate measurement, that, before we could be brought to accede to it, we must see a much stronger case of necessity than any which has yet been made out, and laid before the public. We are not disposed to try this tremendous experiment upon national character merely to put forward the cause of education by a few years.

I advance another step in the argument: I submit, that the transference of educational movement, so warmly urged, from the basis of Voluntary exertions to that of law, is not only a change of inconceivable vastness, but one which carries us in a backward direction. It deliberately sentences the nation to sit on a lower form. Hitherto, the progress of humanity has been upwards— from passive submission to power, to cheerful and willing obedience to truth. Just in proportion as the wise and far-reaching combinations of Providential government have developed man, just in that proportion have they elevated him into the region of individuality, and taught him to find his impelling motives in his own conscience and affections. That he might be governed by truth rather than by power, would seem to be the leading purpose of revealed religion. Hence, Christianity has exhibited to him in forms of loveliness so attractive, of adaptation to his want so complete and cognizable, of mastery over his affections so potent and transforming, that, wherever it is received, it supersedes the action of law from without, by implanting a stronger and more generous law within. And it is worthy of remark, that all the arrangements of Providence are adjusted upon the principle of calling out into daily exercise this inner and individual life. The stage upon which we are placed is crowded with opportunities inviting it to action— all its appropriate exercises are accompanied by pleasure—all its neglects entail penalty. Within the range of his capabilities, each man is made responsible for the progress and welfare of the world; each has his post, his influence, his power over other minds, his share of social importance. The first, the most natural, and, in the long run, the most effective, appeal of want and misery for help and alleviation, is to individual sympathy and sense of social obligation. No favourable response to that appeal can be given without improving and ennobling the nature of him that gives it. Society trained up under such an arrangement—encouraged, on the one hand, by the ample rewards which follow the discharge of obligation, and disciplined, on the other, by the sharp penalties incurred by neglect, gradually gets the better of its selfishness, becomes more thoughtful, acquires a greater sensibility of conscience, and drops, one after another, as not only useless but cumbersome, most of those severe restraints and appliances of coercion which it once judged to be absolutely indispensable.

Looking at the nature of the human mind, at the general principles of Providential government, and at the spirit and tenor of heaven-born Christianity, it may be safely affirmed that law, as law, is "a beggarly element of the world;" that in its operation upon human nature it advances none of the great ends of man's probation—elicits none of his active virtues—ripens in him none of the germs of truth. To the whole extent to which it displaces individual sense of obligation, it sends him back from manhood to infancy—from the world to the nursery—from a moral dispensation to a dispensation of physical force.

Now, I confess, that I augur no lasting good to society from the very general disposition of the present age to merge individual responsibility into that of civil government, and to perform our duty to our neighbour by a sort of public proxy,—thus attempting to evade the penalties of our own indolence and selfishness, by purchasing a joint-stock substitute for fulfilling our solemn trust. If peril arises to our social security and our free institutions, from the growth in our midst of a formidable excrescence of ignorance and vice, does not that peril warn us for some nobler purpose than that of going back to coercive principles, and of renouncing our reliance upon all the higher motives to exertion? Is that a wise, is it a becoming use to make of the punishment of our past neglect, to put ourselves into a position which exiles us from the region of future virtue, and ministers to our safety only by degrading us from the category of agents into that of tools? When Providence affixed to our social selfishness and inactivity the appropriate penalty of danger to our social interests, was it with the design, think you, of spurring us forward to increased vigilance, generosity, and concern for others, or of driving us into a resignation of the high and honourable charge committed to us, into the hands of civil government? The men who counsel us to consent to a legal provision of the means of education for the poor, point to the consequences resulting from many generations of delinquency; and instead of deducing therefrom the most cogent argument for instant, earnest, and self-denying activity, tell us that virtue must be abandoned as inefficient, and that we must seal our own humiliation by invoking the interposition of force. I object to this, as treachery to the moral dignity of society. I protest against this hasty revocation of the commission it holds—or, rather, this passionate and unmanly transfer of it to other hands. I challenge the right of any people, however unanimous, to shift the responsibility which God has imposed upon them as individuals, upon the shoulders of a mere Committee for the whole. And I am compelled to wonder whither has fled the respect of Christian men for their own nature, to say nothing of the genius of the religion which they profess, when, in a matter so vital as the training up of childhood, they ask that their country shall be relieved from any further trial of the law and dispensation of moral obligation, and shall be subject, henceforth, to the law of brute force. Why, it is nothing less than condemning a community—on account of some awkwardness in its earliest attempts to feed itself—to a perpetual infliction of the bib and the spoon. It is a concession made to laziness; one of those short cuts by which national sloth hopes to save itself the toil of a tedious journey—the vulgar impatience which cannot wait to untie a knot, but calls for a knife to cut it—the puerile officiousness which, distrusting the influence of sunshine and rain to open the rose-bud, pulls it open with rude fingers, and thinks to hasten it to its blushing and beauteous maturity. It bodes no good; it bodes, I fear, darker and drearier times, this itching propensity to go down to Egypt for help—to run for shelter from the land of promise, to the land of horsemen and chariots. If we take not heed, it will put back the moral destinies of the world for many generations.

Before we can be expected, in reason, to acquiesce in this great change, or to beat a retreat upon a principle which, in such a matter as education, we cannot, either as freemen or Christians, occupy without shame, we ought, at least, to be well assured that the special advantage which, by such means, we hope to purchase, will be fully obtained. That it should be as extensive as it promises— substantial, and not hollow—permanent, and not transitory—is the *least* demand we are entitled to make. But, to my judgment, no guarantee has been yet offered us, that the demand will be satisfactorily met. This legal provision of educational means may possibly prove a failure. I confess, I, for one, have my doubts—doubts strong enough to drag me upon the very confines of disbelief. In the first place, the real disease appears to me to lie far down beyond the reach of *any* system of educational means. When you have placed your school, your schoolmasters, your books and apparatus, in every parish or district, just as you have provided your church and your clergyman, is there not ground to fear, that abject poverty will operate to prevent the use of them by the children, in the one case, as it does by the parents in the other? That undermost *stratum* of English society, in our large towns especially, upon which ignorance squats contented, and crime crawls about unconscious of its own hideousness—that too rapidly increasing class, in fact, which has stirred men's fears, and provoked the cry for Government interference,—will that be reclaimed, or even touched, by any instructional machinery which coercion can furnish? I will not say—far from it—that *no* mental and moral light can be let in upon this more than Egyptian darkness; but I do say, that, if there be any constancy in the laws of human nature, this numerous herd of outcasts from comfort and civilization, these familiar companions of squalor, filth, and brutality, can be attracted from their cellars and their garrets by no light but that which is warm from sympathizing hearts. I fear that nothing but burning love, like that of Him who *went in search* of the lost sheep until he found it, will be able to do much good in that grim region of desolation and the shadow of death; and that the unclean spirit which possesses and vexes that hapless section of the community, is of a sort that will not go out but by prayer and fasting. Glowing hearts and liberal hands must pioneer the way through that jungle, for alphabets and primers, books and pens.

And, then, as to the industrious poor,—the main body for whose benefit a legal provision of school means is claimed,—are we quite sure that, on the whole, and in the long run, they will be gainers by this plan? I refrain from speaking with perfect confidence on this point; but I beg to throw it out as a problem well worthy of mature consideration, whether, in the pursuit of any great social ends, moral in their kind, as contradistinguished from physical, the last result is not always an equivalent, neither less nor more, of the amount of will which has been employed to achieve it? For my own part, the older I grow, and the more I observe, the less am I disposed to place reliance upon the power of mere machinery. Given, a certain amount of social interest in the work of education: and you will have, in real social value, a result equivalent to that amount. And no extension of machinery, which it does not itself make and sustain, will enable it to realise more than this equivalent. The facilities which aid it to cover a much larger surface, will also prevent it from giving the same degree of watchful and superintending care to the wider sphere which it did to the narrower. In process of time, when novelty has exhausted itself, the whole series of instrumentalities,—committees, inspectors, schoolmasters, and assistants, will become the medium of transmission to so much efficiency, and no more, as public interest in the matter will supply. A self-moving and self-improving apparatus, let no one expect! As is the man, so will be his strength. As is the life, so will be its development. As is the value at which society estimates the education of the poor, so, with or without Government interference, will be the ultimate value of the effect it will produce. All beyond that will turn out to be an imposing sham, or, in the words of the Lord Chief Justice of England, "a delusion, a mockery, and a snare."

It is, moreover, worthy of remark, before we quit this branch of our subject, that moral vitality seldom augments, either in intensity or in volume, as the result of being provided with a large stock of ready-made facilities. The will of man to do good is usually most lusty and vigorous when compelled by circumstances (pardon the homeliness of the phrase) to "rough it." He who wrestles with difficulties, is most likely to exhibit a brawny development. Action, antagonism, re-action, growth, is the order of things settled by Providential law. Where all is smooth and mechanical, the spirits soon flag. Of all the roads that one can walk upon, that which is straight and level is the surest to induce weariness. Many a man, charitable to the full extent of his small means, has speculated upon the immense good he would do with a princely fortune; and, pretty generally, where a legacy to a large amount has dropped into the lap of such a one, his benevolence has not expanded with his opportunity of expressing it. I have a grievous suspicion of all "royal roads" to great moral ends, and I feel a qualm come over me when I see inscribed upon any plan, "National Education made easy." Whatever else may be the effect of such a system, sure I am that it will not brace up the now existing amount of intelligent and disinterested care about the matter. Spontaneous virtue, which grew and flourished out of doors, will be none the stronger for being removed into a greenhouse. Mind may make opportunities, but opportunities seldom make mind.

These considerations have carried conviction to my judgment, that the proposed change from "you ought" to "you shall," in reference to the education of the poor, vast as it is in its character, and retrogressive in its spirit, may, after all, fail to work out the permanent extension and improvement of the means required, with a view to which we are asked to adopt it. But this is not all. The substitution of legal authority for philanthropic zeal in this matter, will, if there be any constancy in the laws by which human hearts are swayed, or any truth in experience, inflict deep and irreparable injury upon the intellectual and moral prospects of this empire. I know how puerile it would be to utter such an opinion at random. I have not done so, and I proceed to submit to this audience, with all the brevity which the question will allow of, the train of reasoning which conducts me to this conclusion.

The advocate of a legal provision for the education of the people would do well, I cannot but think, calmly and patiently to revolve in their minds the question how far, in matters relating to the intellect, the character of every movement depends upon the point from which it starts. Commence, for example, with compulsion, in the shape of an educational rate, and all your machinery must necessarily be constructed with strict relation to the original moving power. Thereafter, nothing whatever can be safely left to any force but a compelling one. From the first step to the last, all must be kept in motion by pay, and regulated by authority. The ability, industry, and perseverance of the master; the due supply of the material of instruction which he is to employ; the efficiency and regularity of inspection; the worth of periodical examination—all the details of arrangement, must be legislated for on the presumption that you have unwillingness to deal with. At no stage of the process can you pass into the region of Voluntaryism. Nowhere will the mechanism admit of the introduction of spontaneity. It must needs be pervaded throughout by compulsion. The system must be destitute of inherent vitality. The force which sets and keeps it in action must, in every instance, come from without. Upon this hypothesis all provisions and regulations must be framed. Now, we do not believe that indifference can be made, by any series of evolutions, to work out the same ends as Voluntary zeal. The problem to be solved is the vivifying of national intellect; and the solution proposed is a galvanic battery. We have no faith in it. Like begets like. The stamp answers to the seal. Where all the appliances of mastership are but a graduated scale of external restraint, the general features of scholarship will be sure to exhibit traces of the same character. To teach up to the point absolutely required by law, will be all that the first will attempt; to learn as little as such instruction will demand, will be all that the last will profit. To minimise trouble will be the ruling motive of all parties. The object to be accomplished—an object, let it be borne in mind, which is expected to raise the character of the rising generation—is thus entrusted to an organised army of functionaries whose leading idea it will be to accomplish it to the least possible extent. Compulsion ought always to suppose a natural antagonism between the obligations it imposes and the inclination of the instrument it employs.

We are convinced that a greater misfortune cannot befall a people than to have their intellectual habits gradually encroached upon by this spirit of authority. We can conceive of no condition more certain of terminating in disastrous results than one in which "you shall" is promoted to the guardianship of mind and morals. If, in that department of human affairs, there is not freedom; if the training of intellect and of conscience is to be deliberately committed to an authority whose force is official rather than real; if the idiosyncrasy of the nation is to be determined, not by men whose hearts are prompted by spontaneous interest in the matter, but by pay and preferment; if, in a word, all that is truly spiritual amongst a people is to take its origin from the low and sordid motives which endowed officiality inspires, then, as a people, we are undone. All hope of progress is paralysed: all tendencies to growth are doomed to extinction. Everything is after its own order; every seed produces fruit after its own kind. If we can satisfy ourselves with external decency—a state of things which appeals to the eye rather than the judgment—then a compulsory provision for the education of the people may answer the purpose. But if we aim at higher objects—if it be our desire to furnish mind with full and free scope for natural development—if we would have organised institutions to be something nobler than "organised hypocrisies"—if we are anxious for the embodiment of the true, the real, and the living, as contradistinguished from the false, the nominal, and the dead—if the expansion of a God-begotten thing be dearer to us than the extension of a mere form of human device, then we shall patiently work the principle of willinghood. The immediate results may not be showy, but they will be solid. There will be less outward decency, perhaps, but more life. The body, for a time, will not be comely, but it will be quickened by a soul. And this, after all, is what we want—life—reality—conscience. The mechanism which undertakes to fill up the vacancy which these ought to fill will be found, in the end, to be an impediment rather than an assistance.

Meanwhile, who will furnish us with an estimate of the deteriorating influence likely to be exerted upon the public spirit of our people by this transference of responsibility? The value of moral obligation as a moving force is to be computed,—in the secular, as well as in the religious education of our countrymen,—not merely from the direct results to which it conducts, but also from the indirect influence of the process which it employs. Dwell upon it a moment or two! Society, suppose, is conscious of some urgent want—lives on in the neglect of its obligations, and reaps the penalty. Anon, here and there, men of sensitive consciences, large hearts, and indomitable resolution, are inwardly impelled to cast about for a remedy. Here is life to begin with. The germ may be as "the smallest amongst seeds," but it is a living one. The unostentatious philanthropists, each in his own sphere, become "preachers of righteousness,"—inculcate upon individuals their responsibility and their duty—hold up before society the light of some forgotten truth, and commend it, by persuasion, to the notice. Presently a few kindred spirits wake up from previous torpor, respond to the appeals with which they are addressed, and, gathering about the original nucleus, swell the amount of life. So much mind and feeling are now awake in reference to the particular object. Combination follows—concert—co-operation. The press is employed. Arguments are collected, marshalled, and sent forth to invade and subdue the general indifference. Triumph after triumph is achieved; not, however, without hard labour, great self-denial, and unflinching perseverance. New domains are won from the vast territory of public listlessness. The spirit of moral conquest becomes contagious. Whole classes are seized by it. Activity grows to be as universal as it is spontaneous, and by the time the end is gained, one is at a loss to decide which is most important—the object accomplished, or the tone and habits of the public mind, nurtured by the process of accomplishment.

I assert, without the fear of contradiction, that it is to the action of this moral force, to the gradual working out of its ends by the power of "you ought," and to this alone, that Great Britain is indebted for whatever public spirit it can boast of. Devolve upon the principle of compulsion the social obligations which are now spontaneously, or from inward impulse, assumed by the philanthropic, and patriotism would shrivel up into a senseless prejudice—a mere chattering, boasting, self-glorifying passion. The men who work, because the voice within them commands them to work—who act up to the extent of their capacity and means, without waiting to see what others will attempt—who seek their happiness in the discharge of duty, and who cultivate responsibilities which others willingly permit to perish of neglect—these are the men who preserve the social body from actual putrefaction. One such, in a district, will create a silent public opinion, which renders further degeneracy all but impossible. In his own sphere, one such will diffuse just enough light to make sleep uneasy, and to compel all sorts of noxious things, which else would have lived and gendered there, to crawl away into completer darkness. Not a few of these practical patriots and philanthropists have been disciplined by their moral obligations, in every part of the empire. To them most modern schemes of social amelioration and progress may trace their origin. They are to be found in every Committee-room in which a good work is to be done, for the mere pleasure and the utility of the doing of it. From them goes forth, through various channels, a powerful influence to modify the opinions, principles, and modes of action of all classes of society. They are the life, the conscience, the heart of the body politic. Senators may be ignorant of them; the public press may know nothing of their whereabout; the wealthy may hear of them only through some appeal for pecuniary contribution; but, after all, these are the men upon whom the higher interests of manhood rest—the springs which keep the world in motion towards a brighter and a happier destiny. If, therefore, it could be proved that the country would gain, from a legal provision of educational means, a large increase in the amount, or a considerable improvement in the quality, of the book-learning imparted to the people, the advantage would be dearly purchased by the loss, or serious diminution, of the class we have attempted to describe. And yet this, in our judgment, would be the certain and disastrous issue of the introduction of compulsion in aid of education. The two principles "ought" and "shall" are antagonistic, and cannot well run in couples. The Irish *Regium Donum* is the most modern proof of that. Make the erection of the school-house, the maintenance of the schoolmaster, and the superintendence and direction of education, the business of authority, whether national or local, and the active and earnest advocates of popular enlightenment will die out in a generation or two. For a brief period, those who took an interest in the work will take an interest in it still. But their occupation will be gone. Their hold upon the conscience of the community will be lost. Their arguments will want cogency—their appeals, pertinence and power. Mechanism will have displaced life, and mere doing will supersede all care for the mode and spirit in which it is done. I characterise any approach to such a consummation as a great national calamity. The moral sympathies of society, rendered comparatively useless by the constant presence and action of legal authority, would shrivel up like an unexercised limb. Supersede the necessity of philanthropic effort, and the *vis vitæ* of the nation will become extinct. We can derive no permanent advantage from aught that is not capable of spontaneous growth amongst us; we can ensure only evil by counteracting providential laws. Communities, as well as individuals, are under the merciful sentence, "By the sweat of thy brow shalt thou eat bread." All attempts to evade our responsibility will terminate in disappointment and in sorrow. Indolence, however ingenious its devices, will bring home to us at last sickliness and shame. Increased sense of duty is more to be desired than increased knowledge. Let us beware lest, in the ill-considered methods we adopt to enlighten the understanding, we harden the conscience, and breed a canker in the heart.

I pass on to observe, that a legal provision for the education of the people is condemned by experience. I am prepared, of course, to see this decision controverted. Instances will be adduced whose testimony in favour of resorting in this matter to the compulsory powers of law, many are disposed to accept as worthy of confident reliance. So far as they apply, let them, by all means, have their weight. To me they do not speak in very convincing accents. Where time enough has elapsed to allow of the full influence of the system upon national character, results have not been such as alter my judgment. A wide, or even universal, diffusion of knowledge, when accompanied by a general intellectual pugnacity, servile submission to ancient standards, and a rigid attention to mere shows of propriety and decency, and, at the same time, unattended by superior morality, deficient in generosity, devoid of all high-toned principle, and quickened by scarcely a breath of spirituality, may have its charms for utilitarian philosophers, but will never do much, I fancy, to help on the right in its struggle with might, or to make conquest of any large domains of human nature for virtue and religion. I may be a heretic for saying so, but I would rather have an ounce of heart, than a pound of brains. And where the experiment is going on amongst a newly-settled people, whose amplitude of territory produces more than enough for all, and by whom, consequently, pinching poverty need never be known except by the hearing of the ear, no proof is afforded me that the much which is now done by law, would not be accomplished as easily, as surely, as efficiently, and with greater satisfaction, and nobler rewards in the doing of it, by the dimple force of moral obligation. The experience, however, to which I refer, lies at our own door. We have had, for centuries past, a legal provision for the instruction of the people—for training up the nation in morality and religion,—I allude to the Established Church. It has enjoyed ample revenues—it has secured the services of highly educated functionaries—it has distributed them with skill over the entire breadth of the country—it has wielded immense influence—and it has had time enough to develope all its capabilities; and what has been its success? I do not ask, what sort and measure of Christianity it has diffused among the people, because I shall be told in reply, that the question is irrelevant—that the nature of religion elevates it above the reach of assistance from law—and that spiritual ends were never likely to have been promoted by any merely secular machinery. I will not therefore press for a reply *quod* vital godliness, nor dwell, in accents of commiseration, upon the evidence daily thrust before our eyes, of the strange uncomfortableness exhibited by the genuine Christian spirit which unfortunately has got entangled with this unlikely system of means, and which, if it were to utter its complaint in Scripture language, could discover no sentence more appropriate than that exclamation of the Apostle, "Oh, wretched man that I am, who shall deliver me from this body of death?" But then, if reference to the failure of the Established Church, in so far as spiritual Christianity is concerned, is pronounced to be beside the mark, it may claim to be admitted as pertinent, up to the limits of all that is merely intellectual and external. If it be anticipated, that legal compulsion will diffuse abroad some accurate knowledge of Julius Cæsar, surely I am not out of order in inquiring whether it *has* communicated to the poor an historical acquaintance with the life of Jesus Christ. Revelation consists, for the most part, of facts, narrated with inimitable simplicity, and instinct with marvellous interest. How comes it that, with such ample provision for their instruction, the poor of this country, by tens of thousands, are represented as utterly ignorant even of these facts? The doctrines of the Gospel may be understood, as mere propositions, by the most unlettered. Whence happens it, that they know nothing of them even as propositions? The precepts of Christianity will be admitted to be sufficiently plain and comprehensive. Why, then, do you marshal before us troops of ragged children who, on your own showing, can scarcely distinguish between right and wrong? If your immense system of means and appliances for religious instruction, as by law established, cannot convert men's hearts, it might, at least, have informed their minds, and have imparted to them the first elements of religious truth,—a mental cognizance of its facts, dogmas, and principles. Now, has it really done this? Have its vast resources and peculiar advantages been made to conduce to even this narrow result? Withdraw our Sunday schools, the most precious of the embodiments of moral force, from our villages and hamlets, from our districts and haunts of the poor in manufacturing towns and great cities, and how much Scriptural information, think you, will be left in their midst? What proportion of the residue can be fairly traced up to the legally authorised source? And yet men, who would blush to answer these questions as conscience dictates, would fain persuade us to repeat and enlarge the experiment. Because an elaborate and richly-endowed national system, constructed and kept in motion to civilize and moralize the people, by instructing them in the leading facts and doctrines connected with the life and death of Jesus Christ, has utterly failed in its duty, we are desired to set up a similar and supplemental system, to compass the same point, by teaching children the history of Socrates or Julius Cæsar. Why, it is really a tax upon our patience to reply to so preposterous a demand. If you rely upon a pecuniary provision and a staff of able teachers, as sufficient to humanize the destitute by instruction, have you not got them in the Established Church? If any kind of information let in upon the intellect is calculated more than another to elevate, to purify, to refine, is it not just that kind which there are already the most ample compulsory means for imparting? And, in the face of egregious failure, are we to be taunted with indifference to the mental and moral progress of our poorer countrymen, because we decline to be parties to the erection of *more* machinery, on precisely the *same* principles, but intended to work up far inferior stuff? I really wonder where the wits of some of our good friends have fled! If they had half the faith in the Voluntary Principle which they appear to have in the Compulsory, or half as keen an eye to the shortcomings of the last as they clearly have to those of the first, Dissenters at this day would have presented an unbroken front against the advance of a principle which has already cost them so dear. . . I have now laid before you the course of reasoning which has compelled my judgment to pronounce against any system, however modified, which would provide means of education for the poor on the principle of compulsion. I need hardly point out to you that my arguments, if good for anything, cut away the ground on which every plan, admitting the aid of law, must ultimately rest. Indeed, it has been my aim to steer clear of all plans now before the public, and to strangle the error itself rather than any particular form of its development. It was open to me to have reached the same conclusion by a widely different path. I might have commenced with an examination of the legitimate objects, powers, and functions of civil Government; and have gone on to show, that the care of mind does not fall within the range of its duties, and cannot be assumed without injuring the people it is professedly taken up to serve. But, as I have already hinted, the occasion appeared to me to demand, that the argument should be built up on high moral considerations, rather than on a basis, however solid, of merely logical deduction. My object has been to drive at conscience, for it is possible to take the understanding captive without touching the will.

With a brief summary of the whole case, as I have endeavoured this evening to present it, I will close my observations. The substance of the question submitted for examination was:—"Is it expedient, is it wise, would it be conducive to national well-being, to provide for the education of the destitute by the interposition of the authority of law?" To this question my answer has been, "No.;" because Voluntary benevolence, prompted by sense of obligation, universally admitted to be superior as a moving force, is already largely engaged in the work, prospers in it, and promises to complete it. "No;" because to abandon moral for legal force, in so important a department of social duty, is fraught with contingencies of peril, and may involve effects upon national character, which no man can accurately estimate. "No;" because the change proposed is nothing less than social retrogression—a retreat, without necessity, upon "beggarly elements." "No;" because we have no guarantee that the surrender we make of a high position, will insure even the specific advantage for which alone it could be given up. "No;" because, even if we had, the good attained would be counterbalanced by the greater evil, of damage to our intellectual character and to our public spirit. "No;" because experience warns us to anticipate an egregious failure. "No;" because the step recommended cannot be taken without trampling upon the claims of justice. "No!" finally and emphatically, because we cannot adopt such a course without a virtual impeachment, and immediate counteraction, of the manifest design, scope, and principle of God's moral administration. On these grounds, leaving out of sight the nature and purpose of civil government, which conduct us to the same conclusion, we offer our protest against any interference of the Government with popular education.

10

"The Connection of Religion with Popular Education"

Algernon Wells

From *Tracts on Popular Education* (London: John Snow, 1852)

Algernon Wells (1793–1850), per the will of his late father, attended a Quaker grammar school. Thereafter he lived with an ironmonger and, under the influence of some Congregational ministers, decided to pursue a career as a preacher. In early 1815, Wells enrolled in the Hoxton Dissenting Academy. After graduating he became the minister at the Congregational Church at Coggeshall, in Essex—a position he held for nearly 20 years. In 1837, Wells took the position of Secretary of the Congregational Union of England and Wales, and it was in this capacity that he exercised influence on the Nonconformist crusade for

Voluntaryism in both religion and education. He insisted that no Congregational schools should accept government funds. At a meeting of the Union in 1843, Wells proposed a resolution that any Congregational school that accepts government funds should be disqualified from receiving any voluntary aid from the Union. Wells's resolution read:

> That this meeting, utterly repudiating, on the strongest grounds of Scripture and conscience, the receipt of money raised by taxation and granted by Government, for sustaining the Christian religion, feels bound to apply the principle no less to the work of religious education, and considering that the education given by the Congregational Churches must be religious education, advises most respectfully, but most earnestly, that no Government aid be received by them for schools established in their own connexion, and that all funds confided to the disposal of the central committee, in aid of schools, be granted only to schools sustained entirely by voluntary contributions.

In his Crosby-Hall lecture, "On the Education of the Working Classes" (1848), Wells said the question is not "How can we obtain Government money?" but "How can we avoid it?" Wells was keenly aware of the self-interested bias generated by government subsidies to teachers and school administrators. State employees will be extremely reluctant to bite the hand that feeds them by criticizing the state school system.

[Dissenters] must ever be equally free to act and speak. They must hold themselves entirely clear of all temptation to ask, when their public testimony is required,— How will our conduct affect our grants? The belief of many Independents is that, from the hour they received Government money, they would be a changed people— their tone lowered—their spirit altered—their consistency sacrificed—and their honour tarnished.

In his 1848 "Inaugural Discourse" at the opening of a Congregational normal school (a school for the training of teachers), Wells again stated the fundamental principle of Voluntaryism.

The originators of this School have arrived at a decided judgment upon it. They believe Government money and power, employed in popular education, to be not only dangerous to liberty, but injurious to the object it is designed to promote; they are persuaded it must and will work to the deterioration of schools; and for the sake equally of education and freedom,—two of the noblest of human interests,—they gather few in numbers, and feeble in resources, but strong in principle, to make a stand, which they are sure will not be in vain, for purely Voluntary Education.

Wells drew a direct link between the efforts of Dissenters to establish voluntaryism in religion and voluntaryism in education, and he conceded that Voluntaryists were fighting an uphill battle.

We are Dissenters in education, as well as in religion: separated in the one great interest by our own act equally as in the other, and for that act, in both cases, disliked and despised. The same principles and objects, the same strength and weakness, the same satisfaction and difficulties, attend us in both these highest and most sacred departments, not merely of national, but of human welfare. We find our conclusions on the question of Government interference almost universally condemned.

The selection reprinted here was published posthumously in *Tracts on Popular Education* (1852). As Wells saw the matter, it was ironic and depressing that at the same time that freedom of commerce, freedom of the press, and freedom of religion were on the march in England, state control of education was being advocated at many points on the political spectrum. Wells, like every Voluntaryist, viewed freedom of education as on a par with civil liberties in other spheres. Certain human activities should be beyond the reach of government power, regardless of the good intentions that may motivate calls for intervention, and education is in the front line of those activities. Once again we see the common Voluntaryist appeal to principles that should limit the extent of government power—abstract barriers, defined in terms of individual rights, that no government should be allowed to cross. Unfortunately, as Wells and other Voluntaryists clearly understood, principles rarely play a role in political decisions, but such principles were worth fighting for nonetheless.

At any time it would be unwise to treat the subject now to be discussed in an abstract form, aiming only at the settlement of principles; but just now it is manifestly but one branch of a great practical controversy pursued for the sake of immediate action. The merits, therefore, and indeed the meaning, of the question for consideration, cannot be fairly brought into view without some previous notice of associated topics, facts, and opinions.

The great controversy, to which this paper is a humble contribution, has for its object to decide, and will help to decide, whether Government shall interpose in the education of the people, or whether that great national interest can be safely confided to the people themselves. And it is sought to settle this question, not incidentally, and as a point of temporary expediency decided by a judgment on present circumstances; but rather on the ground of principle, and by the discovery of a settled rule for general and permanent application. Such fixed rules and general principles for the regulation of human affairs, no doubt, exist in the nature of things, and are discoverable by experience and reason; and once discovered and established, are of infinite benefit and value to nations.

Some such truths have already been brought into clear light, and are advancing to universal acknowledgment. Their effects already have proved most salutary. The hopes they inspire for the future peace and welfare of mankind, animate and gladden every enlightened and benevolent mind. That they have been discovered in what seems a late period in the progress of our race, and at the cost of woful lessons from previous errors, is but in harmony with that great law of gradual development under which mankind exist, and strengthens the hope that the great social system is moving forward, slowly but surely, to better and brighter times.

No one can doubt that civil governments must be placed under some limits as to their functions, no less than in respect to their powers: they are not to be omnipresent any more than omnipotent; they are not to intermeddle at their discretion with every social interest. Some things they *must* do, because they exist to do them. Some things they must *not* do, for these are quite out of their scope and department. No less can any thoughtful person question but that a wise settlement of the boundaries within which civil governments can work legitimately and beneficially, is a matter of vast consequence. The powers of the State are so great, that when they are carried into affairs for which they were never intended or adapted, the disorder, injustice, and mischief they occasion are in full proportion to their vast force and wide operation. Among the evils inflicted on mankind by governments, a large and conspicuous place must be assigned to those occasioned by their intrusion into affairs not within their province. These misdirected attempts to do good have often worked out results no less disastrous than crimes and neglects within the legitimate province of the magistrate. And therefore it is that the province of government requires to be defined and bounded by rules that shall have the force of law and the inflexibility of principles; so that when seeming expediency would tempt the hand of force to interpose beyond its bounds for the aid of a suffering interest, or for increasing a benevolent power, the fixed conviction that unvarying obedience to a general law is the truest of all policy, may be at hand to restrain from well-meant but ill-working intrusion.

This nation seems working its way to the exclusion of Government from interference with its trade by settling as a principle, fixed, general, and permanent, that it is not the province of the State to foster commerce by bounties, to uphold it by monopolies, or to shelter it by protections. In spite of proposition, this will come to be the law of England and of the world. The press has won its freedom from Government control: the principle is now established that it is not the province of the State to determine how men shall think, or how they shall utter their thoughts. Religion is struggling for a like emancipation. It is asserting independent powers and franchise. Many are contending that this sacred interest lies far above and beyond the province of human legislation, and of its coercive force. Minds as wise as they are ardent, as enduring as they are hopeful, picture to themselves a fair future, when the traffic of nations, the publication of thought, and the worship of God, shall at last be freed from the law, the force, and the wrong of human power, "standing where it ought not." Others, fewer in numbers, but well-assured that they have mighty truth with them, are toiling to place education in the same freedom alike from the help and the control of the State, and under the same salutary influences of liberty and competition. They believe education is not a department of State law and administration—that the interference of the State will not advance, but retard, this great interest—that it is not in harmony with sound analogy to leave trade, the press, and religion free, and yet to put education under the power of Government—that the free action of the people, ever growing while free, will make the surest and the best provision for this great want of society. These advocates of free education are not shaken by the fact that great names, ancient, modern, and contemporary, are found all ranged on the other side—or by the confessed difficulties of lifting up a people to self-reliance, self-government, and self-education; because firmly persuaded that their principle is true, and that adherence to a true principle is the one sure path to human welfare and advancement.

Now the reason, apparently, why many are at this juncture contending for the exclusion, from daily schools for the people, of religious teaching and influence in all dogmatic forms, is thereby to facilitate the action and interference of Government in their support. It is conceded that funds raised by taxation or rates, and the power of the State, would be misapplied, would be unfairly employed, in teaching either one set of doctrines and forms objected to by great numbers of tax and rate payers; or various sets of doctrines and forms, each approved by comparatively few, and each rejected by all the rest of the community. Therefore it is suggested—Exclude religious doctrine, that you may admit State money and State regulations: let general education so far cease to be an affair of religion that it may properly become an affair of taxation and coercion. The end and the means, as thus stated, are equally objected to. The admission of State money and power into schools for the people— the exclusion of religion from them in any form which the supporters of the schools and the parents of the pupils may approve—are viewed as great evils, social wrongs, and impediments to education.

The grounds on which these proposals rest are in part facts, in part assumptions, and both overstated. It is urged, that great numbers of children are still uneducated—that the education at present given is very imperfect—that the low quality of the schools for the people is one chief reason why children are not sent to them in greater numbers, and for a longer period. The truth of these representations, when abated of the grossly exaggerated form in which they are often made, is admitted. Then it is assumed—"Admit the action and resources of the State, and schools will be improved." This is very much more than doubted; it is denied, if the meaning be that they will permanently improve, or that they will improve more under Government care, than under the free influence of competition and benevolent effort:—and, if this is not asserted, nothing at all to the purpose is advanced. On the contrary, it is contended that all Government action tends to abuse, to stereotyped forms, to perfunctory discharge of duties, to the minimum service that will secure official approbation, to the maximum negligence that public apathy will tolerate. This, let it be said without offence, because with truth (unless, indeed, as is too common, the more true so much the more offensive), this has been the result of all past experience, equally in Church and State. When, or where, were salaried officials found to be a class noted for zeal, open to popular influence, prepared to promote or even adopt improvements? Were they ever seen heading progress, and conducting forward to reform? Has not their station been always far behind, retarding every movement, clogging every effort? When was the inspection of superiors found to kindle public spirit, or even to prevent dead apathy, and mere hireling service? Are we to have a great class of education officials, such as all other officials ever have been? And why should they permanently differ?

Will a school be more inspiring than a church, or will a Board for Education be of course permanently more energetic, than one for building ships, or governing colonies? Who can believe this, except on that solid ground of confidence, the wish that it may be so! Now nothing that does not energise and animate will improve education. It is an affair of mind, of knowledge, and of virtue. It is not a material interest, nor a thing of forms. Education can be promoted only by means calculated to arouse and to elevate the general mind of a country. This never was, and never will be, permanently the effect of Government administration. There is a thorough conviction that education, to become universal and effectual, must be constantly improved. There is an equal conviction that Government interference will not produce constant improvement in education, but the exact contrary. Therefore is Government education strenuously opposed, as surely fatal in the long run to the object it is intended to promote. Government can build schools, advance money, employ masters, commission inspectors, and distribute books; and it can so cover the land with the means and the aspect of education, but it cannot educate. Soon all this will be found obstructive machinery, cumbering the ground. Change will be impossible. School books will be as unchangeable as church books, and for the same reasons—their fixed use and immense numbers. A vast interest will be created, and stand as an insurmountable obstacle to spontaneous effort and improvement.

Moreover, nothing is more obvious than the fact, that as nations become populous and advanced, the power of Governments to deal with their economics proportionally lessens. Then the department of the legislature and the State becomes necessarily more limited to political and judicial functions only. A free people has then outgrown pupilage. No powers the State can create and wield, no resources the State can command, are any longer adequate to manage the affairs, and to supply the wants of a great people, in many departments quite within their scope in a ruder period of society, when a thinly scattered population live and die inactive and incurious, with small possessions, few activities, and no complex interests. What censorship could oversee the modern press? Has not the poor-law in our own time almost broken down, threatening to engulf all property? Were there no voluntary religion in England, how could the taxation be borne, necessary to supply the place of its vast apparatus of means? Had we no elective municipalities, what an army of officials must we encounter? A nation of our numbers, wealth, and activity—could such a nation exist otherwise than amidst our freedom—that received its local administrators, its clergy, its schoolmasters, all from central authority, would be burdened with an intolerable load of influence and corruption, aggravated, beyond endurance, by inefficient, formal, and sluggish administration. Now England, true to the natural developments of a free country, was in full progress to supply the want of general education, by voluntary effort. Great exertions had been made, and were ever producing greater. Discussion brought to light deficiencies, and new discovered wants roused to new labours and appliances. Sunday schools called forth daily schools—both led on to Mechanics' Institutes, lectures, libraries, and people's classes. While the movement spread and rose, it descended also. Like a true natural force, it worked in every direction. The outcasts of society were explored, and Ragged Schools were invented and established for their rescue from brutality and crime. What should have stayed this everspreading energy, which still increased by progress? We hear a voice, alas! From true, but mistaken friends of education and liberty, calling on the ardent and growing multitudes of zealous labourers in this great word—"You cannot do it." "Invoke the aid of Government." "Have recourse to the public purse." "Admit the force of law, and the power of coercion." "Lean on the arm of the State." To accept this counsel would be to ruin this fair promising work. Nothing seems more nobly illustrative of the real tendencies of genuine voluntaryism than the fact, that this proposal is by many rejected—that it stirs controversy, brings facts and principles to the test, promises, by the opposition it encounters, to serve the cause it proposed to supersede. No. Teach nations to be self-reliant, self-governed, self-educated. Widen the base of the social edifice. Add not to the superincumbent pressure of governing power, but to the supporting foundations of general independence. Already too much, not too little, is done for general education, even by voluntary efforts. This comes of a necessity. But both the necessity, and the over-help it occasions, are to be lamented. There ought to be vast numbers of schools in England for the common people, sustained by no subscriptions, governed by no committee, but undertaken by the enterprise of private masters, in the midst of competition, with nothing to uphold them but their own excellency, subject to no inspection, except that of the intelligent parents, who should send them their children, and pay them their money, on their own judgment and satisfaction. Well will it be if our voluntary efforts work in this direction—if they make way, and give way, for more purely independent, competing schools. Ill will it be if they work in the contrary direction, and yield their ground rather to Government schools, and compulsory education. For they are the true friends and instructors of the people, who teach them to think, and act, and pay for themselves. In truth, as already observed, they are becoming too multitudinous for charity, either private or public, either compulsory or voluntary. And there are no bounds to the wants found or created by the friends of State education. It has been stated, by an advocate of the Lancashire scheme, that four and a half millions of money per annum are required to educate the people. Could the worst enemy of education devise a proposal more surely fatal to it than this? Who can imagine or depict the sinecures, abuses, neglects, jobs, and malversations, of which such a sum of money would be the sure and prolific parent! In this immense heap of patronage, education would be stifled and buried. Here and there a true-hearted teacher might remain, but in every instance by virtue of individual character and energy, in no case as the genuine and natural product of the system. Are we never to profit by experience, or to learn by failure? Can a worse evil be inflicted, than to teach reliance on Government? Is there no such place as Ireland? As the ancients feigned their islands of the blessed for their joyous solace, have we feigned an island of the miserable, from our more melancholy genius, or for the mere charm of novelty and surprise? *There*, if all we hear be not fiction, is a people taught to lean on Government—for school, for work, for bread—for magistrate, for police, for overseer—for everything: and it has become the shame of Britain, and the wonder of Europe. England oppressed the land cruelly for ages. England has helped the land profusely for two generations. The oppressions of ages were not so pernicious as have proved the doles of fifty years. The people struggled against wrong, and became at least strong to endure. They sink under help: paralysis forbids exertion, despondency breaks down even endurance.

It falls within the scope of these preliminary thoughts to observe on a strange misconception, not to say misrepresentation, of the views propounded by the friends of voluntary education, by which they are made to claim for themselves the instruction of the whole people, and to assert their own competence for the work. Then the little they, the pure voluntaries, have effected, and the inadequacy of their resources for the entire work, are pointed to as fatal to their system and their principle. They were never so foolish. They never so magnified themselves. Their argument is, that the nation will best educate itself on the voluntary principle. They reckon all that effort in this work voluntary, which is not coerced or sustained by the State—all that parents expend or do for the education of their children—all that minds athirst for knowledge accomplish in self-instruction—all that is effected by libraries, institutes, and lectures to diffuse intelligence—all the schools originated and sustained by munificence, private or associated—although such labourers in the common work may not hold the voluntary principle, but only be pressed into the effort by the competition of which it is the parent. This is all, in their view, voluntary. It is already immense. It might become universal. It is maintained that it certainly and speedily would become universal, if not interfered with by Government.

The nature and tendency of such voluntary efforts are seen to work powerfully for propagation, and spread. Indeed, it is obvious that one real objection to the voluntary principle—for nothing is perfect, and, therefore, nothing quite free from objection in human movements—is its tendency to excess, to over-supply. Now, it is maintained that these voluntary agencies, thus working their unimpeded way through the land, would educate the people for intelligence and virtue, freedom and vigour, far beyond what could be accomplished by any State system that could be devised. And there is this powerful presumption in favour of this view, that the voluntary principle will bear the most thorough application, but this the compulsory system will not. The more thoroughly you apply the voluntary principle, the more efficient for its end it appears, and the more harmoniously it is perceived to work with all related interests: but the further you carry the compulsory system, the more rigid, formal, and inoperative it obviously becomes, and the more hostile altogether to the genius and action of a free people. Hence the advocates of compulsory education generally show anxiety to confine its operation within the narrowest limits, to admit as little of it as possible, to retain the largest amount of voluntary action that can be secured. Carry out the voluntary principle to its extremest application—imagine universal spontaneity of effort to secure instruction for the people—parents freely seeking it for their children, and freely making sacrifices to secure their training in knowledge and virtue—instructors free under competition for every effort and every improvement—all men of religion, philanthropy, and patriotism, concurring in voluntary efforts, because none other are admissible, or to be hoped for.

Does any man doubt that by such a thorough-going, all pervading voluntaryism, education would reach the highest point of extension, excellence, and efficiency? But suppose the compulsory system worked out and applied thus universally; the money supplied by the State at first in small proportions, but as the deadening effect of this on voluntary supplies came to be felt, the proportion from the two sources continually altered till all, or nearly all, the pecuniary support of schools was derived from taxation; then instructors, trained, appointed, directed, and inspected by authority; then coercion in some way laid on employers and parents to send children to schools; then public sympathy and care withdrawn from this, as from other departments of parochial or public administration—and where are we? What point have we reached in national education, the highest or the lowest? Have we a great and free people, all alive to thought, improvement, and progress? Or, rather, have we not a people snared and trammelled in a great net of centralised, coercive, fettering officialism? Say that such a state of things cannot be reached in England? God send that it may prove impossible! But it is surely a fair test of a principle to inquire how it will work the more it is applied, and the further it is carried. Step by step the voluntary principle shows to more advantage, and leads on to better hope. Step by step the compulsory principle appears less applicable, excites more fear, and diverges more widely from all the other conditions of a free people. Nor can it be admitted that the two systems will blend and co-operate. They are incoherent and incompatible. The one will extinguish the other. Nor do the friends of voluntary education hesitate to express fear that their plan would sink in the unequal conflict. They do not deem this admission a slur or blow on their plan. Far otherwise, they know that their system can be maintained and worked only by virtue. This is its glory. It is the offspring and the exercise of virtue. Its springs are benevolence, public spirit, self-denial. Now virtues and their issues are in this world wrought out by effort and difficulty—most of all is it so with virtues that have the public good for their object. Too happy are most men to gain exemption from such duties, by seeing their objects made the professed care of the State, and lodged in the hands of hired officials. Add, then, this to all other difficulties of rousing a people to benevolent care, bounty, and labour, that they can plead the intervention of the State in the objects for which they are solicited, and you certainly commence a course of constant diminution in the supplies derived from benevolence, and of constant increase in dependence of those supplied by coercion. The friends of voluntary education, who invoke the help of the State, will discover their mistake. The State cannot be, ought not to be, a great subscriber to a voluntary fund on equal terms with other subscribers. Its bounty will not stimulate generosity. Its co-operation will not call forth activity. Force and freedom work not together. The State must command, and therefore must pay. It must go first, and, therefore, in the end must go alone.

Whoever looks at this nation, and at all nations, must surely say, "Something is wrong, much is wrong. Change is wanted, great change. Governments have not answered their end, institutions have not wrought out right results. There must have been great mistakes in principles, as well as great delinquencies in persons. The world remains dark, wicked, convulsed, and suffering.

In what quarter does any gleam of light appear, kindling hope, promising improvement?" Surely, if anywhere, in the great spirit of voluntary effort and self-action among the people. If anything is to benefit the human race, it must be diffused effort, wide-working energy, self-reliance. To lean on Governments for what they cannot do; to expect from them what they cannot give; to quarrel with them for failing to meet unreasonable desires—has been long enough the bane and curse of the world. Let the people be at last roused to help themselves, to advance themselves. It is the last hope of humanity.

11

"On the Parties Responsible for the Education of the People"

Richard Winter Hamilton

Crosby-Hall Lectures on Education (London: John Snow, 1848)

Richard Winter Hamilton (1794–1848) was a highly respected Congregational minister and a Radical Dissenter who defended a wide range of civil liberties. He studied at the Dissenting Academy at Hoxton, and began his career, in 1815, preaching for a Dissenting congregation at Albion Chapel in Leeds. He was a founding member in 1821 of the Leeds Philosophical & Literary Society and an influential member of the London Missionary Society. In 1844, Hamilton received the honorary degree of LLD (Doctor of Laws) from the University of Glasgow; and later in the same year he was awarded the honorary degree of Doctor of Divinity from the City University of New York.

Hamilton became active in the British Anti-State Church Association (later known as the Liberation Society) shortly after its formation in 1844, giving many talks in Leeds and other towns calling for the complete separation of church and state. Like other Voluntaryists, Hamilton applied the same principles that he used to justify the separation of church and state to the separation of school and state. Consider his reaction to a parliamentary measure, passed in 1847, that increased government funding to schools. At a meeting of the Congregational Union, Hamilton insisted that the many voluntary schools established by Nonconformists should refuse all such aid.

> We, who object to all establishments of religion, could not foster a new one. We, who refuse all Parliamentary grant for religious purpose, could not accept this. We have been overborne;—but our resistance has not been in vain. Public inquiry has been aroused. Men begin to search more keenly into the scope of government, and into the province of legislation.

In his book *Institutions of Popular Education* (1845), Hamilton presented some of the same arguments for voluntary education that he later repeated in our selection. Especially interesting are his views on the "right" of children to receive an education. Hamilton agreed with many advocates of state schooling that children have a right to an education, and that this right imposes a corresponding duty, but he went on to argue that the latter is a "social duty," not a political duty. He wrote:

> Many a social duty exists, however, apart from the ruling power . . . . Social and political duties are not necessarily convertible. The political must be social, but the social need not be political.

The duty to educate children belongs principally to parents, according to Hamilton; but if parents are unwilling or unable to provide that education, the duty "falls on others"—either relatives or through the "voluntary contributions" of members of a society. "This duty belongs to that large class of morals, which includes the love of our neighbour." If it is said that people may contribute to the education of children not from a charitable motive but because they fear the social consequences of ignorance, Hamilton sees no problem with this. In addition to charity, the motives of "policy and self-interest" have social value. Under no circumstances, however, should the state interfere in activities that should be purely voluntary. To replace the virtue of charity with "legislative design" would be to lessen that "perennial spring of kindness and pity, which now sends forth such abundant and healing streams." This argument, to the effect that state schools would seriously erode the charitable motive to contribute to the education of poor children voluntarily, is also found in the writings of Herbert Spencer and other Voluntaryists.

Hamilton opposed all schemes of compulsory education, which is "a wrong to all liberty." To argue that liberty should be abrogated in this case for a greater good is short-sighted. There is no greater good than liberty. "There can be no greater good. It is not a simple means, it is an end."

———————

Our selection is from the *Crosby-Hall Lectures on Education* (1848). We see here a different style than we find in Hamilton's written works. In this selection, the transcript of a lecture delivered before an audience of around 500 people, Hamilton drew upon his extensive experience as a Congregational minister and used a pulpit style of exhortation.

———————

It is the People which the present examination respects,—a wide, generic, term. Statistically considered, they are the subjects of a sovereign power. The term knows nothing of classes, orders, differences: it is the patent of simple citizenship. "High and low," "rich and poor," "small and great," are the same in this category. No man can aspire to any nobler rank. He who springs from the people can never pass beyond them. All ambition ranges within this fellowship. Everything is great only as it is popular. Prerogative is but the borrowed loan of the people. Aristocracy and commonality are but spontaneous marshallings of the people. The crown is but the badge of the voluntary service of the people. There is no right which the people can surrender or transfer. They have no power of alienating aught of their manhood or of their civism, one particle of human or social claim! All power is in them, all honour,—all that they can do in reference to those possessions is,—not to cancel them, that were their political annihilation,—not to sell them, that were their moral slavery,—but to entrust the power for particular administration of public affairs, and to invest the honour for particular reward of patriotic virtues. Let neither be parted with! If that people be great, if they would become greater, let them keep in mind and in hold the original compact; let them remember, that this outward condition of things is mere arrangement and compromise,—that the signiory is native and necessary to them,—that it cannot be pawned by venality nor betrayed by abjectness,—that it not only immediately reverts, but never can be relinquished,—and that while their lien is maintained upon whatever they have allowed the use of to some for the benefit of all, the equality is absolute, and the fee-simple of this glorious inheritance is only and for ever in themselves.

In speaking of the people, I would not refuse nor hesitate to apply the term in the universal sense. It may predicate our kind. And as we both desire and foretell the extension of every blessing to the species, to every member and portion of the human family,—it would not be an improper treatment of the thesis, though inconveniently large, to demand, What parties are responsible for the education of the race? I trust that we should not be behind, in our benevolence of definition, the philanthropy of toast which a warm-hearted man, once suddenly called upon to give one, most candidly and impartially proposed, "All people that on earth do dwell." A difficulty, indeed, occurs in all such inquiries, whether more restricted or comprehensive,—What those parties can be that are to educate the people? Are they not themselves the people? And if so, who are to educate them? *"Quis custodiet custodes?"* Whence do they kindle their torch?

We do most repugnantly allow the term to denote the labouring multitude. We envy and grudge them such a distinction. They are no more the people than ourselves. It is to our shame if they have won propriety in it. Deeply will it mortify us, should we be compelled to resign our share. Not as a refuse, at least, can they so be called. Theirs is the majesty of numbers. Not as lower orders can they be figured, save as the rustic work of the palace, or the plinth of the Corinthian column. In them is productive wealth, and that which multiplies value tenfold. They are strength and life to a community. All besides are for them; they are for themselves. Without them capital is not wealth, and knowledge is not power. Not that they are selfishly divided from the rest. They sustain and elevate. They are not the trunk on which flower and fruit are grafted, but which bears them after its kind. We cannot, therefore, speak of them in scorn. Scarcely know we pity. We burn at their wrongs. We sicken at their abuses. "This people!" cried the ancient hypocrites: "the people," thus a vulgar refinement describes them. A philosophy, cruel as Herod, scowls upon their birth, as though they intruded upon nature's festival, and incommoded lordly guests holding banquet there. Thus are their practical applications computed. To what account can they be turned? Mechanism can be made almost intelligent: why should not intelligence be made almost mechanical? They are the inferiors! Coarser clays to be rudely shaped into the vessels of dishonour! Born for menial drudgery,—sound into their ears incessantly their destiny and doom! To hope to be otherwise, is a quarrel with a fixed law, an inexorable fate! They are the tools of gain, the conscripts of ambition, the materials of luxury!

It is somewhat a new doctrine that the people, as they are styled, ought to be instructed. Time was when the opposite doctrine was favoured and impressed. They could not know too little, or be left in a too contented ignorance. They were bound to let others think for them; they had nothing to do with such privileged things as government and religion. But it is now discovered that they must be taught. That which was maintained to be the spring of their industry, the preservative of their virtue, the mother of their devotion, is not discarded. The truth is, that the people have found for themselves an education, and have acquired the art of thinking,—and these parties do not approve of the spiritualism of that education and the independence of that thinking. They would take both under their management. They would give it their own direction. Hence their sudden conversion and new-born zeal. They would unsting the evil. They would wield the power.—"That it spread no further among the people!"

It is necessary that we should fully and distinctly inform ourselves of what education consists. The education of the people may suggest to different minds most different ideas. If it be a business of mere instruments,—for reading and writing are only means, and not ends,—we should take very little interest, and certainly no share, in the controversy. We would not run a tilt or a gauntlet for the sake of alphabets,—we would not know an ebullition for pothooks, nor bare our bosom for hangers. Ours are deeper, more solemn, views. We look upon man. We seek to educate him. He must be developed and expressed from inward capacity; he must be directed and disciplined for an awful future. He must be interpreted aright. He must be properly placed. With at least as careful study as with which we examine the instinct, the habitude, the habitat, of bird, or beast, or fish, we are bound to search into the true nature of man. Like other existences, he is marked by a fixed nature. All hearts are fashioned alike. But there is not that inflexible certainty of acts which may be affirmed of the mere animal. The creature of reason and volition cannot be foreseen by us in his doings. We must, consequently, allow in him for moral eccentricity. Yet may we define what he is. Man is something more than matter,—he is a spiritual being. He is accountable for the exercise of his liberty, possessing a choice of conduct. Death is his enlargement and enfranchisement to immortality. He lives for ever. These are the views which make him great and dread. To draw out such a being for his duties, and his beliefs, and his prospects, must be a religious task. Any attempt to educate him, save religiously, is a mockery and an insult. It is like the prophetic picture, the "roots in the earth, with a band of iron and brass." It is depreciation and repression. We cannot, indeed, conceive of an education of man's nature without a constant appeal to his relations towards the Deity, and to the influence of rewards and punishments over him. What is defended as secular education is most superficial, considering the depths of his soul; most incidental, considering the laws of his being; most temporary, considering the revolutions of his duration. Such a secular education need not say, there is no God! but it must not say that there is one. Such a secular education need not say, that Christianity is a lie; but it must not say that it is the truth, and no lie! Such a secular education need not denounce the faith of an hereafter; but it, as a thing of an earthly *seculum*, must never point to *secula seculorum!*

But we admit, that the children of the poor are placed under serious disadvantage. If every man has a right to education, if education be due to every man, if he must be educated to be properly the man, then indigence does interpose a great restriction, and handicraft demand a vast diversion. And we also admit that, upon this showing, there is a class to which the labouring poor may look up for help in the matter of education. It is a proper indemnity to them. They who owe to them the means of wealth, leisure, and knowledge, ought to pay back to them not only the wages of labour, but that priceless possession of which labour tends to deprive them.

In saying this, we are aware that there is an appearance of concession. The right of man to education needs to be well considered before it can be allowed. Upon whom of his fellows is it to be enforced? If it be his due, of whom is it to be required? These researches might only conduct us more circuitously to our thesis, and but clog our discussion; for they, in some sort, would be a *petitio principii;* they would anticipate and assume what we have to prove. Nor would the *desirableness* of education establish its right and due. Many other advantages might be pleaded for the same consideration. If there be any claim of man, it is such as he may assert, and which he may be left to himself to win. The original title to education is of the child on the parent: the gentle *Desdemona* could thus address her father, *Brabantio*—"To you I am bound for life and education!"

I am anxious, before any other party be admitted, most suppositiously, in the education of the people, to defend and hallow the parental constitution. This is the grand provision. Society is based upon this law, the earliest law. It cannot be imitated. It cannot be transferred. It cannot be superseded. All nature cries aloud, by a common instinct, against interference with offspring. No outrage is so universally resented; no bereavement is so bitterly rankling. Say what men please against its too arbitrary power,—it is the only check to a tyranny, not like itself, possibly capricious, but necessarily and only oppressive. Say what they will against its transmission of error and prejudice,—it is the only new independence to break up the conceits and presumptions which otherwise would be perpetually secure. Say what they will against its engendered evils,—it contains the solitary corrective and remedy of every evil. The scheme which would repair its mischief, would indefinitely multiply mischiefs, all of them indefinitely more portentous. There is not a fouler treason, than to gainsay this original institution. A distrust of it is a traitorous spirit. Trace it where man is worst—amidst his worst habits and temptations,—still where could you replace its tenderness, its care, its guardianship, its sacrifice? Those brawny arms of toil speak its strength, alike with the softest arms of embracing love. Intrude upon it, and society stands still. The incentive of labour is gone. We live no more in the future. Come once between parent and child, and the golden band which knits all together is snapped asunder. What is that— call it State, conspiracy, rapine—which affects to take charge of my offspring? My other acquisitions are conditional; my other treasures are alienable; my civil rights are things of covenant and arrangement; these have been earned, inherited, or won! But I have another property and propriety in my children; these are imprescriptibly my own—they are myself! Parenthood is their protector! It is the vulture which tears the broodling from the covering wing! Traverse the length and breadth of the land. Enter its cabins and its hovels. Judge not according to a sentimental romance, but judge righteous judgment. There are abuses, grievances, cruelties. These mark themselves. They stand out. They force themselves into notoriety. They are noted—conned. What are they in figures, what in exceptions, to domestic allegiance and regularity? Count them against the rural peasantry of the village and hamlet, going forth to their work and their labour until the evening, when the housewife spreads the dimple repast, and the children greet the return! Count them against the, perhaps, ruder crowds who, at the reverse of the curfew, hasten to the factory, but eat their meals in their adjoining cottages, and, when the shadows lengthen, there lie down to rest! The brawl of the street is rare. Nightfall, in its stillness and in its peace, vindicates the domestic character of the people. Those homesteads of poverty are, after all, though slandered and reviled, happy dwellings—tabernacles of joy. I have faith in the great workings of Nature; in the tenacious links of parent and progeny; in household order, and rule, and influence. I deprecate whatever would tamper with it. There cannot be a substitute for it. Its *penates* are worth a whole mythology besides!

I do not allow, by any of the previous admissions, that labouring habits are incompatible with a considerable share of education; nor that they are unfavourable, except for their consumption of time, to self-cultivation. To allow this would be fatal to the question; for it is a chimerical idea, that the poor shall cease out of the land, and that engrossing occupation shall be no more needed. It may be requisite, in some future conditions of society, that every man, like the ancient Jews, shall learn a trade. The world will never refine into a learned leisure. If education be destined to universality, it must consist with hardy, as well as skilled, labour. We want to be disabused of our artificial prepossessions. We ought to feel that there is no unlikelihood nor contrast between Araunah and the threshing-floor,—Elisha and the plough,—David and the sheep-fold,—Amos and the sycamore-tree,—Peter and the fisherman,—Paul and the tent-maker.

We shall surely concede to the labouring poor, not only the full parental investiture, but the right, in common with ourselves, to depute the educating power where they please. If they cannot teach their children, they are entitled to choose those instructors whom they prefer. They are not to be shut up to this or that. If it be replied, that they will not avail themselves of any, the fact is ostensible, that poverty is generally extravagant in this. There is a pride which overcomes a very parsimony,—or if it produces parsimony, for its sake, in all else, cheerfully abides the strait. If it be replied, that they are unfitted to discriminate between rival claims, the tact which guides them to the best leech and lawyer will be adequate to direct them to the best schoolmaster. It is the old dogma,—the people can know nothing about religion, and it must be dictated to them. But so the religious mind of Britain was never created,—it is self-formed and self-renewed.

We may be expected, on our known principles, to protest against forcible, compulsory, education. We only passingly notice it for future observation. It is surely little to say, that liberty is more precious than education; that education could be no counterbalance to the disturbance of any right; that the reluctant parent, embittered by the violence, would thwart any contingent good; that the deported, abducted, child would participate the parental rancour, and nurse his little revenge; and that this would be a civil war to the very hearth, we do not believe that, whatever pains be taken to blind and corrupt the people, the nation's heart will ever be so craven and so sunk as to endure the indignity.

It is now asked by many, What is to be done? Who are to be evoked to do it? we proceed to the answer,—but by no means conceding that parents have generally failed in their responsibility, or that there is any great dearth of the educatory apparatus.

That which is public mind is often long in being stirred to public opinion. It is commonly inert and stagnant, loves a careless ease, settles into a dreamy notion, until its fears are alarmed and its interests endangered. Then its short-sighted stupor is roused, and its activities may only become too eager. Public opinion is slow in its formation. Great general principles are commonly elicited and matured upon them. They are wrought in studious abstraction. They resemble not the experiments of the forge, the crucible, and the retort. They are tried, and tried again, in another laboratory. They, like mathematical truths, must be the same at every time and in all possible circumstances. They resemble the gold vein, the richest of ores but the latest of minerals. Think Adam Ferguson or Adam Smith (such first and foremost men deserved the original man's patronymic!) sitting with wrinkled brow and wasting lamp in their deep meditations. They have mused long and searchingly. The problem at length is solved. They have found it! They cast some greatly simple principle into the public mind; it is not quickened except it die, or seem to die; it is buried in seeming death. It takes hold of the surrounding soil, it spreads its givre, it strikes its root, it bursts the surface of the ground, it multiplies on every side of the furrow into which it fell, it waves to heaven! We may not be ruminant as they. We cannot boast their far-seeing sagacity. But we have come by a greatly simple principle. We have found it, we have found it! We see how the people can be educated, and how they only can. It is in struggle. That is what we want. It cannot henceforth be overlaid by indifference and scorn. It is opposed. It must then be heeded, sifted, agitated. This is good for truth and right. The harrow is as necessary as the share. Tremendous interests are stricken. A shattering blow has fallen upon ancient and mighty foundations. We are prepared for a death-grapple of sides. The terms are most unequal. The odds might affright the stoutest nerve. But we are so assured of the principle, that we should sin against it were we to falter in its maintenance or to despond of its victory.

We have seen false maxims, once deep-seated in the public mind, once strongly fortified by the public opinion, yield to argument, and shrink before truth. Few, some brief years ago, doubted that the ratio of wages was to the price of food. It was assumed, it was not discussed. Once brought into question, the theory was quashed. It was contrary to common sense. The wages of labour could only be ruled by the standard of labour,—by its worth or by its demand. It is exploded, it is extinguished,—it cannot come into human thought again. As little do we doubt that very popular, very plausible, very enticing, assumptions, touching the question of education, are even now about to receive condemnation, and are hastening to inglorious exposure. This, at furthest, is the beginning of their end! No sentiment seems at present more rife and attractive in certain quarters, than that it is the province of the Government to educate the people. This is the statesmanship of the times.

We may venture to inquire, What is Government? Many make a mystery of it. They hedge it with a divinity. Now, none are better satisfied, more profoundly convinced, than we, that He, who is not Author of confusion, wills the social order of men, adapts them to it, and has ordained its larger outlines. The duties of the ruler and of the subject are given a general interpretation and enforcement. From the inspired code, we ascertain that the things of God are eternally distinct from the things of Cæsar, that earthly jurisdiction cannot encompass thought, that faith and conscience go together, that the civil sword is not borne in vain in regard to well-doing and evil-doing, but that it is borne in vain, that it is a very vanity, "an air-drawn dagger," when it is brandished over the soul!

It is not necessary to argue the abstract proposition. We are not timid of it. We do not shrink from it. Were a people unanimously to invest a Government for this purpose, we deny that they could give it this right. They could not thus transfer to it parental duty. They could not convey the requisite power and capacity. So far as it was attempted by the deputed party, it must be wretchedly performed. It will suffice, however, for our present argument, to contest the question in simple reference to the elements of our Government and the principles of our Constitution.

To try the question, whether this be the province of the Government, we must apply various tests. Let us examine our own. Is it, in this case, enacted and provided? Is it in the bond? I love not to hear my fellow-subjects speak doubtingly of the Constitution,—where it exists,—what it is. It is an understanding, an intelligent covenant, something better than dusty archives, or engrossed parchments,—which guards property, liberty, life. Its reign is that of law. Its tribute is that of suffrage. Look at your statute of treason, your trial by challenged jury, your Habeas Corpus. Its principles are avouched and inviolable. It may not be consistently carried out. But it is in itself a wondrous thing. Every republic looks to it, even for its model. Our fathers devised it, upheld it, and shed their blood in its defence. But, we demand, knowing that in its spirit it is a trust had and held of the people,—when, in this great compact, again and again renewed, sometimes at the sword's point and the cannon's mouth,—in Council-chamber, in Aulic congress, inaugurated at Runnymede, and rallied at Chalgrave,—by oath, by blood,—where does the people, in what clause, surrender to the State the responsibility of their education,— and where in what clause, does the State undertake it? Show us the statutes at large. Apply to them the constructive latitude of exposition. Let court-lawyers and constitutional lawyers be summoned to give judgment. We are appellants to them, and let them answer our appeal. What tribunal speaks? What juris consults respond? What grey-beard ancestry calls up the remembrance? From what remote antiquity comes a voice? Out of what depth of ages resounds the oracle? We are constantly reminded of the wisdom, of the foresight, of the providence, of our fathers. They bear authoritative names. We venerate their urns. On which part is their prescription? To whom do they give their sanction and bequeath their experience? Education was a part of their religion. None honoured it more than they. "Ever witness for them" their schools and their colleges! How they spread the means of learning over our land! Did they abandon the task to Government?

Did they crouch for extraneous and public aid? Their endowments, the broad stripes of their estates with which they cheerfully parted, their princely bequests, prove how olden a principle is Voluntary self-reliance. Descend to nearer times. Unwind the scrolls of your best patriots, senators, magistrates, true to prerogative, yet ever most on the side of the people. Listen to your Somerses, your Newcastles, your Chathams, your Burkes, your Camdens! Talked they of the right or duty of the State to educate? It coalesces with none of those high principles which gradually develop themselves in the constitutional history of our country, which season the very forms of our legislative and juridicial institutions, which seem to thread themselves, like as the nerves which rise almost imperceptibly from the human brain, until they are foliated and knitted into the organs and instruments of the manly frame.

Government Education is the crudest novelty. It was not attempted until 1833. It is not fifteen years old. Is it so proved, so clear, so efficacious, that it must disturb and subvert all that centuries have confirmed and achieved? Is the upstart to scatter all that is rooted and well tried? Is the Grecian monster-toy to be trusted rather than our anciently enshrined Palladium?

But whether it rank among modern platitudes or not, let us examine its pretensions,—let us canvass its merits: is it right or is it wrong? Is it strong in truth, and benevolence, and policy; or is it unhealthy and untenable?

Putting from us all the mystery of things,—acquainted nothing, however high and holy, into which we may not inquire,—we address ourselves to the simple question, What is Government, as it obtains among a free people? We know nothing of its arcana,—we will hear nothing of its State-craft,—we do no wor-ship to heaven-born Ministers, though we have often prayed that they had been heaven-retained, and had never quitted their birth-place. Government is—we employ the term with no sneer—the creature of the nation. It is a trust. It can possess no legal compe-tence to do otherwise than the nation's will. If it assume an inde-pendence of that will in some great peril,—amidst some gross popular delusion,—still at its own hazard, still awaiting its own account,—we might even see a heroic virtue in the act. Our idea of the most liberal Government is far higher than delegateship. It may be obliged to resist momentary outcry. But we deny that it can introduce a new principle into the code, much less into the constitution, without an appeal to the nation. It must be put to issue. When has such a convention been held? When have popu-lar meetings, and municipalities, and petitions, declared for the principle? Some have approved aid, some have sought it,—none have been bold enough to avow the principle. Nay, they have charged us with morbid sensitiveness and cruel wrong in suspect-ing that such a slavish principle could anywhere, or by any one, be possibly entertained.

Before the State can fairly take upon itself the work of pub-lic instruction, it should establish its peculiar capacity for it. We say no more concerning the distance at which hitherto it has stood, and the delicacy with which it has hitherto refrained, from this work. It has all to begin. It finds no machinery to assist its operation. It looks around in vain for a minister of education. It can go to no board, no bureau, no portfeuille. The wisdom of our ancestors has left no such appendage to a Cabinet. All is to be created. The ministry sets about it. There is a chief,—he is a Cabinet minister,—and then an array of clerks and inspectors, who certainly are not of the Cabinet. The whole is irresponsible. But the justifying allegation is, that a Government, from its high position of intellectual superiority, should guide the mind of the people. In what does this superiority consist? Scarcely in literature. Its speeches and its manifestoes lead to a rather painful distrust of its peculiar aptness to teach the art of eloquence and the syntax of composition. Scarcely in politics. It invariably lags behind the questions of the day, always carried from without ere they receive its support and stamp. Scarcely in religion. Perfect respect sometimes fails to follow its expositions of doctrine; nor can a true holiness invariably warrant even certain points of practice. Heaven does not uniformly hear our prayer to "give unto the Lords of the Council grace, wisdom, and understanding," nor to "teach our senators wisdom." We are compelled to conclude, that the people are generally in advance of those who govern them, in all the higher elements of a true education.

It may be objected, that this is an inversion of things; that a paternal idea is involved in the State. That this is sometimes averred, we know,—and we know, that the supposed duty of teaching the people is suspended upon it. But all the parental duties are then implied; and we must not stop at one. Well! can the State carry out all? It is thus that figures are abused. "These sheep," said David, "what have they done?" The metaphors of the family and the flock are beautiful—but only beautiful—metaphors. No argument can be raised upon them. They are not literal truths. Children owe their existence to parents. But the people exist independently of the State. If it be said, that only political existence is intended,—be it so. We are helped. The people is here the parent; it is the author of political existence; it is before all other things; it is the source of all relations, and the origin of all institutions: it begets the State, it feeds the State, it clothes the State, it revises the State, it checks the State, it chastises the State, it may outlaw the State! It finds, no doubt, a forward child and a forgetful pupil. But it has the means of discipline. It has the key of the wardrobe of velvet and ermine. It has the charge of the refectory of tribute and revenue. It has not, however, concealed, quitted its hold of the rod. In extremity, it may turn the prodigal out of doors. If the question be stirred, who shall educate?—who is the better qualified?—at least the respective postulants must submit to a previous examination!

Rights and duties, it is allowed, are not always correlative. I may have a right, and yet it may not be my duty to press it. Things lawful may not be expedient. Still is it scarcely conceivable that the rights of a Government should lie in abeyance. Such rights, if genuine, if beneficial, if unselfish, are for use. How can it be a right to educate, and not a duty? Be it remembered, that this is not a business of personal rights, inherent and connate in the individual,—but public, the trusts of public investiture, the pledges of public benefit,—not like those which are private, under the control of a circumstantial prudence. We, then, infer that, if it be the right, it must be the duty, of a Government to teach. Two consequences will be granted. First, that it ought to enforce obedience. Law needs an executory principle. Be the penalty some disqualification, some deprivation, it is force as much as mulct and imprisonment. No matter what,—sanction is required, and it is the duty of the Government to see that its behest is obeyed. But, secondly, if the obligation be in Government to teach, the obligation must be on subjects to learn. If such were a theocracy, God would have made these duties parallel. If a nation has formed its Government with this provision, that nation is bound to take the attitude of the scholar towards its own anointed instructor. Let us see where we now are. Let us weigh the corollaries. These parties cannot lawfully think in different ways. Teacher and learner must act in common. All, in the condition of subjects, cannot but yield. This is the foot of intellectual tyranny; but we have bowed our necks to the sole of that foot. Nor is this all. There are other and more serious consequences. Education must be religious. Numberless awakenings rise in the course of it, which can only be religiously answered. If Government has found out the true religion, and can insist upon infusing into education some parts of it, why may it not insist upon its whole? Indeed, it has always seemed to me, that if Government is seised of the right, and laid under the duty, of establishing a religion, all toleration is inconsistency. From such right and such duty persecution becomes the clearest of all rights and duties. Doubtless, we may rejoice in every degree of religious sufferance or liberty,—but it is only a relief, a mitigation, under a state of things which never should have been.

A true moral philosophy, blending with a hardy logic, deals with certain questions, not only on their own principles, but pushing them to their necessary difficulties and natural results.

The pecuniary assistance of the State—the lowest, though perhaps not the least, exercise of this supposed right and duty—must have its conditions. It cannot be flung idly away: it must be accounted for. Now, if this boon cannot be equally divided, or if it must be accompanied with invidious distinctions, then is there partiality. And let us never forget, that all this money is the people's money, and that they all have an equal right to it. Why should a religious section be preferred? Why should it be turned into a bounty upon particular opinion? Why should some parties be altogether denied their pittance of a share? We complain not of these consequences, we tax them not with injustice,—they are inevitable—they belong to the responsibility of managing a public expenditure; but we do thus convict such measures of injustice when they, of their own nature, debar and force back impartiality.

That statement is good for nothing which proves too much. The statement that Government ought to educate a people, is general. Does the whole educational system of the country properly attach to it? Is the entire nation comprehended? Some will qualify it, and say that they only intend the poor. Then there is one law for the poor and another for the affluent. Then, too, poverty and affluence—mere accidents—are rendered the types of ignorance and wisdom, which are mental states. But it is not impossible that some shall contend to include the wealthier classes. I am free to declare that this is my opinion, the case being allowed. If Government be authorised to teach any, let it teach all. Let it study hard, and begin with itself, for self-cultivation often bears a full ripe fruit. A Normal-school for courtiers would be worth a visit of inspection. An Infant-school for those of noble blood might elicit that sweetness of common nature which fictitious manners so soon disguise. A Finishing-school for placemen and pensioners, would afford a rich exhibition of supple joint and sinew. A very gymnasium might open its gates, teaching by its poles how to climb, and by its hoops how to bend, until curved backs and itching palms should fill the scene. Here, too, might be taught the many sports of shooting pheasants in *battu*, or of evicting tenants by almost as summary a process, without which how could proprietors live on their estates or endure their homes? Oh, let it go round! Let the State do its duty by all alike. Teach the poor for what they were born. Teach the rich their proper destiny. Discern between the delf and the porcelain. There must be no exception. None must play truant. The nation's forms are set! The nation's tasks are appointed! All in! all in! (as some of us urchins used to say at school.) Seems this absurd? It is but a legitimate dilemma.

• • •

If it can be shown that the aid of Government leads to the discouragement and extinction of the Voluntary support of education,—its only imagined or argued support until a few most recent years,—many would esteem it, so far, an evil. It must ever be a generous and elate emotion which springs from independence. It is something to bear a weight alone. We summon all our strength for it. Let us be *helped*, and the strenuous effort is relaxed. Its glory is snatched from it. Atlas would drop his load of earth, and sink under his burden of heaven, were a brother Titan to interpose. Now, when the Exchequer opens for us, the consciousness of pressure upon us ceases. It may be said this is but to incite us. It is not according to the laws of human motive that it should. For a time we may maintain it, because the aid is measured out in strict proportion to it. But we are tempted to withdraw, not believing the threat that Government will withdraw. The school is built,—the master is appointed,—the pupils are gathered. Shall that school be left to decay,—that master to starve,—those pupils to become outcasts? Government has expounded its responsibility to us; and we have reliance, though we decline, that it will remain true to it. If it be its duty, it is a pitiful mode of performing it. To require a bribe before it will act at all, would seem to show little heart for it. It would seem, upon a triple calculation, that it has reached the conviction that its duty in this affair is as one to three, and that of the people is as two to one!

I have no wish to impute any sinister design, but many men about Government avow the policy of getting the mind of the nation under an unitive system of education. They would torture all into shape, and fix that shape for ever. It is against such a Machiavelian, Austrian, Chinese archetype that we contend!

A concession is sought to be wrung from us, in respect to certain departments and classes, among which it is affirmed that the State only can be the educator. We are pointed to our prisons, to our troops. Government, in these cases, is said to stand *in loco parentis*. Little welcome may be given to Voluntary instruction in such instances. Still has it found its way. Where gyved hardihood and profligacy yelled with bestial strength and gnashed with bestial fury,—where sympathy was derided and kindness spurned,—was found a better teacher than the State! The State was the keeper before the door, and kept the prison; but an angel of the Lord came upon those wretched and branded inmates, "and a light shined in the prison." Elizabeth Fry sat, prayed, persuaded, wept, there, *in loco matris.* She was to them more than a parent; and, as they listened and as they gazed, they were as those whom their "mother comforteth." Where is the gaol, to which we might have access, that should want a Voluntary education? Our distant soldiers and sailors find evangelists, teachers, pastors, in those noblest of Voluntaries, our Missionaries.

The argument for the jurisdiction of the State in popular education often halts, but still more frequently betrays and neutralizes itself. Its advocates will rarely assert that it ought to ply its jurisdiction, the people being already educated. But this proves that this interference might not be necessary, that the object might be otherwise attained. If it ought not to interfere, its tasks being accomplished by others, then it may either depute its duty or suspend it. The common plea is, that it ought to educate the poor, because the parents of the poor cannot, or will not. This is to make it but a succedaneum. It reserves to itself an *ad interim* power. Its present right or duty grows out of the neglect of the rights or duties of others. Then it has not the primary, the inherent, vocation. When parents all attend to these rights, or duties, the Government is superseded, and reverts to its natural irresponsibility. The argument is complete. We, at the same time, deny the assumption on which it proceeds,—that these parents generally are chargeable with such inability or negligence.

Then, who are to do it? Do what? We believe that a very large bulk of the people are now under instruction. But there is defect. We feel that there is much to overtake. The sentimental, or the partizan, cry of them who never expressed a care, or took a part, for education until now, shall not turn us to indifference. I do not think any can be over-educated. I wish every man understood geometry as well as Barrow, and the stars as Newton. But, first of all, let the people trust to themselves. Let them seek all that is withheld from them, by the force of knowledge, and virtue, and religion. These are the only weapons with which they must contend, with which they can succeed, in the conquest of their immunities. Much of education is in their power. The thirst, the effort, the resolve, for it cannot be in vain. Mind enlarges with these dispositions. Thousands of ways are open, thousands of means are at command. They never want help who will help themselves. Let the vicious vulgar,—let the low dissipation,—let the contented ignorance,—let the hopeless apathy,—be eschewed. Let the people, the mighty fold of labour and industry, lift themselves up. The ocean-coasts more generally sink than rise; but some have been known, without convulsion, to rise,—nobler headlands than before, while the billows recede and sink. So shall the true elevation of the people be hailed by all the good! Its swelling rampart shall not appal, but only more firmly beat off the waves. And now, let all true-hearted and Christian philanthropists show themselves ready to this good work, zealous of these good works. They have every augury in the state of the public mind. They, on every hand, may read note and presage of onward movement. I do not say that Christian ministers, as ministers, Churches as Churches, are peculiarly obliged to lend an impetus to it. But all that is benevolent in them, all that breathes warmly for our humanity, all that is refinedly and expansively Christian, assuredly does. It is no superfluous, no gratuitous, duty, to desire and pursue the weal of our race. We must love our nation. We must honour all men.

We must condescend to the man of low estate, the brother of low degree. We must not despise one of these little ones. Let us act, with others, if it might be a national league. Let us act, but only when repulsed, alone. Let us keep the cause before the world.

It is wrongly objected, that we withstand others in doing the work which we will not do ourselves. We only withstand a noxious principle, which we believe to be destructive of the work. We do not boast, but of that work we hope that we emulate our share. Yet we are likened to the dog in the manger. We never were in the manger. We keep watch at the stable-door. We guard the entrance against the intruding steeds which would eat our master's hay and corn, and the pilfering varlet grooms who would abstract it. We raise the alarm by our deep baying. We should be caressed if we took the bait thrown out to us,—were we dumb dogs that would not bark, lying down and loving to slumber.

• • •

We do not conceal from ourselves our disadvantages. We cannot soon forget our proud sacrifices. We love education, but there are things which we love better. For them we have suffered loss and rupture of the oldest and the dearest ties. It was, indeed, a taunt which we had not deserved, when Education was inscribed on the standard of our foes!

We see arrayed against us that love of money which makes stooping sycophants and crawling mercenaries, called into action by bribe and bounty. The teacher and the child are to be bought. It is a small beginning: the wedge has one side thin. Commonly, to give it power, you must strike hard if you would drive it to its head; but this works its own way, for it is a wedge of gold. *"Virtus post nummos."*

We see in all such measures a tendency to pauperize education. It is already made too eleemosynary. Where it is paid for, it is always more thankfully estimated. Any aid which is now proposed, so vain is the scheme, will not originate a school, nor cheapen one; but then it is known that the Government has power over it, yields support to it, and each child will be thought its foundling.

We see in these tamperings with a higher independence more than a tendency to destroy the self-reliance of a people. It is but an experiment and reconnoissance. It is a precursor. A system is avowed, of which this is little more than a symptom. It is publicly recommended to take all general interests into the State, and to stipendize all who superintend them.

We see strengthened, by these means, that ghostly power which seemed well-nigh laid,—once more ruling by superstitious fears, now beguiling maiden simplicity and sensibility,—then extorting the miser's hoard. The cowl and the crucifix insinuate themselves. The infant mind is brought under the control of those unscrupulous agents, who are the hirelings of one Church, but the familiars of another.

We see an insatiable rapacity which millions of sterling cannot appease, grasping at more. It knows not Balaam's check, though its house is full of silver and gold. Not the little addition makes it happy, but the prospect which that addition opens! It sees it with a gloating eye! Its joy for it is almost riotously elate! It "grins horribly a ghastly smile, to hear its famine shall be filled, blessing its maw, destined to that good hour."

We see a centralization which is always to be deprecated,—not as accidently, but necessarily, tending to abuse,—an over-riding of the country by inquisitors, a multiplication of officials,—new sources of a corrupting influence in seduction and in intimidation. It is an insidious attempt upon the independence of the electoral constituencies. It is to be a quietus to the rising claims of the poor.

We see in it a futurity of evil. The nation will blindly lend itself to an accrescent power. We shall have a new pension list, a new national debt. Claims thicken and seize on a perpetuity. It is "little," it is "small." But,—for it is not the pecuniary cost about which we comparatively care and fret,—so is the alligator's egg, and the lion's cub. "It is but a scratch; marry, 'tis enough. No; 'tis not so deep as a well, nor so wide as a church-door." The well of truth they would not sink, and the church-door is wide enough for all our renegades.

We see a fetter forged for the restriction of educational freedom and competition. Left to its native strength, committed to its true independence, mind will grow up under it variegated and prolific. When the culture is cramped, there will be a dwarfish and barren growth. There will be an organization of ideas. A very concrete of dead intelligence only will be left. Nothing will be created to inform the life within, or to enrich the world beyond. That which should liberate will rivet; that which should develop will straiten. There will be no laying open of the soul of man. In a modern instance of statesmanship nothing very great is contemplated—though visions are made to play before us of a more artistic laundry and a more mathematical excise!

But I do not despond, much less despair! It will be hard to bow the mind of England! There are too many historical glories, too many constitutional safeguards, too many free institutions, too many popular habits, to justify a drooping thought. It is a serious struggle; but struggle is the price of all momentous victories. At present the few must stand against the many; but "the fewer men, the greater share of honour!" I pity the schoolmaster who is set over boys to teach them servility and slavery. There is, ground and kneaded into our native temperament, that enthusiasm for freedom and erectness, that this may be a hapless fate. One of this order, among the ancient Falisci, brought his pupils with him to betray them to the Roman general, Camillus, who was then besieging that people. Revolting at such treachery, though in his own favour, the generous conqueror spurned him; and, arming the boys each with a rod, sent back the traitor, with a strict command to them to flog him all the way. I trust they stoutly obeyed. I hope they settled all arrears. What would I have given to have claimed the opportunity of reprisals upon some who reared my tender thought with little commiseration of my tender skin! So may every school, turned into a house of bondage, be in an uproar,— and such taskmasters learn, from a well-swinged experience, the peril of insulting their country's mind and independence!

The retrogressions of social and religious truth are illusory, and not real. No step is lost. All—though it seems to waver, or even to recede—truly advances. It must make way. Whatever surrounds it, must make way for it. We might have thought that this battle had been decisively fought. We were prepared to claim the field. We had well-nigh shouted the victory. But it is happy that the strife has been rejoined. We may rejoice that it is once again put to the issue! The whole of the question was never before placed in sight.

The entire gage is only now thrown down. And though we may deem the repetitions of error and sophistry tiresome,—though we might have hoped that the common places of vulgar ignorance and obtuseness were worn out,—yet this has always been the trial of those who would forward the race, and amend the world. It is to be done, and to be done again. But thus only can that which is achieved be consolidated. There is no giving way—no yielding. The giant plants his foot a little farther back to take a more mighty spring, and to deal a more conquering blow. There is no mere turning round—no circle. Like the seven ledges of Dante's Mountain-cone, we travel no ground again: each curve is a spiral ascent, and each winding lessens as we rise!

At least we have one *"Patriot"* with us. That is a patriotic host. It has stood firm with us amidst frown and menace. Its high and eloquent intelligence has been of the greatest stead and service. Its "leaders" might be manuductions to the age. Now up with the *"Banner!"* I am not content with a flag-staff, with its drapery reefed and furled! Where is the meteor streaming forth of its folds? Where the breadth of the shadows it might fling? Where is the battlemented height on which it should be planted,—a signal known afar? It wants but one device to its emblazonments, but one motto to its legends,—Free, self-sustained, self-advancing, Education. Then, what will be its gorgeous field? Then, what will be its triumphant flight? When will the meridian hour strike?

Our ranks may even thin. Truth may fall in the street. Men may ride over our heads. Our natural allies may turn to be our bitter foes. Whig, Reformer, Free-trader, whom *we* never forsook in their evil hour, may desert us. Where we cannot find consistency, we call ill hope gratitude. We grudge the delay for our generation. For ourselves, we can bide the time. We do not seek, with Malcolm, "some desolate shade, and there weep our sad bosoms empty;" but rather say, with Macduff, "Let us hold fast the mortal sword; and, like good men, bestride our downfallen birthdom." Galileo was not more convinced of his principle than we. Somewhat like his is our persecution. Others would bring the sun of knowledge to wait upon them. We would bring them to wait upon the sun of knowledge. If the earth will catch its light and warmth, the earth must move, and move round it. The mechanics of the universe were always right. The laws of mind have been disturbed. But they once were duly obeyed, and shall be obeyed again! Look forth upon the spiritual, moral, universe! The sun is high; and if it moves, it moves not to us, though it may draw us with it into some more glorious depth of splendour, into some mightier firmament of power. The earth circles it, in tribute and for regeneration. Let the people, like the planet, know their duty. As she relumes herself at the great urn of solar fire, let them seek their true enlightenment. It will not revolve for them: let them secure for themselves this only peaceful and holy revolution. Still, with Galileo,—we proclaim, The Earth must move! Does move!

12

From Reasons Against Government Interference in Education

Anonymous

(London: T. Ward and Co., Paternoster Row, 1843)

———————

Very little is known about the writer of the treatise excerpted here. No name is attached to the manuscript. We know that he wrote much of this treatise while ill and that he died (1841) before completing it. The treatise was published posthumously by friends who wished to make the writer's observations available to critics of the Factories Bill then under consideration in the British Parliament.

———————

Chapter I.: That there is a party in Britain disposed to give up the direction and superintendence of Education to the Government.

It will perhaps be necessary that I should adduce a few facts in support of the above proposition, for state direction or guidance in general, and more especially in education, is so inimical to British institutions, so *un*-British, in a word, that some will be inclined to question my assertion. However, that there is such a party, appears evident from the multitude of books and pamphlets which have been published during the last ten or twelve years on the subject of National Education, a topic which has become the daily theme of declamation at our public meetings, and of occasional discussion, even from our pulpits. It is called the all-important question—the momentous question—the "question of questions." It is looked upon as the panacea, the universal cure for all the ills that betide humanity. We cannot open a newspaper but the words "National Education," in large capitals, immediately meet the eye. National Education—National Education is echoed and re-echoed throughout the length and breadth of the land. Now all this would be very well if the word "education" were simply used alone. No man has a firmer and fuller faith than I have in education, as a means of improving and moralizing the whole human race; but this can never be done nationally, above all, in Britain. It is the attempt to make a national concern of what should remain a local one—I was going to say, a family concern, and to a certain degree, an individual one—which paralyses many otherwise praiseworthy exertions.

While it may be doubted whether many of the National Education men know what they would be at, it is manifest that their leaders are quite clear upon the subject. What *they* aim at is, to establish a system of National Education, the direction of which is to be given over to the State. They wish to create a separate ministry for the thing, the chief of which is to be called, "The Minister of Public Instruction." Mr. Wyse, the able advocate for Educational Reform, now a Lord of the Privy Council, a man with whom I sympathize on most other points, tells us plainly that his object is to connect education with the State. And he wishes government controlment, not only over elementary and primary education, but also over what he calls the *superior,* the *supplementary*, and the *subsidiary,*—that is, university education, adult education, and the education imparted through the medium of museums and libraries. In justice, however, to this high-minded and warm philanthropist, it must be told, that he would still allow the people, at least for the time being, to have some share in the management of their own educational concerns. But even thus modified, the principle is bad enough, as I hope to show before I have done. His plan of National Education for Ireland is briefly this:—That a Board be formed under the Secretary of State as its president (Minister of Public Instruction), the Board to be his council, and to consist of a Protestant and Catholic archbishop, a Presbyterian clergyman, and five lay members.

We find the author of this plan, in Manchester, Cheltenham, Sheffield, and other parts of England, haranguing crowded audiences in support of a similar scheme for that kingdom. Such is his present scheme; but he speaks of a *gradual interference of government,* which implies that he would allow the State further power over individual freedom as soon as practicable. "The elements of social progression," says he, "which are now scattered in many directions, must be brought to bear with a concentrated force upon the public, and every British child be provided from infancy with a good, useful, intellectual education by the State, free from superstition and sectarianism." This passage needs no comment.

. . .

The thing aimed at is evidently the establishment of government direction, both in *what* is to be taught, and in the *methods* of teaching it. Alas! for Britain, if ever this takes place.

. . .

The government scheme of national education for England scarcely deserves the name; for, after all, it simply amounts to the appointment of a Committee of the Privy Council to superintend the application of any sum voted by parliament for the purpose of promoting education. At first sight this appears to be a very harmless interference; but its very want of fixedness, that is, its want of definite organization, renders it more dangerous than if the law were fixed and well known; for while we may be happy enough to know what principle is followed the present year, we can never know what shall be followed the next. The Board may be influenced by party feeling, and, of course, changes take place. Where are these to stop? May not the pretended government improvements be evils? Teachers' colleges, too, are to be established. Of what religious and political creed are the rectors to be? Again, the committee are enabled to grant gratuities to such teachers as put themselves most forward in advancing government methods and objects of education; but what, I ask, are these methods and objects to be?

Nevertheless, lest it should be thought that I object to the government plans for England and Ireland, on any other ground than that of their just being government plans, I here declare, once for all, that, as State schools, I consider them as the best that could be devised in existing circumstances. But this being the case, it must be owned that their failure is a demonstration that government plans of education, in Britain at least, must ever by unsatisfactory and inadequate. Meanwhile, I hope it will be allowed that sufficient evidence has been adduced to show that there is really a party within this empire disposed to give up the direction and superintendence of education to the government.

Chapter II: That Education has most prospered in those countries where it has remained a family and a local concern.

In France, education has always been more or less under the direction of the government; and during the last fifty years it has been exclusively so.

[After providing details about the French system of state education, the author continues:]

. . . In short, the exertions of the French government for the advancement of education, and the money expended, must appear to Englishmen almost incredible. But what is, perhaps, most worthy of notice, is the care which is taken that nothing but sound doctrine shall be taught. The teachers of the primary schools are required to have a schoolmaster's diploma of capacity from examinators appointed by the University. Each school has for itself a special committee of surveillance; which committee, again, has another body of a higher order to watch over it, and so forth, until we come to the Grand Master of the University and his council, who watch over all. Moreover, there are thousands of books, together with a great many journals, quarterly, monthly, and weekly, published with the approbation of the Royal Council, and patronized by the Minister himself, the object of which is to make known and propagate good methods, good doctrine, and good books. Nay, more; the University is supposed to be enabled, by her laws and organization, to prevent the spread of bad methods, books, or doctrines, as well as to propagate good ones—to prevent and suppress error, as well as to enforce truth, inasmuch as she has all the education in France, even from the professor of transcendental philosophy down to the most illiterate schoolmaster, under her hand. None can teach even gratuitously without her permission, nor use a school-book without her consent. In short, the French have not educational freedom—every kind of teaching being entirely under the censorship and direction of government.

I had almost forgotten to mention that the French government, considering theatres, botanic gardens, monuments, and musical science, as a means of education, and of propagating sound doctrine, exercise a sovereign influence over them all, and annually grant considerable funds for these purposes.

Such is the external organization, or the instrument of State education in France; and though I abhor it, I hope no one will say I have set down aught in malice; but that, on the contrary, I have frankly and fairly stated what it is, as far as I have been able.

I now proceed to examine the results which French State education has produced; for results, after all, ought to be the touchstone of this, as of all else. Every tree is known by its fruits. What, then, are the fruits of State education in France? Give ear, all ye who prefer facts to theories—*the French labourers and peasantry are among the most ignorant of any that cover the face of the globe.* There are spots even in the East Indies, whole kingdoms in priest-ridden Italy, and provinces in monkish Spain, more enlightened than many a province in France. We learn, from the excellent reports of the Statistical Society, that the state of education is more deplorable in the boroughs of Manchester, Liverpool, and Salford, than anywhere else in the three kingdoms; still, even in these places, we find about one-half of the population more or less instructed; whereas, in France, there are hundreds of parishes where the only persons able to sign their names, are the mayor and priest, and sometimes the latter only. In the above-mentioned boroughs, it is true, the dames' schools are generally in a deplorable condition—damp, dirty, and unwholesome; but these are exceptions in Britain, whereas the majority of French communal schools are equally as bad, and even worse—a fact which is proved by the most authentic documentary evidence, and of which, besides, I myself can have no doubt, because I have seen several of these schools with my own eyes.

The first primary school I entered in France was in the department of Cher. The school-room served at once for the bed-room, kitchen, and work-shop; the schoolmaster, being a cobbler by trade, was actually mending a shoe when I called to see his pupils, and inquire into his system of teaching. I learnt afterwards, that out of the whole working population in the parish, not more than thirty read, and about half that number were able to write. But, indeed, the ignorance of the French peasantry, and other working classes, is so well known to all those who are any way acquainted with educational matters, that it is needless to adduce any new evidence on the subject. There exists such a multitude of reports on this point by government, societies, and private individuals, that any man who chooses may satisfy himself. . . .

• • •

Such is education in France, directed and managed by the central government. It is now time to take a view of those countries where this matter is managed by families themselves, or by local committees, as in the United States of America, for instance. All the world knows that there is no minister of public instruction there, and that so far from having a uniform system, there are not two States which are alike in this respect; yet the Americans have done more for popular education in fifty years, than the French have done ever since the days of Charlemagne. In short, it is incontestable, that primary instruction is six or seven times more diffused in the United States than in France. In the non-slaveholding States, principally in Massachusetts, for instance, no citizen is to be found but who can read, write, and cast accounts. I wish the French would tell us how all this has been brought about without government direction and superintendence.

The Scotch, too, the first, and, for more than a hundred years, the best educated people in the world, required no minister of public instruction, nor government superintendence, to reach that elevated position. The Scottish system may be objected to on several points, but the good it has effected is so well known, that any attempt to prove it would be superfluous; and to compare the

Scotch peasantry with those of France, is to compare light with darkness. Now, here again, it is for the partisans of government direction to tell us how the people of Scotland have attained that high intellectual and moral character, for which, by universal consent, they have been so long and so honourably distinguished. Whence come the habits of reflection, and solidity of judgment, for which they and the natives of the northern states of America have been so often noted? How does it happen that they seek after knowledge, and love it for its own sake; whereas the French refuse it when it is offered to them? And above all, how does it happen that they think far more for themselves than the French do? O freedom! thou art indeed a "noble thing!" Thy absence or thy presence explains all. In education the French are not free—that is the mischief. Government not only does this work for them, but actually prevents them from doing it themselves.

In primary instruction, the Belgians have far outstripped the French; and in Belgium educational freedom exists; there, too, education is for the most part a family and a local concern.

In Austrian Italy we find a well-informed peasantry, with a primary and an infant school, in every commune; and there, too, popular education, at least, is a local concern.

Look to the Basque provinces—they are far more enlightened than the rest of the Peninsula, or France; and they, too, have never yet been subjected to the central government in education or in aught else.

In Switzerland, too, people of all ranks are well educated and intelligent; and here again educational liberty exists.

In Iceland, even, the people are far more enlightened than in France. In fact, almost all can read and write, and yet they have no public schools there; nor can this be otherwise in a country where the inhabitants live so far from each other; but then every *boer* or cabin is a school, and every mother a schoolmistress. The children of the poor and the orphans are placed in such families as are willing to take them, and paid for out of the poor's box. No doubt, one cause of good education in Iceland is, the rule that no one can receive confirmation unless he can read and write; but it is not for us to explain this matter; it is for the French and the supporters of French ideas to explain to us how these poor people are all enabled to read their Bibles without government direction and aid.

The organization of public instruction in Denmark Proper, in many points bears a resemblance to the Scottish system. There, too, the proprietors have been compelled by law to erect schools in every parish, and to maintain a schoolmaster; so that every one may be enabled to read and write, the king coming in aid of such localities as are unable to provide for themselves. The superintendence of the school is intrusted to a local committee, consisting of the minister and two of the principal inhabitants of the place.

Such are the means provided for the training of the poor. As to the higher schools, and gymnasiums, although they are under the superintendence of a committee named by the king, the institutions themselves cost the government nothing, many of them furnishing more than the means of defraying their own expenses. Others have considerable revenue arising from estates and donations.

It is true every man who wishes to set up a school must ask permission from the educational committee of the town, who always grant it, and who seldom interfere with his method of teaching, or books, although it must be owned they have the power to do so.

Here, again, is a State that has no minister of public instruction; that expends but little out of the public funds for educational purposes, and whose working classes are yet incomparably better educated than those of France.

In Sweden, too, education is mostly a local concern; the schools being left to manage their own affairs under local inspection. In fact, the budget in this country is so small that the government can really give no aid worth mentioning. There is a great deal of family education by the mothers, as in Iceland, which has produced the same results; for in Sweden, too, you will hardly find a man of sane mind but who has received a good moral education. No doubt, one cause of this is the fact, that no minister will publish the bans of marriage unless the parties can read and write. Be that as it may, here again is a country with no minister of public instruction, with hardly any government interference or aid, with only one normal school, and that one founded by private individuals, possessing a working population infinitely better educated than the French of the same class.

In Holland, the central power—that is, the king, is very slightly felt, and, as a natural consequence, we find the local spirit of municipal self-government everywhere pervading; and, as may be supposed, education is more under local and paternal direction than in the centralized countries of France and Prussia. In short, in Holland there is little of the French unitive impulse—no minister of public instruction, nor royal council, yet the Dutch, as a nation, are now one of the best educated in the world; and for this elevated position they are indebted to the exertions of a celebrated association known by the name of *La Societé du Bien Publique,* founded in 1784. Nevertheless it must be owned, the *power* of miseducating the people, and of doing immense evil, does exist in Holland, seeing the general inspection of schools is in the hands of a king who is almost absolute. I beg, therefore, once for all, to remark, that I am very far from giving Holland or any other country where the liberty of teaching does not exist, as models to be imitated; my present business is, not to show what is the best system, but merely that education has prospered most where it has remained a local and a family concern. Whatever I have said here concerning Holland is applicable to Denmark, Sweden, and almost all the German States.

Come we now to Prussia. In this monarchy there is a minister of public instruction, a hierarchy of State-paid trainers, together with a series of normal schools—the whole system in many points resembling that of France. In some particulars it is even more despotic than the French system. For instance, parents are compelled by law, under pain of punishment, to send their children to school, from the age of seven to fourteen. Not only the right of setting up schools does not exist, but, in towns, all teachers, even such as give lessons in families by the hour, are subjected to the educational authorities of the place. Notwithstanding, it cannot be denied that the labouring population of Prussia possess at least as great an amount of knowledge as any other in the old or new world.

At first sight, therefore, it may appear to some that Prussia furnishes an argument against the proposition I am endeavouring to prove. Now, supposing the education itself, I mean the thing taught by the Prussian government to the youth of the Prussian monarchy, to be altogether unobjectionable, which I am very far from granting, still that would only prove that Prussia is an exception, for it is impossible to point out any other country where such a system has prospered well. But I never denied to any government, much less to despotic ones, the *possibility* of teaching its whole population certain prescribed branches of knowledge; but I do now assert, that there is a great deal of very important knowledge which a despotic government can neither teach itself nor allow others to teach within its jurisdiction. The Prussian government cannot teach, for instance, several of the natural, inherent, and unalienable rights of man. It cannot teach—

That all men are born equally free;

That all power is inherent in the people;

That they have an indefeasible right to alter, reform, and totally change their government, when their safety and happiness require it;

That it is supremely unjust to compel a person of one belief to pay toward the support of the teachers of another.

No State-paid schoolmaster can ever teach such truths as these. And yet he who has been morally trained, and who at the same time knows and feels such truths as these, even though he be ignorant of almost all else, is in my mind *better educated* than the Prussian peasant, who may possess ten times more knowledge, but who is scarcely allowed to know that he is a man, and who still imagines that princes and kings are something more.

But as the Prussian system is the boast of the centralizers, and as it is frequently offered for our imitation, if not for our adoption, I must examine its claims to our attention a little more fully.

The first thing that strikes me in this discussion is, that the admirers of the Prussian system of education, to be consistent, must also be admirers of the Prussian system of government, because Prussian education is not only conducted according to the spirit of that government, but it really constitutes one of its main pillars. Education is a means of governing the people by what the king's minister causes to be taught, and also by what he prevents others from teaching. He thus possesses the means of doing evil as well as good, by commission, omission, and prevention. What an immense power! As long as the king possesses it, he has nothing to fear—the first duty of his teachers being to inculcate the principle of blind obedience, and train his subjects to habits of servility. It is quite natural that such a government should cling to monopoly as men do to life: to grant educational liberty would be to commit self-slaughter. And yet there are men, and free-born Britons too, who praise the Prussian system to the skies, and who offer it for our imitation.

But still, it will be urged, with all its faults, this system has made Prussia one of the best educated countries in the world. Now, I am willing to grant this, if to be well educated means to be well instructed in reading, writing, arithmetic, geography, grammar, &c., and in the doctrines and discipline of the church to which the learner belongs. If a knowledge of these branches, learned in servitude, be education, then, most unquestionably, the centralized system has succeeded for once. But it is but for once, as I have already shown, seeing nowhere else a similar system has prospered so well. Prussia is, then, an exception, and an exception, too, easily to be accounted for.

It is well known that the Prussian, as well as most of the German governments, promised its subjects constitutions and freedom as long as it needed them to fight against the tyrant Napoleon; but it is equally well known that none of these promises were kept. In 1814 and 1815, says old Lafayette, the King of Prussia talked of nothing else but free institutions, charters, and the sovereignty of the people; but Napoleon was no sooner in surety in St. Helena, than all was hush! something was wanted to lull the people to sleep, and make them forget their rights; so, among other things, the prudent monarch gave them State education, and a minister of public instruction. This explains, at least, half the success of the Prussian system. But what guarantee, I ask, have we for the continuation of this State education, such as it is, when the effect for which it was established shall have been fully attained? Nay, more, supposing the king to have been absolutely disinterested in this matter, and the system to be all-perfect, still what security have we that the king's successor shall have the same views of popular enlightenment?

I have said that government education has never prospered well except in Prussia, and I have already partly explained the cause of its success there; but there is another cause, which is, that even in Prussia, although the general direction is in the hands of the minister, still the details of primary instruction are left to the management of local bodies. School funds are provided in the place, not from the centre; and the universities themselves manage their affairs according to certain fixed laws. In short, despotic as Prussia is, there is yet more self-government in that country than in France.

• • •

Chapter III.: That a great many inconveniences and even dangers are ever attendant on Government interference in such matters.

Having demonstrated in the preceding chapter that education has most flourished where it has remained under the direction of families and local bodies, I now proceed to point out some of the dangers which have accompanied government interference. But, in the first place—Did ever any government exist which was master of the education of the people, and which did not abuse that power, either by teaching them errors, or by keeping them in ignorance? This I consider a most important question; for if the partisans of State education cannot answer affirmatively, the subject would seem to require but little further discussion. The danger of government interference would thus be proved incontestably by facts. And, indeed, I might here honourably close this debate; for I know full well that it is impossible to point out a single government possessing such power which has not employed it for the attainment of its own ends, by teaching errors, or by concealing truths.

This assertion is confirmed by the whole history of education in France. Previous to the first Revolution, the instruction of the people there, such as it was, was entrusted to the clergy and universities—and a fine work they made of it! The grand thing was the political direction given by these bodies to the public mind. Implicit belief and passive obedience were everywhere inculcated. In a word, during the old regime, education was catholic and kingly; and indeed the very end of education, under such a government, must ever be to keep the people slaves to the king and the priest, to form their hearts and minds according to monarchical and catholic doctrines. The clergy and the universities were well rewarded for their pains in thus training up the youthful Frenchmen; but the University of Paris seems to have received the greatest marks of favour. Besides having several privileges, she was called the eldest daughter of kings, the mother of science; and one of the popes styled her a paradise of delights. Such as she was, however, she had, according to Rollin, who is a standard authority, three grand objects in view; which were, to teach science, morals, and religion. Of course, it was stoutly maintained that the Greek and Latin taught within her walls were only channels to all the knowledge under the sun. This same Rollin looked upon her as the home and the fortress wherein the *antique* taste was to be preserved for ever against the *fury* and dazzling beauties of modern innovations and the injuries of time; and, truly, no innovations were to be feared, except by a revolution; for who ever heard of a paid and monopolizing corporation changing of itself? Accordingly, the priests and the salaried servants of the government continued to inculcate their doctrines of passive obedience, until the Revolution came upon them like a whirlwind, and changed everything in a single night.

During the republic, education was anti-catholic and anti-kingly; in fact; it was republican. But the people were just as much machines as ever, seeing they were still acted upon; nay, forced to receive government republican education. In short, the republican government just did as its predecessors had done: it used education as an instrument to attain its own ends, and even organized it more despotically than before.

Then came the consular government; and as long as it lasted, education was again used as a State engine.

During the empire, public education was martial, imperial, and Napoleonian. It is hardly possible for the mind to conceive a more brutalizing system. I have heard Frenchmen confess, twenty years after their education was over, that, although they did all they could, they had not been able to get rid of the fatal educational impressions they had received under the empire. The truth is, the whole tendency of imperial education was to make the young lovers of glory, war, and Napoleon. Everything was done to effect these ends. The students were marched, drums beating, to and from their meals and recreations. The catechisms were so arranged as to leave the peasant in doubt whether God or Napoleon should occupy the first place in his mind and affections. The effects of this system are well known. The French people, during the empire, were in general mere machines, without any thoughts of their own; they looked up to a tyrant as a kind of god. Leibnitz was right when he said—"Whoever can get possession of popular education may change the face of the world." And Napoleon was right, too, when he exclaimed, at St. Helena,— "Ah! my good University—she was an excellent arsenal of ideas!"

We come now to the first Restoration. It was of short duration; but education had already become catholic and Bourbonian, when Napoleon burst upon France like a thunderbolt, and changed everything again in a few hours. Of course, during the hundred days, education was martial and Napoleonian; but the Allied Powers put a stop to it by bringing back the Bourbons, who immediately set about re-establishing their old catholic and Bourbonian education; and this they continued for the space of fifteen years—that is, until the Revolution of July. During that period, the youths in schools and colleges were obliged to attend mass and confess themselves; and, indeed, to obtain the lowest place under government, it was necessary to produce your *billet de confession*. But this is not all; the government often showed itself hostile to enlightenment altogether; and the clergy deemed it prudent to warn their flocks against the improvements of Bell and Lancaster, which some benevolent Frenchmen were at that time endeavouring to introduce into France. One of these lovers of darkness, a French bishop, actually delivered a charge in which he declared the Bell and Lancastrian systems to be inventions of the devil.

French education is now in the hands of the government of July, which just teaches for its own ends, as all its predecessors have done. It is even reported, that the present rulers are beginning to oppose any further enlightenment of the people; a fact which I am the more inclined to believe, as the present minister of public instruction seems to direct all his attention to his colleges, and the study of classical erudition. Thus the French university has been the tool of every party in turn. At the present moment she is serving Louis Philippe, and the party of resistance, as it is called; and a few years hence she will be serving a new republic or Henry V. Such is the history of State education in France, and such it has always been, wherever it has been allowed to prevail for any length of time. It was so at the present time in the Celestial empire, in Prussia, in Austria, and in almost all the catholic countries in the world. In presence of such facts, will any reasonable man maintain that there is no danger in placing the education of free-born British youths under the superintendence and direction of government. At all events, I hope it will be allowed that these facts clearly prove that State interference in this matter has been pernicious, at least *up to the present time.*

I now proceed to demonstrate by argument that it must, ever continue so under every imaginable form of government; but I perceive I must previously define the words—

CENTRALIZATION AND SELF-GOVERNMENT.

The word centralization is often used in newspapers and modern productions; but it has not yet found its way into any of our dictionaries that I am acquainted with, not even into Noah Webster's, although it contains seventy thousand words. The fact is, we have hitherto had no need of such a word in the English language, the thing being unknown among us. Would that we had no need of it still!

Besides, it is rather a modern thing. At least, the ancients knew nothing of that kind of centralization which was invented by the French revolutionists, and improved upon by Napoleon. Be that as it may, the word comes to us from the French, and in that language it denotes that system of government in which the supreme authority takes upon itself to direct the affairs of the country, by a great number of intermediary agents, leaving the localities but little to do in the management of their own concerns. The French and Prussian governments are of this kind, and the former is so *par excellence*. There almost everything is managed by the central government—roads, bridges, canals, and above all, education. The French have accordingly a minister of public works, another for commerce, another for public instruction, and one also for public worship.

The self-government system is just the reverse of centralization, and therefore requires but little explanation here. It has hitherto prevailed in Britain, the local affairs of each district in that country being chiefly governed by local bodies. As a matter of course, we have no special minister for public instruction, none for public works, nor for public worship. In short, the people in general have a much greater share in the management of their own concerns.

But the grand distinction between the two systems is best seen in that moral influence which centralized governments exercise over the minds of their subjects through the medium of State education. Such governments, through their minister of public instruction, deprive their subjects of all necessity of thinking for themselves, not only by setting up schools, choosing schoolmasters, and deciding what shall be taught, but also in using the power they possess, of preventing them from doing any of this work for themselves.

Such States, in thus supplying all the mental and moral wants of the people, possess the means of giving their minds and characters any turn or form they please. And this is just what centralizers pretend ought to be; for they say children belong more to the State than to their parents, and that therefore it ought to take upon itself the direction of their education.

In public colleges, it is not the parents who decide how much Greek or Latin their children shall learn, nor at what age they shall learn it, nor how they shall learn it, nor whether they shall learn anything else; all this is intrusted to the minister, who regulates the whole by his laws and ordinances. In France, for instance, when the minister of public instruction finds that too much attention is paid to modern studies, at the expense of classical erudition, he immediately publishes an ordinance, requiring the rectors of his colleges to take an hour's study from the one, and give it to the other, and as the minister is supposed to know this, and all else, much better than the parents themselves, they just let him do as he pleases.

The French are thus led to believe that they can do nothing by themselves, that they are minors, as it were, and that the government is a kind of guardian, whose duty it is to impel, direct, and centralize the whole physical, moral, and intellectual energies of the nation. It is the interest of the centralized system to make the people believe this, and it must be owned that the centralizers of France have hitherto succeeded amazingly well; for with the exception of the Lafayette family, and a few others, you will not find a Frenchman but who believes in this degrading doctrine with all his heart. This is indeed a mighty fact. It is a clue to the explanation of a great many things which otherwise would remain for ever inexplicable. It shows us, not only that the French and English must differ in character, but that the character of the former cannot be otherwise than it is. It at once accounts for the well-known fact that the French, as individuals, have little self-reliance, with scarcely any colonies, railways, or commercial companies worth mentioning; the State having hitherto done everything for them, they naturally look up to the State for everything . . . I am convinced that all ameliorations, moral, intellectual, and physical, chiefly depend on individual exertions, and the principle of local self-government. What does the history of Rome, for instance, teach us? That Rome was great and prosperous, so long as she left the government of her provincial towns to magistrates chosen by the inhabitants; and that her decline in morals, and in material prosperity, just kept pace with the encroachments of the central power upon individual and municipal rights, until at last she dwindled away altogether, and was annihilated as a nation. But the clearest demonstration of these great truths is to be found in the events which are passing around us. To what cause, for instance, are we to ascribe the superiority of the British race in colonization, order, and freedom, in whatever quarter of the globe they may be found? To what, but to their habits of self-reliance and self-government? What is the reason that the British possess more useful inventions, more self-taught poets, and self-taught men in general than the French? Because the people of Britain are more left to themselves; because there is less governmental action upon them than in France; in a word, there is less centralization. In centralized states, the individual and the parish do little else, except what they are told to do; hence remain weak and inactive. The centralizers have often complained to me of the backwardness of the French communes, and of their lukewarmness even to their own interests, whence the supporters of the centralized system infer the necessity of governmental action. Now this is a vicious circle: the parishes are inactive, backward, and lukewarm, precisely because the central government has been doing their work for them, instead of leaving them to shift for themselves; for it cannot be too often repeated, that it is only in being left to shift for themselves, and in ceasing to lean upon others, that men collectively and individually can learn to manage their own affairs.

During a long experience, I never yet met with a man, eminent in art, science, or industry, but who had been left to himself at an early age. On the other hand, I have always found daughters, as well as sons, inactive and incapable, whose parents aided and directed them after the years of discretion. The reason is obvious; it is only by the exercise of his faculties that man becomes acquainted with their power and use. Whoever heard of a child who learned to speak or walk without trying it? To expect men to learn how to exercise their rights and duties, without exercising them, is to resemble that father who wished his son to learn the art of swimming before he set a foot in water.

This is foolish enough, no doubt; but not more so than to expect families and parishes to learn the management of their educational concerns so long as their government thinks and manages for them. This manner of replacing the parish by the central power is just the way to destroy the parish altogether, and to smother individuality in the bud.

But indeed the evils attending centralization are innumerable; and one among others is the pernicious influence and supremacy which it gives to the capital. In France, for instance, Paris is everything. Paris is the sole focus of light and knowledge in the kingdom. Paris commands, and France obeys its dictates more implicitly than if they came from the Pope. Nothing can be bad that comes from Paris; for it is the grand criterion of all. It is for this reason that revolutions are so easily effected in France, pass so quickly, and do so little good. When a party takes Paris, France is taken; but also to lose Paris, is to lose France. Then again, if an inventor or literator wishes to come before the public, to succeed he must make his *debut* in Paris, and if he cannot do that for want of money, or on account of distance, he may just go down to his grave in silence, even were he a Shakespeare or a Milton; for in his province he would find none to appreciate or publish his labours. Had Walter Scott been a Frenchman, he never would have succeeded as he did. Had Burns been a Frenchman, he would have lived and died inglorious and unknown.

Another great evil arising from centralization, is its excessive cost, on account of the multitude of officials which it requires. The French have perhaps fifty State-paid servants for every one we have. The offices of the different ministers in Paris, compared with ours, are absolute palaces, filled with mountains of paper, and whole armies of clerks. Now this is not only a vast expense in itself, but it supplies government with an additional means of corruption! What space is here given for jobbing, sinecures, and favouritism! But this is not all, it is not only a means of creating abuses, but of maintaining them; for the agents, who alone could tell the truth about it, remain silent for fear of losing their places or retarding their advancement. Another evil, and a great one too, is the swarms of ambitious and hungry place-hunters which it produces, ten to one of whom are necessarily disappointed, and therefore naturally become one way or other disturbers of the public peace.

But it is chiefly through the medium of State education that the centralized system is degrading in the extreme. In this respect it is a circle from which there is no getting out, except by a revolution; for all those who wish to rise in the world—engineers, military men, barristers, physicians, &c.—are compelled to receive their education in the schools of the government, and of course to admit government impressions. It is impossible to conceive a better plan for enslaving the human mind, and eternising errors and abuses.

All these evils are avoided by the adoption of local self-government. This of itself is surely an immense advantage; but there are others. The exercise of municipal rights and duties is an excellent means of political education; a good apprenticeship to the art of electing proper members of parliament. But the grand advantage of this system is, that it keeps alive the principle of self-reliance, and stimulates all the moral and intellectual energies of every individual in the State; whereby instead of having a few only who concern themselves about social ameliorations, we have tens of thousands and millions. And this late-mentioned advantage will appear more important, if we bear in mind that all the amelioration we possess, including those of Christ himself, were really effected by individual energy or voluntary association. But indeed, who ever heard of any real political or religious reform, invention, or improvement, coming from a central government? On the contrary, does not the whole experience of the past teach us, that no central power ever yet existed but whose general tendency was to make its subjects stand still and often to retrograde. To increase individual energy and voluntary associations, then, is to accelerate the onward march of humanity; whereas to give way to centralization, is to retard it . . . But, for the sake of argument, let us suppose the existence of a thing that was never yet seen in this world—a central government directing and managing all the people's affairs better than they could do themselves. Well, then, still I would consider this as an immense evil, because, while it might make them for a time materially happy, it could not fail but to smother their intellectual faculties, and at the same time to prevent them from learning, through the free exercise of these faculties, the art of self-guidance, without which, as I have already endeavoured to show, whether we consider man individually or collectively, no national progress is to be expected.

The two government theories I have been trying to expose are founded on two views of human nature, which differ very widely from each other.

The one is, that man, under Providence, possesses within himself, and in surrounding circumstances, the means of self-guidance and self-improvement.

The other hypothesis is, that man does not possess such means, and that therefore he requires to be acted upon by some *human* authority, governmental or religious.

The first view might be personified in Lafayette; the second in Napoleon. In fact, what is now called the Napoleonian idea is just another name for French centralization.

These two views of human nature really appear to be quite irreconcilable.

The first bears a strong affinity to true Protestantism. The second to genuine Popery.

The supporters of the former view have a lively faith in man's moral and intellectual faculties; and while they admit that, in exercising these, mistakes and abuses are unavoidable, they look upon them as the errors of his apprenticeship to the art of self-government, and of course transitory. They even think that it is better for men to govern themselves badly for a time, than tamely to submit to an arbitrary regulating power, whatever may be its nature, and however good its intentions.

Before proceeding farther, it may not be amiss to note down here the following useful and important inferences, which may be fairly drawn from what has been said on this matter—viz.:

That the centralized system is every way destructive of the best interests of mankind.

That governmental education is at once the most important feature of that pernicious system, and the chief cause of its perpetuation.

That all ameliorations, physical, moral and intellectual, chiefly depend on individual exertion and the adoption of local self-government.

• • •

There can be no mistake about the thing here intended; what these gentlemen [proponents of State education] want is, that the government of the majority shall form the national mind, belief, will, and character. To attain this end, positive and negative means are to be employed; state teachers, on the one hand, and on the other, laws to restrain man's natural right of teaching. With an educational monopoly of this kind, government would be enabled to get possession of society altogether, and give it any form it pleases, as the potter does the clay. Family and individual rights are entirely lost sight of, and if we object that this despotism, the centralizer answers that the social edifice stands on the principle of the sovereignty of the people, that we are under the government of the majority, and that the more strength and the more authority such a government has, the better; for it will thereby be enabled to do the more good.

It must be owned, the republicans find more plausible reasons for centralizing than any other party can, precisely because they centralize and educate, not in the name of a minority faction, but in the name of the majority. I grant this at once, and I may even add that if any government under heaven could be justified in thus interfering with individual and family rights, it would be a republican one; but there are eternal, and, in my opinion, unanswerable objections to such interference, under every imaginable form of government.

First objection.—an interference of this kind must ever be a formidable impediment to individual exertions and the adoption of local self-government, on which, as has been already seen, all ameliorations, material, moral, and intellectual, chiefly depend.

I think I have sufficiently proved this proposition in a former part of my work; but, indeed, the thing is almost self-evident. How can man learn the art of self-guidance and the parish that of self-government, when a central regulating power acts and thinks for them both? The centralizers tell us, forsooth, that it is their system alone which can establish regularity, unity, and uniformity, inherent to all organized and salaried bodies, which is to be deplored. It is chiefly on this account that no new method of teaching or educational improvement of any kind was ever yet discovered by the French University, and, I may add, or ever shall, unless her present organization be radically changed; for, how can unity and innovations co-exist? How can uniformity and reforms live together? The truth is, uniformity may be an excellent thing in weights and measures, and a few other particulars; but that its tendency is to keep down original thoughts and individual exertions is as clear as the sun at noon-day.

But official teaching has another evil attending it, which is equally inimical to individual enterprise, and, of course, to progress and improvement: it wants the vivifying principle of competition. Who ever heard of useful innovations and reforms without that? Are there many teachers, think you, whose salaries are fixed and independent of their efforts, who innovate and improve upon their art? For my part, I never met with one out of a thousand. And this fact not only helps us to understand why the French University never yet made any discovery in the science of tuition, but also why she has never ceased to shun and oppose all kinds of innovations and reforms, and why at this very hour she still cleaves to her privileges and errors as the oyster to the rock.

Second objection:—The majority is not infallible.

The majority may do wrong—the majority may teach error. The republican centralizers always argue as if this were not the case,—nay, as if the contrary had been granted to them. In this respect, they reason just as the Romanists do about their church and the pope. Thus they tell us that the more power the majority has the better, and that they would not hesitate to restrain paternal authority and the right of teaching for *the sake of unity and the general good*; but the first thing they should do is to prove that the majority is infallible, that it can do no wrong; for if it be otherwise, the more power you give it, the more you may be enabling it to do harm. And who will say that it is uncharitable to distrust governments in general, when the present and past history of the whole human race can hardly furnish us with a good one. At all events, it is for my opponents to prove the infallibility of the government of the majority; until they can do this, surely no wise man should entrust his son's education to its care. But why do I ask the proof of this, when I know that it is impossible, and that the contrary is even demonstrable? The truth is, the majority may not only be wrong, but it has hitherto *been*, and still *is* most shamefully wrong, in matters of the greatest importance to mankind, in education, politics, philosophy, and religion. In the United States, the majority is slave-holding. In Italy, Spain, and Portugal, it is so intolerant that Protestants are not allowed to build a single place of worship, nor speak a single word against the established religion. In France, the government of the majority, in its wisdom, allows the faithful of but four religions, and no more, to worship God according to the dictates of their own consciences, and compels a strong minority to give away its hard earnings for the teaching of religious doctrines it detests and abhors. Nay, if we look back on the past, we find that the few were generally right, and the many wrong—witness Columbus, Galileo, Luther, &c., and Christ himself. All these were right, and all differed in opinion from the whole world. Now this is one of the chief reasons why education should be free. Men should be as free to teach as they are to breathe, in order that no impediment may be thrown in the way to improvement, genuine knowledge, and truth. And this is one of the reasons, too, why we must beware of the unlimited authority of the majority in popular governments. What think you would happen, for instance, if Jesus Christ himself were in Paris at this moment endeavouring to teach the people, whether in a school or in the market-place? Why, the police agent and the municipal guard would instantly lay hold of him and carry him away to prison, as of old; and remember this, they would, in doing so, have the law of the majority on their side. Jefferson was right when he said, "The tyranny of the legislature is the danger most to be feared." Nevertheless, I am a warm, though unworthy advocate of republican institutions, because I am convinced that it is through them alone that order, justice, and liberty, can be established throughout the world, and the aspirations of good men realized; but then I do not mean the unitive and centralized system of revolutionary France, which, in the name of a despotic majority, trampled under foot the most natural rights of man; what I mean is, a republic, in which our local privileges shall be preserved, and the encroachments of the legislative power fully guarded against. For why should we democrats dissemble the fact, the great danger of such institutions—the rock on which they will split, unless avoided—is the despotism of the majority; a tyranny, in my mind, not a whit less odious than the tyranny of a single despot. To guard against it, there appears to be but one means, which is, to enumerate explicitly, in a charter or declaration of rights, all those things which should for ever be excepted out of the general powers of government, and one of those things, in my opinion, should be education, because, once more, in giving it up into the hands of government, we supply a fallible majority with the means of preventing much good, and of doing incalculable evil. I think I have sufficiently proved this already; but to be convinced of it, we have only to look at Austria, papal Italy, or any other country where education is official, and to ponder well the following words of the celebrated Adam Smith:—"When the teacher is the salaried servant of the government, the governors have in their power to train up the public to habits of servility and prejudices, and thus crush within them every free and manly thought." The centralizers are always talking about the danger of allowing parents to teach their children errors of all kinds, moral, educational, political, and religious; and M. Dubois says, that if government did not examine the school-books, dangerous ones might be put into the hands of youth, whereby such impressions and prejudices might be engraven on their minds as would be extremely difficult to efface. Now it is strange that it never occurred to M. Dubois that a French minister of public instruction might also happen to be a propagator of errors, and that he too might sanction a set of school-books whose perusal might also engrave baneful impressions and prejudices on the minds of youth. This, however, was surely a most important consideration; for under a system of freedom, if some parents teach error, others may teach truth, whereas the errors of a minister of public instruction, when education is not free, become the errors of the whole community. Now it happens that there is no fact more certain and better known than this, that all French ministers have been, up to the present hour, almost all propagators of errors and pernicious doctrines. What I here assert can be proved even to a demonstration. About nine or ten biases, all differing widely from each other, have been given to the minds of youth in France, through ministers of public instruction, within the last fifty years; but as truth is one, nine at least of these ministers must have been teachers of errors. And, indeed, this is just what they all say of each other. M. Dubois himself bitterly criticises the educational systems of the Empire and the Restoration; but he ought to know full well that the system which he now defends will be as bitterly criticised by the future director of the normal school, should another restoration take place.

Third objection:—It is utterly impossible for any united body like a government to administer education to several millions of individuals of divers religious persuasions.

Let us suppose, for the sake of argument, that the government of the majority is indeed infallible, and that it has somehow or other really discovered the whole truth on whatever relates to the matters to be taught, still this would be of no avail unless the governors be able to *convince* the nation that it is so. But this, it is to be feared, would be no easy matter, seeing the parties to be *convinced* and brought to unity of opinion are Jews, Deists, Rationalists, Pagans, besides Catholics and Protestants, and about seventy other sects of Christians. Some are for the Bible, the whole Bible, and nothing but the Bible; others are for it with notes and comments; others, again, are for excluding it altogether. One parent wishes his son to be taught that Luther was a great and good man; another wishes his child to learn that this celebrated heresiarch was one of the greatest monsters that ever existed. While one father wishes his family to read histories as represent the Reformation as the most *fortunate* event that ever occurred in the word, another, on the contrary, will be for his children to read such histories only as represent it as the most *unfortunate*.

One mother, wishing to inspire her daughter with a hatred of all deceit, will be for having her taught that she ought never to tell a lie, were it to save the life of her nearest relation, nor speak deceitfully, even for God—and Sir Walter Scott's Jeannie Deans will be pointed out as a model; another mother will be for having her daughter to learn that a little evil may be done to procure a greater good, and that lies, in certain circumstances, are quite justifiable.

One father will have his children to learn that Jesus Christ was the Son of God; a second, that he was solely the Everlasting, the Lord God, and none else; a third, that he was a prophet; a fourth, that he was an impostor. But I have surely said enough to show that the notion of the State teaching Catholics, Protestants, Jews, Unitarians, Quakers, Swedenborgians, Independents, &c., religion, history, and morals, is absolutely farcical and absurd.

If further evidence were yet necessary, I would refer the reader to the catechisms used by the different sects for the education of their youth.

Fourth objection,—It is impossible for government to establish State education in Britain without committing something worse than highway robbery. This is a bold assertion; yet there is nothing more true. We have seen how utterly impracticable it is for the State, by its *unitive scheme*, to impart anything like education to the children of men who differ so widely in their religious, moral, historical, and political opinions. If the State intends to do any good, it must therefore either make a choice of one of the existing religions, or invent one of its own. Let us suppose the choice made, and for the sake of illustration let the Roman Catholic be the favoured religion. Of course, no Independent, Churchman, Jew, or Unitarian would in this case consent to send his children to the government school, which nevertheless he would be obliged to support through the national funds, although receiving no benefit therefrom. Now, would not this be using the property of some for the benefit of others? Would not this be robbery? Yet this is not all. The dissenters, whoever they may be, would be compelled to pay for the education, therefore, the government would really do something worse than the highway robber, for the latter takes your purse only, whereas the former would not only rob you, but actually use your money to propagate tenets and ideas which you might detest and abhor, and which might tend to undermine the sect or party to which you belong. The folly of establishing official education in Britain appears here in a clear light. No wonder the government plans have met with so much opposition from every sect within the kingdom; from Protestants as well as Catholics; from Lord Stanley, as well as from the Roman-catholic Archbishop of Tuam.

Fifth objection,—State education is a hindrance to the discovery of truth.

It is worthy of remark that the centralizers, in their governmental and educational theories, always reason as if man had already discovered all truth, and reached the highest degree of perfection. This is a fundamental error. As yet, we see truth "darkly as through a glass," and now but in part things moral, intellectual, and material. True it is we earnestly hope henceforward to see truth more and more unveiled, and shortly to wrest from nature a series of secrets and laws, compared to which all our past discoveries and improvements will appear as nothing; but these great ends can never be attained by maintaining unity in the ideas of the people, which is, however, the avowed object of State education. Until truth be discovered, she cannot have a greater enemy than unity. . . .

"The Persecution of the Child by the State"

Alfred Edgmont Hake and O. E. Wesslau

Chapter 14 of *Free Trade in Capital, or Free Competition in the Supply of Capital to Labour and its Bearings on the Political and Social Questions of the Day* (London: Remington & Co., 1890)

———————————

Alfred Edgmont Hake (1849-1916) was born in Bury St. Edmonds, Suffolk, and was the son of the poet and physician Thomas Gordon Hake. A. E. Hake defended laissez-faire capitalism (or "free trade in capital") and was a severe critic of the socialism to which he believed the England of his day was trending. Among his many books were *Suffering London* (1892) and *The Story of Chinese Gordon* (2 volumes, 1884). Hake also contributed articles to the *Dictionary of National Biography*. Hake and Wesslau co-authored two libertarian books, *Free Trade in Capital* (1890), from which this selection is taken; and *The Coming*

Individualism (1895). We were unable to locate any information about Wesslau.

. . . Those who criticise our National School system are often exposed to the accusation of being in favour of ignorance and of a degraded state for the masses. Let us therefore at once explain that we are well aware of the immense value of education, and believe that the duty of every government is to place no obstacle in the way of a good education for every individual in the country.

Nowadays most people would say that it is the duty of the government not only to remove obstacles in the way of education, but to promote it with all its power. Our contention is that when the government has removed all the obstacles that stand in the way of popular education it has done all that is in its power to do, because it will then have established a system under which the laws of Political Economy and Sociology have free play. Should the government introduce socialistic measures into such a perfect system they would not favour national education, but vitiate it. And this because State interference always produces mischief so long as it is not complete, and to really promote popular education by State interference would mean to introduce a complete socialistic system. But, as we shall show in the following chapter, a complete socialistic system is degrading to the individual and consequently destructive to education in its best sense. Far then from being the opponents of education, we wish to demonstrate that popular education can be made far more effective and more genuine than it now is.

As the franchise was extended, the want of education in the classes destined to hold the balance of power in the country caused some alarm among the upper classes. The cry was, 'Let us educate our future masters.' But there were other influences at work in favour of improved education of the masses.

When, in spite of the expansion of trade and the rise in wages, such a large proportion of the people remained in chronic misery, it was surmised that the lowest classes were too ignorant to take advantage of the flourishing condition of trade. Drunkenness, vice, thriftlessness, were attributed to ignorance, and philanthropists became fervent advocates of education. The success of popular schools in other countries, such as Switzerland, Denmark, and Sweden, inspired British patriots with the desire to emulate their systems.

These examples set by other nations had a great deal to do with the form the national education system in England took: for without them it would not have been so rashly decided that education was identical with cramming.

A good education, in its best sense, is the greatest boon that can be conferred on a human being, and it is no wonder that the English people should gladly accept the offer of our politicians to confer this boon on every English child. Parliament spoke of education, but meant cramming. Nothing is more difficult to give than a good education, and the State is wholly incompetent to give it. But any power, anyone in authority, is equal to cramming.

This was the way in which the mere storing of the memories of the children, and the teaching of reading, writing, and arithmetic, were confounded with education. The educational system which had succeeded in the above-mentioned countries consisted merely of schools where these three subjects were taught, and the memories of the children were stocked. It was supposed that as schools had produced so much good abroad, they ought to produce the same effect in England.

The vast difference in circumstances was entirely disregarded. The good effect abroad was experienced mostly among the children of the peasantry; these children were poor—extremely poor—but they lived in the pure air of the country, in close contact with nature, and though their food was coarse, it was sufficient and regularly supplied. They lived in rustic but scrupulously clean homes. Their parents were ignorant, but moral, religious, proud, and strictly honest; bent on setting their children as perfect an example as possible. These peasant children had, therefore, all that goes to make up an education, except schooling. It was no wonder, then, that, when this want was supplied, the result was satisfactory.

Here it might be remarked that the effect of public schools in the country districts of Great Britain should be the same as among the peasantry abroad. But there are marked differences which should not be overlooked. There is no peasantry in England at all. The population is divided into landlords, farmers, and labourers. The two former classes educate their children themselves, and the children of the farm-labourers are certainly not so well provided with regard to food, clothing, and homes as the peasantry of the countries we have named. In Ireland, there is a peasantry, but their position is hardly better than that of the labourers in England; and in Scotland the education of the country lads has for a century stood uncommonly high, thanks, as we shall show later on, to the absence of State interference in other directions.

But when national education was advocated, it was not so much the country districts that were uppermost in the reformers' minds, or referred to as frightful examples of neglected education. It was in the courts and alleys of the large towns, swarming with children, that it was expected to achieve the greatest triumphs. The children of the lower middle class, or of the superior working class, were not the objects of our legislators' solicitude, for these had already some home education and attended some kind of schools.

The aim of Parliament was to confer education on the children of the great mass of poor people, who could ill afford school-money, and whose desperate circumstances made them indifferent to the future of their offspring. If we compare the position of these children with that of the continental peasant's children, we shall find it widely different: instead of plenty of food, starvation; instead of healthy and seasonable clothing, rags; instead of country air and contact with nature, the slum and the gutter; instead of good examples, corrupt surroundings. The educational requirements of children living under conditions so different must necessarily be of an almost opposite nature; and it was vain to hope that effects such as were produced in Sweden, Switzerland, and other countries, should follow from cramming.

If our legislators intended to educate the children of the poor, they should first have provided them with wholesome food, then good clothing, then healthy and pure homes, and so on, placing cramming at the end of the list. The Spartans, two thousand years ago, understood that if the State has to educate the child it must take entire charge of it. This is why we have said that national education, to be successful, presupposes complete socialistic institutions.

And what results can logically be expected from a system which consists in giving children instruction without any other educational care; in sharpening the mind without elevating the character; in developing faculties for the gratification of passions and instincts, without religion, morality, or even philosophy; in arousing desires and yearnings that cannot be satisfied; in overcramming underfed brains, and overtaxing feeble and starved bodies?

The results to be expected are weak bodies, weak minds, weak morals, premature corruption, abnormal cunning, lessened self-respect, false pride, contempt for honest work, gambling propensities, love of literary trash, and inordinate selfishness. If these results have not been more apparent than they are, it is because many of even the poorest children have for parents religious and respectable people, and not the monsters which the advocates of State interference with children seem to suppose; because there is in the English character a considerable element of independence and self-respect, traits which here have been developed, thanks to more individual freedom than that enjoyed by any other people.

That the deplorable consequences of our one-sided educational system are not wanting, will, however not be denied by anybody. Children of twelve to fourteen years, who have already seen the inside of a great many prisons, are modern products. Our Reformatories and Industrial Schools contain now about twenty-two thousand juvenile law-breakers, and if we consider how many juvenile crimes remain undetected, owing to a highly developed cunning, and what a very small percentage of actually detected crime leads to the Reformatory or the Industrial School, the given statistics of juvenile criminals are, to say the least, alarming.

Apart from the influence on the child, there are other hardships to be endured by the poorest children in our Board Schools. Some have to learn hard lessons on empty stomachs, some have to walk a long distance in cold weather, half-naked; and the occasional inability to bring the school pence is a cause of humiliation and moral suffering which all who remember childhood can readily conceive.

As to the parents of the children, the school laws seem to be framed on the supposition that the well-to-do have the monopoly of fine feeling. How would a member of Parliament or his lady like to send their children to a school to be crammed even when the child is unfit for it; to have them associate with children to whom they object, to be taught by people they dislike, to be exposed to ophthalmia and other contagious diseases; to have their homes invaded by inspectors, and not to be allowed to instruct their own children without being called upon for the proof of results?

That is what the parents have to submit to because they are poor. We shall not dwell upon the numerous and very painful cases in which parents have been summoned before the courts, fined and imprisoned, because from sheer poverty they have been unable to conform to the official regulations, for we should be met with the usual reply, that it is the parent's own fault, though in thousands of instances a good defence could be set up for them. It is a slow and thankless task to bring home to bureaucrats that the poor under their power should have any rights or liberties.

The advocates of our present system will here probably ask if it has not produced good and great results, and what would be the state of things if the instruction supplied by Board Schools had been wanting? The reply to this is that the question is not whether the present system of instruction is better than no instruction at all, but how far it can favourably compare with that education which would have been supplied to the children if this country had not suffered from State interference. If State education, even so one-sided and defective as that afforded to English poor children, were the only kind of education that could be had it might be expedient to submit to the evils it involves in order to escape greater evils. This fortunately we have not to discuss. We have simply to show that State interference exercises a baneful influence over the people in every respect, State education not excepted.

We shall presently make clear what kind of education would have taken place if State education, if State interference, had not prevented it, but we must first say a few words about the results claimed by the advocates of the present system, namely, that it has reduced mendicity, crime, and drunkenness.

There is happily a considerable diminution of these evils, but it will be very difficult to determine the relative potency of the factors that have produced it. The Sunday School teachers claim the improvement as a result of their exertions; the teetotallers declare that it is entirely due to the sobriety they have inculcated;

the clergy affirm that it is traceable to Church-work; and the Salvation Army boast that it is due to the safety-valve of excitement they have supplied.

All these may have had a share in the good work, but there are many and powerful causes that alone are sufficient to explain our social improvements. There are, in the first place, all the enormous causes for trade inflation already referred to, such as Free Trade, Joint-Stock banks, development of the Colonies, locomotion by steam, &c., whereby the condition of the working classes has been immensely improved. For prosperity stimulates self-respect—*noblesse oblige*. Then we have a more humane administration of our laws, improved workhouse organisation, more stringent poor laws, an increased and improved police force, a more elevated tone and a greater supply of public amusements, Trades Unions, Provident and Benefit Societies, and the unprecedented and immense efforts on the part of the wealthy classes to influence the lower for the better.

It is, therefore, unreasonable to claim for national education the moral improvement among the masses when so many other potent causes have been simultaneously at work. The fact is that the increased depravity among the young, in face of a general social improvement, does not point to a healthy influence of the School Board system.

To educate adequately the children of a nation by the agency of the State would, as we have pointed out, only be possible under complete Socialism. Apart from the degrading influences of Socialism, it still remains an open question whether State education can ever excel education by the parent.

When we consider that all parents in this country who can afford it, as a rule, strive hard to give their children as good an education as they possibly can, it is only fair and reasonable to conclude that it is only poverty and misery which prevent the poor from giving their children the benefits of education.

We have already shown how State interference with banking inflicts poverty on the majority of our working classes, and if it be granted that prosperity would enable and induce them to give a good education to their children, it becomes evident that State interference is the original cause of the gross neglect of children which we have witnessed and still witness in this country. What we deplore is that one piece of State Socialism—State education—should have been introduced in order to remedy the effects of another piece of State Socialism—bank monopoly.

Had bank monopoly not prevailed, and Free Trade in Capital had accompanied Free Trade in foreign goods, the people would have enjoyed a degree of prosperity which would have rendered compulsory education entirely unnecessary. We should have had all the advantages of parent-supervised education, without the many evils of State education, and there can be no doubt that both the moral and physical condition of the children would have reached a higher standard than under our present State-produced poverty and compulsory cramming.

What is here stated is strikingly confirmed by experience in Scotland. . . . It is a well-known fact, that the poor children in Scotland enjoyed, during the last century and the beginning of this, a degree of education far above that of the poor of any other country. There are no doubt people who will say that education in Scotland was not the effect of prosperity, but prosperity the effect of education. But here again experience is on our side: for though education is generally good in countries where production flourishes and the lowest ranks of the working classes are well off, in the countries in Europe where instruction by State interference has been brought to a high standard, there is very little prosperity among the masses.

In face of the economic and political situation produced by State interference, we would not advocate the abolition of what now are inaccurately called the educational laws: for, unfortunately, one State-socialistic enactment renders others necessary.

When Free Trade in Capital is introduced, the prosperity among the working classes will stimulate in the parents the desire to give a good education to their children, and they will be able to escape the tyranny of the school laws in the same way as the upper classes escape them now. The present educational laws will, like thousands of other Parliamentary Acts, become obsolete without being repealed. They will remain on our Statute Books to be quoted by future students of history as results of the strange socialistic mania which possessed the British nation in the latter half of this nineteenth century.

14

"State Education: A Help or Hindrance?"

Auberon Herbert

Fortnightly Review (July 1850)

Auberon Herbert (1838–1906) studied at Oxford and served in the British army. He was a member of parliament from 1870 to 1874, only to repudiate, under the influence of Herbert Spencer, the political process as a means of bringing about beneficial social change. In 1890, Herbert started his own weekly paper, *Free Life,* which later became a monthly journal, *Organ of Voluntary Taxation and the Voluntary State.* This ran until August 1901.

Herbert popularized the labels "Voluntaryism" and "Voluntaryist," but he used these terms in a broader sense than had previous Voluntaryists, who applied them to the causes and advocates of the separation of church and state and the separation of school and state. For Herbert, "Voluntaryism" signified a political philosophy that we now call "libertarianism." In "A Plea for Voluntaryism," Herbert wrote: "We, who call ourselves voluntaryists, appeal to you to free yourselves from these many systems of state force, which are rendering impossible the true and happy life of nations today. . . ."

Herbert's Voluntaryism was based on the moral principle of self-ownership—a term that was later employed extensively by Murray Rothbard and other modern libertarians. As Herbert explained in "The Principles of Voluntaryism" (1897):

> We hold that the one and only one true basis of society is the frank recognition of these rights of self-ownership; that is to say, of the rights of control and direction by the individual, as he himself chooses, over his own mind, his own body, and his own property, always provided, that he respects the same universal rights in others. We hold that so long as he lives within the sphere of his own rights, so long as he respects these rights in others, not aggressing by force or fraud upon the person or property of his neighbors, he cannot be made subject, apart from his own consent, to the control and direction of others, and he cannot be rightfully *compelled* under any public pretext, by the force of others, to perform any services, to pay any contributions, or to act or not to act in any manner contrary to his own desires or to his own sense of right. He is by moral right a free man, self-owning and self-directing; and has done nothing which justifies others,

for any convenience of their own, in taking from him any part, small or great, of his self-ownership.

In a 1906 lecture delivered at Oxford University, "Mr. Spencer and the Great Machine," Herbert recalled the profound influence that Herbert Spencer had on his intellectual life:

I have often laughed and said that, as far as I myself was concerned, [Herbert Spencer] spoiled my political life. I went into the House of Commons, as a young man, believing that we might do much for the people by a bolder and more unsparing use of the powers that belonged to the great lawmaking machine; and great, as it then seemed to me, were those still unexhausted resources of united national action on behalf of the common welfare. It was at that moment that I had the privilege of meeting Mr. Spencer, and the talk which we had—a talk that will always remain very memorable to me—set me busily to work to study his writings. As I read and thought over what he taught, a new window was opened in my mind. I lost my faith in the great machine; I saw that thinking and acting for others had always hindered, not helped, the real progress; that all forms of compulsion deadened the living forces in a nation; that every evil violently stamped out still persisted, almost always in a worse form, when driven out of sight, and festered under the surface. I no longer believed that the handful of us—however well-intentioned we might be—spending our nights in the House, could manufacture the life of a nation, could endow it out of hand with happiness, wisdom and prosperity, and clothe it in all the virtues. I began to see that we were only playing with an imaginary magician's wand; that the ambitious work we were trying to do lay far out of the reach of our hands, far, far, above the small measure of our strength. It was a work that could only be done in one way—not by gifts and doles of public money, not by making that most corrupting and demoralizing of all things, a common purse; not by restraints and compulsions of each other; not by seeking to move in a mass, obedient to the strongest forces of the moment, but by acting through the living energies of the free individuals left free to combine in their own way, in their own groups, finding their own experience, setting before themselves their own hopes and desires, aiming only at such ends as they truly shared in common, and ever as the foundation of it all, respecting deeply and religiously alike their own freedom, and the freedom of all others.

Like his mentor Herbert Spencer, Auberon Herbert warned against the uniformity that will inevitably accompany a state system of education. "All influences which tend towards uniform thought and action are most fatal to any regularly continuous improvement." Imagine the effects of state-imposed uniformity in religion, art, or science. Progress would grind to a halt. Education is no different. "Therefore, if you desire progress, you must not make it difficult for men to think and act differently; you must not dull their sense with routine or stamp their imagination with the official pattern of some great department."

For ten years we have been busy organizing national education. A vigorous use of bricks and mortar is not generally accompanied by a careful examination of first principles, but now that we have built our buildings and spent our millions of public money, and civilized our children in as speedy a fashion as that in which the great Frank christianized his soldiers, we may perhaps find time to ask a question which is waiting to be discussed by every nation that is free enough to think, whether a state education is or is not favorable to progress?

It may seem rash at first sight to attack an institution so newly created and so strong in the support which it receives. But there are some persons at all events whom one need not remind, that no external grandeur and influence, no hosts of worshipers can turn wrong principles into right principles, or prevent the discovery by those who are determined to see the truth at any cost that the principles are wrong. Sooner or later every institution has to answer the challenge, "Are you founded on justice? Are you for or against the liberty of men?" And to this challenge the answer must be simple and straightforward; it must not be in the nature of an outburst of indignation that such a question should be asked; or a mere plea of sentiment; or the putting forward of usefulness of another kind. These questions of justice and liberty stand first; they cannot take second rank behind any other considerations, and if in our hurry we throw them on one side, unconsidered and unanswered, in time they will find their revenge in the imperfections and failure of our work.

National education is a measure carried out in the supposed interest of the workmen and the lower middle class, and it is they especially—the men in whose behalf the institution exists—whom I wish to persuade that the inherent evils of the system more than counterbalance the conveniences belonging to it.

I would first of all remind them of that principle which many of us have learned to accept, that no man or class accepts the position of receiving favors without learning, in the end, that these favors become disadvantages. The small wealthy class which once ruled this country helped themselves to favors of many kinds. It would be easy to show that all these favors, whether they were laws in protection of corn, or laws favoring the entail of estates, creating sinecures, or limiting political power to themselves, have become in the due course of time unpleasant and dangerous burdens tied round their own necks. Now, is state education of the nature of a political favor?

It is necessary, if discussion is in any way to help us, to speak the truth in the plainest fashion, and therefore I have no hesitation in affirming that it is so. Whenever one set of people pay for what they do not use themselves, but what is used by another set of people, their payment is and must be of the nature of a favor, and does and must create a sort of dependence. All those of us who like living surrounded with a slight mental fog, and are not overanxious to see too clearly, may indignantly deny this; but if we honestly care to follow Dr. Johnson's advice, and clear our minds of cant, we shall perceive that the statement is true, and if true, ought to be frankly acknowledged. The one thing to be got rid of at any cost is cant, whether it be employed on behalf of the many or the few.

Now, what are the results of this particular favor? The most striking result is that the wealthier class think that it is their right and their duty to direct the education of the people. They deserve no blame. As long as they pay by rate and tax for a part of this education, they undoubtedly possess a corresponding right of direction. But having the right they use it; and in consequence the workman of today finds that he does not count for much in the education of his children. The richer classes, the disputing churches, the political organizers are too powerful for him. If he wishes to realize the fact for himself let him read over the names of those who make up the school boards of this country. Let him first count the ministers of all denominations, then of the merchants, manufacturers, and squires. There is something abnormal here. These ministers and gentlemen do not place the workmen on committees to manage the education of their children. How, then, comes it about that they are directing the education of the workmen's children? The answer is plain. The workman is selling his birthright for the mess of pottage. Because he accepts the rate and tax paid by others, he must accept the intrusion of these others into his own home affairs—the management and education of his children. Remember, I am not urging, as some do, the workmen to organize themselves into a separate class, and return only their own representatives as members of school boards; such action would not mend the unprofitable bargain. To take away money from other classes, and not to concede to them any direction in the spending of it, would be simply unjust—would be an unscrupulous use of voting power. No, the remedy must be looked for in another direction. It lies in the one real form of independence—the renunciation of all obligations. The course that will restore to the workmen a father's duties and responsibilities, between which and themselves the state has now stepped, is for them to reject all forced contributions from others, and to do their own work through their own voluntary combinations. Until that is done no workman has more, or has a claim to have more, than half rights over his own children. He is stripped of one-half of the thought, care, anxiety, affection, responsibility, and need of judgment which belong to other parents.

I used the expression, the forced contributions of the rich. There are some persons who hold that the more money you can extract by legislation from the richer classes for the benefit of the poorer classes the better are your arrangements. I entirely dissent from such a view. It is fatal to any clear perception of justice. Justice requires that you should not place the burdens of one man on the shoulders of another man, even though he is better able to bear them. In plainer words, that you should not make one set of men pay for what is used by another set of men. If this law be once disregarded it simply reduces politics to a universal scramble, in which the most selfish will have the most success. It turns might into right, and proclaims that each man may rightfully possess whatever he can vote into his pocket. Whoever is intent on justice must be as just to the rich man as to the poor man; and because so-called national education is not for the children of the rich man, it is simply not just to take by compulsion one penny from him.

No columns of sophistry can alter this fact. And yet, when once the obligation disappears, and the grace of free-giving is restored, it is a channel in which the money of the richer classes may most worthily flow. Whatever the faults are of our richer classes, there is no lack amongst them of generous giving. Take any newspaper and you will find that although by unwise legislation we are closing many of the great channels existing for their gifts, yet the quality persists. The endowment of colleges at one period, the endowment of grammar schools at another period, gifts to religious institutions, and the support given to that narrow, partial, vexatious, and official-minded system of education which prevailed up to 1870, are all evidence of what the richer people are ready to do as long as you do not withhold the opportunities. It may, however, be said, "Do not rich gifts bring obligations, and with them their mischievous consequences?" It is plain that the most healthy state of education will exist when the workmen, dividing themselves into natural groups according to their own tastes and feelings, organize the education of their children without help, or need of help, from outside. But between obligatory and voluntary contributions there is the widest distinction. There is but slight moral hurt to the giver or receiver in the voluntary gift, provided only that the spirit on both sides be one of friendly equality. It is the forced contribution, bringing neither grace to the giver nor to the receiver, which has the evil savor about it, and brings the evil consequence. The contribution taken forcibly from the rich is justified on the ground that the thing to be provided is a necessity for which the poorer man cannot pay. Thus the workman is placed in the odious position of putting forward the pauper's plea, and two statements equally deficient in truth are made for him: one, that book education is a necessity of life—a statement which for those who look for an exact meaning in words that are used is simply not true—and the other, that our people cannot provide it for themselves if left to do so in their own fashion.

I wish to push still further the question of how much real power the workman possesses over the education of his children. I maintain that, setting aside the interference of ministers, merchants, manufacturers, doctors, lawyers, and squires in his affairs, he has only the shadow and semblance of power, and that he never will possess anything more substantial under a political system. Let us see for what purposes political organization can be usefully applied. It is well adapted to those occasions when some definite reply has to be made to a simple question. Shall there be peace or war? Shall political power be extended to a certain class? Shall certain punishments follow certain crimes? Shall the form of government be republican or monarchical? Shall taxes be levied by direct or indirect taxation? These are all questions which can be fairly answered by yes or no, and on which every man enrolled in a party can fairly express his opinion if he has once decided to affirm or deny. But whenever you call upon part of the nation to administer some great institution the case becomes wholly different. Here all the various and personal views of men cannot be represented by a simple yes or no. A mixed mass of men, like a nation, can only administer by suppressing differences and disregarding convictions. Take some simple instance. Suppose a town of 50,000 electors should elect a representative to assist in administering some large and complicated institution. Let us observe what happens.

It is only possible to represent these 50,000 people, who will be of many different mental kinds and conditions, by some principle which readily commands their assent. It will probably be some principle which, from its connection with other matters, is already familiar to their mind—made familiar by preceding controversies. For example, the electors may be well represented on such questions as "Shall the institution be open or closed on Sundays? Shall it be open to women? Shall the people be obliged to support it by rate? and, When rate-supported, to make use of it?" But it will at once be seen that these are principles which do not specially apply to any one institution but to many institutions. They are principles of common political application—they are, in fact, external to the institution itself, and distinct from its own special principles and methods. The effect then will be that the representative will be chosen on principles that are already familiar to the minds of the electors, and not on principles that peculiarly and specially affect the institution in question. Existing controversies will influence the minds of the electors, and the constituency will be divided according to the lines of existing party divisions. Both school boards and municipal government yield an example that popular elections must be fought out on simple and familiar questions. The existing political grooves are cut too deeply to allow of any escape from them.

"But," it may be replied, "as intelligence increases, and certain great political questions which are always protruding themselves are definitely settled, the electorate may become capable of conducting their contests simply with regard to the principles which really belong to the matter itself." Another difficulty arises here. Without discussing the possible settlement of these ever-recurring political questions, it ought to be remembered that, in the case of increased intelligence, we should have an increase in the number of different views affecting the principles and methods of the institution in question; and, as we should still have only one representative to represent us, it would be less possible for him than before to represent our individual convictions. If he represent A he cannot represent B, or C, or any of those that come after C; that is to say, if A, B, C, and the others are all thinking units, and therefore, do not accept submissively whatever is offered to them. He can only represent one section, and must leave other sections unrepresented. But as these individual differences are both the accompaniment and sign of increasing intelligence, this unhappy result follows, that the more intelligent a nation becomes, the greater pain it must suffer from a system which forces its various parts to think and act alike when they would naturally be thinking and acting differently.

"But if this is so, then there is no such thing possible as representation. If one person cannot represent many persons, then administration of all kinds fails equally in fulfilling a common purpose. All united effort therefore becomes impossible."

No doubt effective personal representation is under any circumstances a matter of difficulty; but political organization admits only of the most imperfect form of it, voluntary organization of the most perfect. Under political organization you mix everybody together, like and unlike, and compel them to speak and act through the same representative; under voluntary organization like attracts like, and those who share the same views form groups and act together, leaving any dissident free to transfer his action and energy elsewhere. The consequence is that under voluntary systems there is continual progress, the constant development of new views, and the action necessary for their practical application; under political systems, immobility on the part of the administrators, discontented helplessness on the part of those for whom they administer.

"But still there remain certain things which, however much you may desire to respect personal differences, the state must administer; such, for example, as civil and criminal law, or the defense of the country."

The reason why the nation should administer a system of law, or should provide for external defense, and yet abstain from interference in religion and education, will not be recognized until men study with more care the foundations on which the principle of liberty rests. Many persons talk as if the mere fact of men acting together as a nation gave them unlimited rights over each other; and that they might concede as much or as little liberty as they liked one to the other. The instinct of worship is still so strong upon us that, having nearly worn out our capacity for treating kings and such kind of persons as sacred, we are ready to invest a majority of our own selves with the same kind of reverence. Without perceiving how absurd is the contradiction in which we are involved, we are ready to assign to a mass of human being unlimited rights, while we acknowledge none for the individuals of whom the mass is made up. We owe to Mr. Herbert Spencer—the truth of those writings the world will one day be more prepared to acknowledge, after it has traveled a certain number of times from Bismarckism to communism, and back from communism to Bismarckism—the one complete and defensible view as to the relations of the state and the individual. He holds that the great condition regulating human intercourse is the widest possible liberty for all. Happiness is the aim that we must suppose attached to human existence; and therefore each man must be free—within those *limits which the like freedom of others imposes on him—to judge for himself in what consists his happiness. As soon as this view is once clearly seen, we then see what the state has to do and from what it* has to abstain. It has to make such arrangements as are necessary to ensure the enjoyment of this liberty by all, and to restrain aggressions upon it. Wherever it undertakes duties outside this special trust belonging to it, it is simply exaggerating the rights of some who make up the nation and diminishing the rights of others. Being itself the creature of liberty, that is to say, called into existence for the purposes of liberty, it becomes organized against its own end whenever it deprives men of the rights of free judgment and free action for the sake of other objects, however useful or desirable they may be.

It is on account of our continued failure to recognize this law of liberty that we still live, like the old border chieftains, in a state of mutual suspicion and terror. Far the larger amount of intolerance that exists in the world is the result of our own political arrangements, by which we compel ourselves to struggle, man against man, like beasts of different kinds bound together by a cord, each trying to destroy the other out of a sense of self-preservation. It is evident that the most fair-minded man must become intolerant if you place him in a position where he has only the unpleasant choice either to eat or be eaten, either to submit to his neighbor's views or force his own views upon his neighbor. Cut the cord, give us full freedom for differing amongst ourselves, and it at once becomes possible for a man to hold by his own convictions and yet be completely tolerant of what his neighbor says and does.

I come now to another great evil belonging to our system. The effort to provide for the education of children is a great moral and mental stimulus. It is the great natural opportunity of forethought and self-denial; it is the one daily lesson of unselfishness which men will learn when they will pay heed to none other. There is no factor that has played so large a part in the civilization of men as the slow formation in parents of those qualities which lead them to provide for their children. In this early care and forethought are probably to be found the roots of those things which we value so highly—affection, sympathy, and restraint of the graspings of self for the good of others. We may be uncertain about many of the agents that have helped to civilize men, but here we can hardly doubt. What, then, is likely to be the effect when, heedless of the slow and painful influences under which character is formed, you intrude a huge all-powerful something, you call the state, between parents and children, and allow it to say to the former, "You need trouble yourself no more about the education of your children. There is no longer any occasion for that patience and unselfishness which you were beginning to acquire, and under the influence of which you were learning to forego the advantage of their labor, that they might get the advantage of education. We will give you henceforth free dispensation from all such painful efforts. You shall at once be made virtuous and unselfish by a special clause in our act. You shall be placed under legal obligations, under penalty and fine, to have all the proper feelings of a parent. Why toil by the slow irksome process of voluntary efforts and your own growing sense of right to do your duty, when we can do it so easily for you in five minutes? We will provide all for you—masters, standards, examinations, subjects, and hours. You need have no strong convictions, and need make no efforts of your own, as you did when you organized your chapels, your benefit societies, your trade societies, or your cooperative institutions. We are the brain that thinks; you are but the bone and muscles that are moved. Should you desire some occupation, we will throw you an old bare bone or two of theological dispute. You may settle for yourselves which dogmas of the religious bodies you prefer; and while you are fighting over these things our department shall see to the rest of you. Lastly, we will make no distinctions between you all. The good and the bad parent shall stand on the same footing, and our statutes shall assume with perfect impartiality that every parent intends to defraud his child, and can only be supplied with a conscience at the police court." This cynical assumption of the weakness and selfishness of parents, this disbelief in the power of better motives, this faith in the inspector and the policeman, can have but one result. Treat the people as unworthy of trust, and they will justify your expectation. Tell them that you do not expect them to possess a sense of responsibility, to think or act for themselves, withhold from them the most natural and the most important opportunities for such things, and in due time they will passively accept the mental and moral condition you have made for them. I repeat that the great natural duties are the great natural opportunities of improvement for all of us. We can see every day how the wealthy man, who strips himself entirely of the care of his children, and leaves them wholly in the hands of tutors, governesses, and schoolmasters, how little his life is influenced by them, how little he ends by learning from them. Whereas to the man whose thoughts are much occupied with what is best for them, who is busied with the delicate problems which they are ever suggesting to him, they are a constant means of both moral and mental change. I repeat that no man's character, be he rich or poor, can afford the intrusion of a great power like the state between himself and his thoughts for his children. Observe the corresponding effect in another of our great state institutions. The effect of the Poor Law—which undertakes the care in the last resort of the old and helpless—has been to break down to a great extent the family feelings and affections of our people. It is simply and solely on account of this great machine that our people, naturally so generous, recognize much less the duty of providing for an old parent than is the case either in France or in Germany. With us, each man unconsciously reasons, "Why should I do that which the state will do for me?" All such institutions possess a philanthropical outside, but inwardly they are full of moral helplessness and selfishness.

These, then, are the first charges that I bring against state education; that the forced payments taken from other classes place the workman under an obligation; that, in consequence, the upper and middle classes interfere in the education of his children; that under a political system there is no place for his personal views, but that practically the only course of action left open

329

to him is to join one of the two parties who are already organized in opposition to each other, and record a vote in favor of one of them once in three years. I do not mean to make the extreme statement that it is impossible to persuade either one party or both parties to adopt some educational reform, but I mean to say that one body acting for a whole country or a whole town can only pursue one method, and, therefore, must act to the exclusion of all views which are not in accordance with that one method; and that bodies which are organized for fighting purposes, and whose first great object is to defeat other great bodies nearly as powerful as themselves, are bound by the law of their own condition not to be easily moved by considerations which do not increase their fighting efficiency.

I have just touched upon the evils of uniformity in education; but there is more to say on the matter. At present we have one system of education applied to the whole of England. The local character of school boards deceives us, and makes us believe that some variety and freedom of action exist. In reality they have only the power to apply an established system. They must use the same class of teachers; they must submit to the same inspectors; the children must be prepared for the same examination, and pass in the same standards. There are some slight differences, but they are few and of little value. Now, if any one wishes to realize the full mischief which this uniformity works, let him think of what would be the result of a uniform method being established everywhere—in religion, art, science, or any trade or profession. Let him remember that canon of Mr. Herbert Spencer, so pregnant with meaning, that progress is difference. Therefore, if you desire progress, you must not make it difficult for men to think and act differently; you must not dull their senses with routine or stamp their imagination with the official pattern of some great department. If you desire progress, you must remove all obstacles that impede for each man the exercise of his reasoning and imaginative faculties in his own way; and you must do nothing to lessen the rewards which he expects in return for his exertions. And in what does this reward consist? Often in the simple triumph of the truth of some opinion. It is marvelous how much toil men will undergo for the sake of their ideas; how cheerfully they will devote life, strength, and enjoyment to the work of convincing others of the existence of some fact or the truth of some view. But if such forces are to be placed at the service of society, it must be on the condition that society should not throw artificial and almost insuperable obstacles in the way of those reformers who search for better methods. If, for example, a man holding new views about education can at once address himself to those in sympathy with him, can at once collect funds and proceed to try his experiment, he sees his goal in front of him, and labors in the expectation of obtaining some practical result to his labor. But if some great official system blocks the way, if he has to overcome the stolid resistance of a department, to persuade a political party, which has no sympathy with views holding out no promise of political advantage, to satisfy inspectors, whose eyes are trained to see perfection of only one kind, and who may summarily condemn his school as "inefficient," and therefore disallowed by law, if in the meantime he is obliged by rates and taxes to support a system to which he is opposed, it becomes unlikely that his energy and confidence in his own views will be sufficient to inspire a successful resistance to such obstacles. It may be said that a great official department, if quickened by an active public opinion, will be ready to take up the ideas urged on it from outside. But there are reasons why this should not be so. When a state department becomes charged with some great undertaking, there accumulates so much technical knowledge round its proceedings, that without much labor and favorable opportunities it becomes exceedingly difficult to criticize successfully its action. It is a serious study in itself to follow the minutes and the history of a great department, either like the Local Board or the Education Department. And if a discussion should arise, the same reason makes it difficult for the public to form a judgment in the matter. A great office which is attacked envelopes itself, like a cuttlefish, in a cloud of technical statements which successfully confuses the public, until its attention is drawn off in some other direction. It is for this reason, I think, that state departments escape so easily from all control, and that such astounding cases of recklessness and mismanagement come periodically to light, making a crash which startles everybody for the moment. The history of our state departments is like that of some continental governments, unintelligent endurance through long periods on the part of the people, tempered by spasmodic outbursts of indignation and ineffectual reorganization of the institutions themselves. It must also be remembered that the manner in which new ideas produce the most favorable results is not by a system under which many persons are engaged in suggesting and inventing, and one person only in the work of practical application. Clearly the most progressive method is that whoever perceives new facts should possess free opportunities to apply and experiment upon them.

Add one more consideration. A great department must be by the law of its own condition unfavorable to new ideas. To make a change it must make a revolution. Our Education Department, for example, cannot issue an edict which applies to certain school boards and not to others. It knows and can know of no exceptions. Our bastard system of half-central half-local government is contrived with great ingenuity to render all such experiments impossible. If the center were completely autocratic (which Heaven forbid) it could try experiments as it chose; if the localities were independent, each could act for itself. At present our arrangements permit of only intolerable uniformity. Follow still further the awkward attempts of a department at improvement. Influenced by a long-continued public pressure, or moved by some new mind that has taken direction of it, it determines to introduce a change, and it issues in consequence a wholesale edict to its thousands of subordinates. But the conditions required for the successful application of a new idea are, that it should be only tentatively applied; that it should be applied by those persons who have some mental or moral affinity with it, who in applying it, work intelligently and with the grain, not mechanically and against the grain. No wonder, therefore, that departments are so shy of new ideas, and by a sort of instinct become aware of their own unfitness to deal with them. If only one wishes to realize why officialism is what it is, let him imagine himself at the center of some great department which directs an operation in every part of the country. Whoever he was he must become possessed with the idea of perfect regularity and uniformity. His waking and sleeping thought would be the desire that each wheel should perform in its own place exactly the same rotation in the same time. His life would simply become intolerable to him if any of his thousands of wheels began to show signs of consciousness, and to make independent movements of their own.

But suppose that a man of fresh mind and personal energy were to be placed at the head of our Education Department who perceived the mischievous effect of uniformity, could not this official tendency be counteracted? It might for a short space of time, just as the muscles of a strong man can for some hours defeat the pull of gravitation, but gravitation wins in the end. Such changes would be only spasmodic; they would not be the natural outcome of the system, and therefore could not last. Moreover, for those who understand the value of liberty and of responsibility, it is needless to point out how utterly false the system must be which makes the nation depend upon the intelligence of a minister, and not upon the free movement of the different minds within itself.

I come now to another great evil which accompanies an official system. In granting public money for education you must either give it on the judgment of certain public officers, which exposes you to different standards of distribution and to personal caprice, or you must give it according to some such system of results as exists at present with us. Payment by results has the merit, as a system, of being simple, easy to administer, and fairly equal; but it necessarily restricts and vulgarizes our conceptions of education. It reduces everybody concerned, managers, teachers, pupils, to the one aim and object of satisfying certain regulations made for them, of considering success in passing standards and success in education as the same thing. It is one long unbroken grind. From boyhood to manhood the teacher himself is undergoing examinations; for the rest of his life he is reproducing on others what he himself has gone through. It is needless to say that the higher aims of the teacher, methods of arousing the imagination and developing the reasoning powers, which only bear fruit slowly and cannot be tested by a yearly examination of an inspector—whose fly will be waiting at the school door during the few hours at the disposal of himself or his subordinate—new attempts to connect the meaning of what is being learned with life itself, and to create an interest in work for work's own sake instead of for the inspector's sake, above all, the personal influences of men who have chosen teaching as their vocation, because the real outcome of their nature is sympathy with the young, and have not been drilled into it through a series of examinations owing to some accident of early days, all these things must be laid aside as subordinate to the one great aim of driving large batches successfully through the standards and making large hauls of public money. In our ignorant and unreasoning belief in examinations we have not perceived how fatal the system is to all original talent and strong personality in the teacher. Whether it be a professor at a university or a master in a board school, this modern exaggeration of the use of examinations makes it impossible for him to treat his subjects of teaching from that point of view which is real and living to himself, or to follow his own methods of influencing his pupils. In all cases he must subdue his strongest tastes and feelings, and recast and remodel himself until he is a sufficiently humble copy of the inspector or examiner, upon whose verdict his success depends. Any plan better fitted to reduce managers, teachers, and pupils to one level of commonplace and stupidity could scarcely be found. The state rules a great copybook, and the nation simply copies what it finds between the lines.

I cannot escape a few words on the much-vexed religious question. Under our present system the Nonconformists are putting a grievous strain upon their own principles. Whoever fairly faces the question must admit that the same set of arguments which condemns a national religion also condemns a national system of education. It is hard to pronounce sentence on the one and absolve the other. Does a national church compel some to support a system to which they are opposed? So does a national system of education. Does the one exalt the principle of majorities over the individual conscience? So does the other. Does a national church imply a distrust of the people, of their willingness to make sacrifices, of their capacity to manage their own affairs? So does a national system of education. Does the one chill and repress the higher meanings and produce formalism? So does the other. But everywhere Nonconformists are being drawn into supporting the present school system, into obtaining popular influence by means of it, and, what is most inconsistent and undesirable, into using it as an instrument for spreading their own religious teaching. It is rapidly becoming their established church, and it will have, we may safely predict, the same narrowing effect upon their mind, it will beget the same inability to perceive the injustice of a political advantage, which the national church has had upon its supporters. Such a result is matter for much regret. First, because there is already but little steady adherence to principle in politics; and where a large body of influential men put themselves in a position which is inconsistent with the application of their own principles there is a sensible national deterioration. Second, if school boards are to be instruments of authoritatively teaching subjects of common dispute amongst us, such as the inspiration of the Bible and the performance of miracles, the struggle between the supporters of revealed religion and the different schools of free thought must be embittered. It is the question of political advantage and disadvantage which fans these disputes into red heat. Should this be the case, much of the better side of the present religious teaching will be lost sight of by a large part of the nation under the irritation of the political injustice, and its influence lost at a moment when its influence is specially wanted in shaping the new beliefs.

It may be said that secular education will prevent such antagonism, and that every year brings us nearer to the establishment of it. But secular education, even if it be the most just arrangement of trying to meet the injustice which a state system necessarily brings with it, is at best a miserable expedient. It is as if everybody agreed by common contract to tie up their right hand in doing a special piece of work in which they were most interested. Far healthier would it be for each section in the nation, from the Catholic to the materialist, to regain perfect freedom, and to do his best to place before children the scheme of life as he himself sees and feels it. If the common argument that such separate teaching will produce narrowness of mind and sectarian jealousy, is to be regarded, it should be carried a step further, and the children on Sundays should not be permitted to go to their own churches and chapels, but the state should provide a universal temple with ceremonies adapted for all. I confess, for my own part, that I prefer to see intensity of conviction, even if joined with some narrowness, to a state of moral and intellectual sleepiness, and children waiting to be fed with such scanty crumbs as fall from official tables.

It only wants an effort to shake off the thraldom of familiar ideas and to see with fresh eyes, and then the monstrous fact that all England is placing itself under official restraints as regards that which it cares most about, would be enough to show us that there must be something radically wrong in a system which necessarily carries with it such a disqualification.

"But what are we to do?" is the impatient exclamation of many persons who feel both the pretentions and the poverty-stricken character of our present system? "Could education be supplied without official assistance?" My answer is that it could; that the combining and cooperative power of our people would provide for this great want, as it is providing for their religious and social wants; that money is waiting to flow from some of the richer people, if so plain and good an outlet were left open— money which is at present doing harm by creating scholarships and increasing the power of examinations; that good citizenship essentially consists in those who have learned to value some gift of civilization, awakening the same sense in those who remain indifferent. "But why did not education spread more quickly in the earlier part of the century?" No truly great thing grows like a mushroom. An intelligent value for education can only spread slowly like civilization itself. In our hurry to act we have not seen how much life and movement is sacrificed to make place for an official system. Those who administer such systems wish to get the flower ready-made without any process of growth. They do not recognize in the early and imperfect efforts the first stage of growth from which the better form will spring, but they wish to start at once with that which will satisfy their own rather prudish eyes. A certain uniform standard is fixed, and all that falls short of it is declared infamous. Of course it is always possible to smear education, religion, or anything else over a country, as you might smear paint, by departments or boards, and in five years be able to glorify your great work and to cram your speeches with statistics of what you have done. Every autocrat with ideas in his head has done the same thing, but he has also left it to his successors to moralize over the results of his work. Education when still left to itself did spread, perhaps too rapidly, in the beginning of the century. Presented to the English people by Lancaster, it was received like a gospel of good news; and although many of the early schools were of exceedingly humble and imperfect form, yet the want was beginning to be felt, and the supply was following. Then came the unwise, if well-intentioned, assistance of government. As usual, the political philanthropists could not endure to see a movement taking its own direction and shaping itself. As soon as the idea of government responsibility had taken root the evil was done. It is a mistake to suppose that government effort and individual effort can live side by side. The habits of mind which belong to each are so different that one must destroy the other. In the course of time there fell alike over everybody concerned the shadow of coming changes, and work which would have been done resolutely and manfully, if no idea of government interference had existed, remained undone, because the constant tendency of government to enlarge its operations was felt everywhere. The history of our race shows us that men will not do things for themselves or for others if they once believe that such things can come without exertion on their own part. There is not sufficient motive. As long as the hope endures that the shoulders of some second person are available, who will offer his own shoulders for the burden? It must also be remembered that unless men are left to their own resources they do not know what is or what is not possible for them. If government half a century ago had provided us all with dinners and breakfasts, it would be the practice of our orators today to assume the impossibility of our providing for ourselves. And now, leaving much unsaid, I must ask what practical steps should be taken by those workmen who suspect that state education is but a part of that coercive drill which one half the human race delights to inflict upon the other half. First of all get rid of compulsion. It has been made the instrument of endless petty persecutions. It is fatal to the free growth of an intelligent love of education; to that moral influence which those of us who have learned the value of education ought to be exerting over others; to a true respect of man for man; for each man's right to judge what is morally best for himself and for those entrusted to him. It is an attempt to make one of those shortcuts to progress which end by making the goal recede from us. It is an exaggerated idea—as exaggerated, ill considered, and probably as short-lived as some other ideas of the present moment—of the value of book education, founded on a rigid and official idea that home duties and labors must in all cases be put aside before the official requirements. It is a copy of a continental institution, taken from a nation that, living under a paternal government, has not yet learned to spell the letters of the word *liberty*. The example of Germany and its highly organized state education is not alluring. In no country perhaps is there less respect of one class for the other class, or greater extremes of violent feeling. Where you subject people to strong official restraint, you seem fated to produce on the one side rigidity of thought and pedantry of feeling, on the other side those violent schemes against the possessions and the personal rights of the rich which we call socialism. Careful respect for the rights of others, vigorous and consistent defense of one's own rights, a deeply rooted love of freedom in thought, word, and action—these things are simply impossible wherever you entrust great powers to a government, and allow it to use them not simply within a sphere of strictly defined rights, but as supreme judge of what the momentary convenience requires.

Second, get rid of all dependence upon the central department. If you do not as yet perceive that public money cannot wisely, in any shape, be taken for education, still refuse the grant that the central department offers as a bribe for the acceptance of its mischievous interference. Until individual self-reliance has grown amongst us, let each town administer education in its own way. So, at least, we shall get local life and energy and variety thrown into the work, not the mere mechanical carrying out of regulations of two or three gentlemen sitting at their desks at Whitehall. But do not believe that you will get the highest results in this way. More freedom for action and experiment is wanted than you can get under any local board. Accustom yourself to the idea that men will act better in voluntary groups than if forced into union by external power. Many boards acting freely in a town, and learning gradually to cooperate together to some extent and for some purposes, is what we should look forward to. Perhaps the best step in advance, and in preparation for a purely free system, is to obtain powers from Parliament under which any considerable number of electors, say from one-sixth to one-tenth, according to the size of the town, might elect, and pay their rate to, their own board. Under such a plan there would be imperfections and possible evasions; but it would cast off the swaddling clothes imposed by the Privy Council, and would give a life to the work which would far more than compensate for the loss of mechanical regularity. It is always difficult to introduce freedom into a system that is founded on authority and officialism. You can only escape from anomalies and contradictions by being either rigidly despotic or completely free. But a little life and light are worth getting at almost any price, and will make us wish for more. The final step will be to render the rate purely voluntary, and to give full freedom and responsibility of action, for which the people will never be fit as long as they are persuaded to subject each other to official regulations under the much-abused name of self-government.

15

"Some Socialist and Anarchist Views of Education"

Benjamin R. Tucker

Educational Review (15: 1898)

Benjamin R. Tucker (1854–1939) was arguably the most influential individualist anarchist in American history. (The twentieth-century economist and historian Murray Rothbard would be his only serious rival.) Beginning in August 1881, and for 27 years thereafter, Tucker edited and published *Liberty*, a provocative and highly interesting journal that included contributions from George Bernard Shaw and other prominent writers.

Tucker was a vivid, forceful, and polemical writer. J. William Lloyd (a friend and colleague of Tucker who contributed articles to *Liberty*) said of his style:

> No more fiery and forceful apostle ever put pen to paper.
> A veritable Berserk of dialectics. He was dogmatic to the

extreme, arrogantly positive, browbeating and dominating, true to his plumb-line no matter what was slain, and brooked no difference, contradiction or denial. Biting sarcasm, caustic contempt, invective that was sometimes actual insult, were poured out on any who dared criticize or oppose.

As Lloyd observed, those who only read Tucker's writings without ever meeting him in person would be surprised to learn that Tucker "was the most genial, affable and charming gentleman that that you could possibly imagine, kind, gentle, and always smiling."

Our selection by Tucker was not published in *Liberty* but in the respectable journal *Educational Review*. It is a concise statement of Tucker's opposition to state education and his ideas about how children should be educated. Like other libertarians of his day, Tucker believed that education should be adapted to the wants and needs of individual children. No one method is appropriate for every child, so the single, uniform method imposed by state systems will do more harm than good.

For many readers a curious feature of this article will be Tucker's position on the rights of children. Children before the age of reason have no rights, according to Tucker. Infants are the property of their parents, their human creators, so no third party, including the state, "should be allowed to step in between the creator and his property. If the creator sees fit not to give his child an education, that is his business."

It should not be supposed that Tucker's position was shared by all of his anarchist contemporaries. On the contrary, many individualist anarchists defended natural rights, including the rights of infants, and rejected the ideas of Max Stirner, which had greatly influenced Tucker. A prolonged debate over this controversy appeared in the pages of *Liberty*, along with many other debates of considerable interest to political philosophers.

Do parents have a duty to provide at least minimal education for their children? This was a wedge issue in the debate over what role, if any, the state should play in education. According to J. S. Mill, for example, parents do indeed have a duty to educate their children; and if they neglect this duty, the state may intervene to enforce it. Although Mill believed that parents should be free to teach their own children as they see fit, whether in or out of formal schools, the state should enforce minimal educational requirements through a series of public examinations. Herbert Spencer and other Voluntaryists responded to this common argument in various ways, many of which may be found in other selections in this Reader.

The Anarchists do not believe that education should be furnished to children by the state. We have no objection to philanthropic efforts in that direction,—people voluntarily combining together for such a purpose,—but we do object to public schools supported by compulsory taxation.

So far as education is connected with what is commonly called the "general intelligence" of the public, the Anarchistic idea is that the most intelligent public is the public which is educated to know how to do what it wants to do. The people may always be trusted to find out the means to provide for the instruction they desire. To be worth anything, education must come as the supply responsive to demand. Private enterprise always furnishes anything for which there is demand, provided the demand is a practicable one.

The Anarchist believes that education does little or nothing in the direction of forming the morals of the people. It puts weapons in the hands of those who are criminally inclined, and instruments for good in the hands of those whose inclinations are good. Whoever is educated has power, and that power may be used for evil or for good.

As to what education a child should have the answer is, the education that it wants. Anyone who feels the need of higher education has the opportunity to strive after it and find the means of getting it. Educational enterprise should be, like any other, a commercial enterprise. It offers what is wanted to those who want it at a competitive price; those who want a little education will buy a little, those who want much will buy much. I think the system of manual training in the public schools (which, of course, I object to the state supplying) may have a better effect on the morals of the people than mere book learning. This kind of education fosters the habit of industry and contributes in a greater degree to the formation of character than does the accretion of information; it is more closely connected with the personal habits and conduct of the people than book learning. Perhaps the main criticism that I would make against the public-school system is that it lays down one programme for all; it fits Procrustes to the bed instead of the bed to Procrustes. As to whether or not children are compelled to study too hard, it may be said that any child studies too hard who studies more than it wants to. I claim that all children, by nature, like to study if they are not compelled to. A child begins to study as soon as it opens its eyes. There is no need of discipline to direct the mind of the child. Let the child follow its bent and learn what it wants to. Here, for instance, is a youth who spends most of his time reading novels, to the exclusion of sound literature. There is no occasion for alarm on that account. In order to be able to read novels he had to learn to read. He manifested a desire to be able to read because he saw the children around him reading, and, in order to communicate with them and have feelings in common with them, he must feel a desire to learn to read. He would be an abnormal being if he did not manifest such a desire. However difficult it may be for a child to learn his A B Cs, the task would be undertaken in proportion as the child wants the results that come from it. When children see other children enjoying reading, and talking about it, they must necessarily desire to partake in the same enjoyment themselves.

I make the same criticism against the present educational system that I make against all government institutions: they are all subject to the same incompetency, carelessness, over-drill, too much regimentation, too little spontaneity, too little recognition of individuality—everything run in the same mold.

What is the duty of the parent toward the child? The position of the Anarchist is that there are no such things as rights and duties except so far as they are a matter of contract; and, as there can be no contract between a parent and an unborn child, and as a mere infant is incapable of making a contract, it is obvious that there can be no duty to an unborn child or an infant. Until they are able to assert themselves, until they are able to contract, they are the property of their creators (I mean, of course, their human creators), and such creators should have sole control of them, and neither the state nor anybody should be allowed to step in between the creator and his property. If the creator sees fit not to give his child an education, that is his business. It is to be added, however, that the Anarchist holds that the motive of parental affection is all-sufficient to insure the care of children by their parents.

The only ethical teaching that the Anarchist believes in, for either public or domestic purposes, is the inculcation of the doctrine of equal liberty. The child is more amenable than anybody else to this teaching if taken in hand in the beginning. If his own liberties are respected by his parents; if there is no attempt to interfere with him; if, whenever he wishes to do a thing, he is allowed to do it, simply with an explanation of the consequences that will follow, and if no compulsion is exercised upon him except as it would be exercised upon an invasive adult,—*i. e.*, if the compulsion exercised upon a child was a purely defensive compulsion against any invasive act which the child was going to commit,—the child, then, from its very treatment, would acquire an idea of his own liberties and of the liberties of others, and would learn to insist upon the one and respect the other. Such ideas are carried out by all Anarchistic parents who understand their own ideas and have themselves sufficient strength of character to live up to them.

It is said that all children are naturally disposed to take property belonging to others. A child should be given something as his own, and, as early as possible, should be allowed to earn something as his own, and then care should be taken that his enjoyment of the property should never be interfered with, and the same care taken that he never interferes with others in the enjoyment of their property. In that way he would, at a very early age, get a very clear idea of the sanctity of the individual, of his earnings, and his personal property. And that idea covers all there is in ethics.

Physiology, the Anarchist would teach to boys and girls under the same conditions that he would teach anything else: if they wanted to learn. The Anarchist would probably inform his young daughter about the views that were held about virtue, etc., by the majority of the world, present the pros and cons of the matter, and allow the girl to come to a decision for herself. The Anarchists do not accept the usual views and prejudices in regard to so-called virtue in women, but they consider utterly repugnant the relations of the sexes when they are made the matter of bargain and sale, whether it is done legally, under the name of marriage, or illegally.

END

Index

Note: Page numbers with letter n indicate notes.

Libertarianism.org

Liberty. It's a simple idea and the linchpin of a complex system of values and practices: justice, prosperity, responsibility, toleration, cooperation, and peace. Many people believe that liberty is the core political value of modern civilization itself, the one that gives substance and form to all the other values of social life. They're called libertarians.

Libertarianism.org is the Cato Institute's treasury of resources about the theory and history of liberty. The book you're holding is a small part of what Libertarianism.org has to offer. In addition to hosting classic texts by historical libertarian figures and original articles from modern-day thinkers, Libertarianism.org publishes podcasts, videos, online introductory courses, and books on a variety of topics within the libertarian tradition.

Cato Institute

Founded in 1977, the Cato Institute is a public policy research foundation dedicated to broadening the parameters of policy debate to allow consideration of more options that are consistent with the principles of limited government, individual liberty, and peace. To that end, the Institute strives to achieve greater involvement of the intelligent, concerned lay public in questions of policy and the proper role of government.

The Institute is named for *Cato's Letters*, libertarian pamphlets that were widely read in the American Colonies in the early 18th century and played a major role in laying the philosophical foundation for the American Revolution.

Despite the achievement of the nation's Founders, today virtually no aspect of life is free from government encroachment. A pervasive intolerance for individual rights is shown by government's arbitrary intrusions into private economic transactions and its disregard for civil liberties. And while freedom around the globe has notably increased in the past several decades, many countries have moved in the opposite direction, and most governments still do not respect or safeguard the wide range of civil and economic liberties.

To address those issues, the Cato Institute undertakes an extensive publications program on the complete spectrum of policy issues. Books, monographs, and shorter studies are commissioned to examine the federal budget, Social Security, regulation, military spending, international trade, and myriad other issues. Major policy conferences are held throughout the year, from which papers are published thrice yearly in the *Cato Journal*. The Institute also publishes the quarterly magazine *Regulation*.

In order to maintain its independence, the Cato Institute accepts no government funding. Contributions are received from foundations, corporations, and individuals, and other revenue is generated from the sale of publications. The Institute is a nonprofit, tax-exempt, educational foundation under Section 501(c)3 of the Internal Revenue Code.

CATO INSTITUTE
1000 Massachusetts Ave., N.W.
Washington, D.C. 20001
www.cato.org